NEVER AGAIN THE BURNING TIMES
PAGANISM REVIVED

LORETTA ORION
Hofstra University

WAVELAND
PRESS, INC.

Prospect Heights, Illinois

For Hekate

For information about this book, write or call:
Waveland Press, Inc.
P.O. Box 400
Prospect Heights, Illinois 60070
(708) 634-0081

Acknowledgements

I am deeply grateful that throughout the long evolution of this book Dr. David Hicks has helped me to adjust my course. His enduring confidence in my work has sustained me. I continue to benefit from the guidance I received as a graduate student at State University of New York at Stony Brook from Dr. Daniel M. Fox. I am indebted, also, to the Neopagans who trusted me with their story, and to Debbie Light who introduced me to them. For assistance in the most difficult part of this project—processing of the data collected with my questionnaire—I thank Gary Piatt, Mary Graves, and Dave Bock. For typing previous drafts of the manuscript I am grateful to Sandra Ferguson and Suzanne Peiffer. Also, I praise the patience of my students and thank them for the clarifying effect of their response to many of the ideas presented here.

With extraordinary talent my editors, Jeni Ogilvie and Carol Rowe, guided the many revisions of the manuscript and eased the process of producing it. As permissions manager, Steve Dungan skillfully monitored the flow of external resources into this work. Because it took three times longer to complete the project than I expected, I thank all my friends at Waveland Press for their help and patience.

Without the support and encouragement of my husband, Hugh King—who is a constant source of delight and comfort—this book would not be.

iii

Contents

Chapter One

Introduction

W hy do some individuals in American society resort to the magical beliefs and practices of the occult[1]—a hidden spiritual tradition that has long existed in Western culture—while the majority do not? Contemporary witches say that witchcraft is a revival of a European pre-Christian religion called *Wicca*. Practitioners of Wicca believe the world is alive, interconnected, and responsive to attempts to manipulate invisible (occult) forces. These efforts constitute their magic, the "craft" of witchcraft. In the United States, Wicca has become the core of a collection of other pagan traditions, religions, and magical systems that together are called *Neopaganism*.

Conservative estimates suggest that approximately a few hundred thousand[2] individuals participate in Neopaganism. Their interpretation of the character of witches and witchcraft differs radically from the conceptions of nonbelievers. The witches believe that they are healers and that the kind of witchcraft they practice is *benevolent* magic.

Anthropological studies have generally taken the perspective of those who fear witches and accuse others of witchcraft. In this book we will explore the topic from the unusual perspective of self-identified witches and magicians, and we will have the opportunity to learn what kinds of individuals engage in radical thought movements such as this one. We can view the ideas of witchcraft and magic from the vantage point of those who profess to be witches and *practice* magic. An ethnographic description of the demographic characteristics of the group combined with an analysis of their complex and sophisticated belief system will provide insight into the unusual behaviors shared by participants in this subculture within American society. With such a foundation, we will have a better vantage point to discover the premises underlying their view of the world and the behaviors that follow from it.

I have recently come to understand why this research was difficult—

as well as exciting—and why I seem always to be defending my position relative to my subjects, my discipline of anthropology, my motivations, and my methods. Anthropologists have only recently begun to apply the ethnographic method to subcultures within their own societies. As a result of projects such as this one, the nature of ethnography and the relationship between anthropologists and their subjects has been rapidly changing. For instance, we find that acquiring informed consent from all of many hundreds of subjects is impossible. Many other ethnographers have been discovering, as I have, that it is more appropriate to approach the individuals whose culture or subculture we study not only as our teachers, but as collaborators in the project of presenting what has been learned. And, when the subjects are members of one's own society, they are present and vulnerable to the outcome of the use we make of what they teach us.

My anthropology became sociological and historical. How could I account for the discrepancies in the beliefs and practices of this large and diverse population except by resort to survey techniques? Yet the result of these techniques falls between the cracks, neither proving dependable probabilities nor accounting for the full diversity of the unique population I studied. At best I have been able to circumvent guessing at generalizations by allowing my subjects to speak for themselves and be counted. Nor could the motivations of my collaborating subjects be rendered meaningful without grounding them in the context of contemporary Western society.

It proved quite impossible to explain the resort to the witch as culture heroine without following the roots of that perennial character not only around the world through the ethnographies of my colleagues but into the depths of the history of Western society. In order to understand the present resort to magic, this study had to be historical as well, for magic has a long history not only in the shadowy peripheries of Western society, but it has wound itself into the major transitions in Western culture all the way back to ancient Egypt and Greece. For these and other reasons this is a thick book, and a strange tale, stranger in many ways than the ethnographies of remote societies my predecessors tell, precisely because it takes place here, at home in contemporary American society.

Still, this book addresses several fields of anthropological inquiry: cultural revitalization, religion, witchcraft, magic, and medicine. The grounding in history helps to clarify the origins of the contemporary movement which has its roots in cultural radicalisms in the United States and Europe. The most immediate ancestor is the Wiccan revival that originated in Great Britain in the 1950s. We will look at the introduction of that revival into the United States and the transformations it sustained under the impact of American culture. First, it will be helpful to clarify some terms.

We will see that the witches use their craft of magic to transform themselves and their relationship to their society by modifying and shifting allegiance among elements of expressive culture, specifically, myths, religion, and magic. It is important to realize that the Neopagans regard culture as *continuous* with nature. In contrast, many social scientists think of culture, together with the society within which it exists, as being *distinct from* nature. A classic definition formulated by Edward B. Tylor, for instance, states that culture is "that complex whole which includes knowledge, belief, art, morals, law, custom, and any other capabilities and habits acquired by man as a member of society" (1871, 1). Thus, culture was, to him, distinctly social and separate from nature.

Society is the organization of individuals into culture-sharing groups (Kroeber 1952). Social institutions are behaviors and activities (units of culture) that are standardized within a society. These definitions establish the continuity between culture and society as human inventions and set them in opposition to nature. From this perspective, nature is all that must be classified and subdued by culture so that humans may establish the terms of their difference from it, set themselves apart from it, in order to live more conveniently with one another in society.

This view of society as separate from nature is the unique product of the Western mind. We might go so far as to locate it in time—the modern age—when nature came to be regarded as hostile and requiring "perfection" by the efforts of humans, i.e., "progress."

Pagans see the function of society as imbedded in nature. Natural processes are affected by the acts of humans just as human life depends on harmonious integration with nature. Witches and Neopagans speak of the "web" of life to express the idea that all kinds and levels of life within nature, including that of humans, are interwoven into the unity of the universe. "Life" implies the ability to move and change. Until humans invented such products as non-biodegradable plastics, pagans could think that nothing is devoid of this quality. To apply this view of an integrated living universe to definitions of culture and society, we may say that culture—which includes all that Tylor attributed to it—is an element within an organized collectivity of humans (society) which is in turn a subsystem of the vast, complex, interrelated living cosmos. Significant among the many social institutions through which culture is expressed are religion and mythology.

The persuasive power of religious symbols is expressed in Clifford Geertz's idea that religion is, "a system of symbols which acts to establish powerful, pervasive, and long-lasting moods and motivations in men by formulating conceptions of a general order of existence and clothing these conceptions with such an aura of factuality that the moods and motivations seem uniquely realistic" (1973, 90). *Myths*, among other things, are the stories through which people communicate a system of symbols, and they serve as the text for religious rituals.

According to Émile Durkheim's definition, "a religion is a unified system of beliefs and practices relative to sacred things, that is to say, things set apart and forbidden—beliefs and practices which unite into one single moral community called a Church, all those who adhere to them" (Durkheim 1915, 62) This definition implies that religion is a conservative and unifying force that reflects and validates the social order. On the other hand, Firth (1954) and Leach (1967) recognize that religion is potentially dynamic. Individuals may manipulate myths and produce variants that promote their individual interests, and the gradual accumulation of individuals' choices produces a continually changing social order. At times efforts to construct a more satisfying and meaningful moral order by resort to religion are undertaken collectively. Anthony Wallace (1956) contends that all religions have been devised by the same systematic process that he named "revitalization." I would argue that when religious beliefs and practices contribute to the transformation of societies in conformity with the wishes of individuals or groups of individuals within society, they more accurately constitute magic rather than worship.

Although magic is generally regarded as the opposite of religion, it is more accurately distinguished from religion by virtue of being a form of *behavior* while religion is a set of *beliefs*. Like acts of worship, magical behavior is based on beliefs regarding the nature of the world according to which those actions seem appropriate.

Worship and magic can be seen as two different approaches to the sacred. Worship consists of acts of supplication, entreaty, or propitiation to the gods and cosmos, as the group agrees they exist. Such religious actions reiterate and reinforce shared beliefs. *Magic*, on the other hand, expresses assertive, creative actions, an intent to effect a transformation. It expresses the intentions and beliefs of individuals which may or may not be in conflict with those of the collectivity.

Keith Thomas (1971) has remarked that nearly every primitive religion offers the prospect of a supernatural means of influencing the earthly environment. The history of early Christianity offers no exception.[3] The Anglo-Saxon church's exclusive claim to supernatural powers was an essential element in the indictment against paganism. Nor did missionaries fail to stress the superiority of Christian prayers to heathen charms.

In the distinction I am making between worship and magic as the two functions of religion, the desire to effect *change* by what appears to be *supernatural* control of the environment (to the uninitiated) constitutes magic. In established religions, the magical aspects of religious practice are generally reserved for priests who perform healings or intercede with divinities for other practical purposes on behalf of the members of the congregation. When individuals pray or make offerings in an effort to bring about some change in themselves or their environment—in terms of the distinction I am making—they are performing magic. This way of thinking helps us to avoid the impulse to dismiss magic as an antisocial (Durkheim 1915) or deviant (Mauss 1950) action; erroneous science or defective religion (Frazer 1907); substitute for effective action (Malinowski 1948, Marett 1909); or plain superstition.

Magic is easily confused with superstition and prayer. For our purposes magical actions will be distinguished from superstition on the basis of the systematic nature of the beliefs relative to the supernatural realm on which magic *is* based and superstition *is not*. It is useful to think of prayers that seek to effect change—such as healing, or the gaining of confidence or strength—as magic. This way of distinguishing magic from worship allows us to ask with an open mind, "What exactly is magic?" rather than judge the legitimacy of any action relative to the supernatural realm. Entreaties for help from deities of institutionalized religions are generally regarded as prayer, an acceptable religious behavior. To request success in love from the goddess Venus might be dismissed as superstition, or even heresy. The distinction I make between two basic types of actions that are motivated by religious beliefs frees us from prejudice that is irrelevant to our purpose.

To summarize: magic is religious practice undertaken by individuals, alone or in concert, on their own or another's behalf to effect some transformation in themselves or the environment. These actions may be based on the society's shared religion or an alternative belief system that serves as the religion of the magician.

The exploration of the beliefs and practices of the witches and other Neopagans that follows will, I believe, persuade the reader (as it has convinced me) that magical practice is based on a very clear and sophisticated conception of the nature of the cosmos that unifies those who share that understanding into a group, or congregation, such as Durkheim described in his definition of religion. Once the premises of the Neopagans are accepted, magical intervention seems as feasible as prayer in any other religion.

Given these considerations, I define religion as a unified system of beliefs and practices relative to sacred things (Durkheim 1915) that are powerful and persuasive and that motivate (Geertz 1973) actions, both worshipful and magical, and provide for all those who adhere to them the foundation for a sense of unity based on their sharing of these common beliefs. Revived Wicca is, according to this definition, a religion, albeit a radical religion.

Efforts of individuals, or groups, to change themselves and the world in which they live through religion can be classified as magic if (1) the views and desires of individuals vary from those of the larger society and (2) *change* is invoked by processes that operate on a different order of cause and effect (*supernatural*) than those normally accepted by the majority of members of mainstream society. In this respect, we may consider revived Wicca a magico-religion that shares a common purpose with revitalization movements. That is to say, individuals are empowered to effect transformations in their culture and ultimately in their society.

When comparing Neopaganism to other radical religions, the most striking differences that emerge are the importance of creativity and the lack of a guiding prophet for Neopagans. Every member is theoretically a prophet, and nearly every individual in the movement is a practitioner of some art or craft. It is readily understandable, then, that the members of the movement would think that: (1) witchcraft is benevolent creativity and (2) they, as witches, are healers and culture reformers. The craft or "magic" in this version of witchcraft is nearly indistinguishable from the artistic creative process.

Wicca fosters the acquisition and use of the faculties of creativity: imagination, will, and the "craft" or skill of making things. Their magic takes the creative process beyond the mere fabrication of works of art into the creation of the conditions of their personal and social lives.

Revived Wicca and Neopaganism share with other radical religions the goal of revitalizing culture. However, the numerous discrepancies between Neopaganism and the movements that anthropologists have observed in preliterate societies has convinced me that the present movement represents a uniquely Western phenomenon.

Rather than the sudden emergence of a bizarre cult, the new witchcraft and Neopaganism represent parts of a continuum of a generally submerged (occult) tradition within Western culture. For hundreds of years the occult tradition has been a repository of beliefs, techniques, and ethics relating to the creative process deployed to achieve spiritual refinement. It has surfaced and been more visible during historical periods when efforts at cultural revitalization were important.

Blended with my anthropological perspective is my interest in healing that resulted from my former career of professional nursing. Thus I have a special interest in a significant feature that the Neopagan movement shares with this long tradition: the concern with healing individuals and society. The new witches say they are healers. This book is devoted to discovering what they mean by magic and healing and to discovering the relationship of these to the creative process.

Physicians figured prominently among the enemies of those who were persecuted in the European witch hunts of the sixteenth and seventeenth centuries. The ethnohistory of the witch hunts combined with the ethnographic literature on witchcraft beliefs around the world provide a context for the Neopagans' idea of witchcraft. Taking a structural perspective, we learn that the witch serves Neopagans as a symbol of the opposite of "right" or "proper" society, just as he, or more generally she, does in all the societies in which this negative character is believed in. By linking their benevolent practices with the evil character of the witch, the Neopagans reveal that they see themselves as the opposite— and victim—of the socially approved healer, the physician. We will explore the contrasting roles of the witches (and their magical healing) and physicians (and the official American health care system). What benefits do such interpretations have for coping with problems in present-day society?

Neopagan witches share a pervasive disenchantment with the prevailing health care system with many others in mainstream society, but Neopagans are more daring than most in their solutions. Their alternative therapies represent efforts to address problems that the troubled health care system has not recognized or been able to solve. The willingness of Neopagans to be more self-sufficient and to experiment with alternatives to the health care system suggest possible ways of reducing the uncritical reliance on expensive, technologically intensive medicine that impairs the economy of this country.

I have benefitted from three earlier studies of the Neopagans. Margot Adler, a journalist and witch, conducted several years of fine participant observation among the Neopagans and published her insightful reflections on these experiences in her book, *Drawing Down the Moon: Witches, Druids, Goddess-Worshippers, and Other Pagans In America Today* (1979). J. Gordon Melton compiled a bibliography, *Magic, Witchcraft, and Paganism in America* from the files of the Institute for the Study of American Religion (1982) in which he describes the Neopagan community. An earlier study of Neopagans was made by a team of sociology students headed by Dr. R. George Kirkpatrick, at San Diego State University.[4] The sociologists and sociology graduate students who conducted the study sampled what they called "informed networks of pagans," focusing on three categories: "revivalist witches," whom they defined as Gardnerians (practitioners of a conservative Wiccan tradition); participants in the Aquarian Age counterculture; and practitioners of revived, feminist witchcraft combined with "shamanistic Goddess worship" (Kirkpatrick 1984). This population coincides with the national community that is the subject of my study—although my terminology differs.

My study is based on an extensive analysis of the relevant extant literature together with fieldwork complemented by interviews carried out since 1983. My effort to present a clear image of the Neopagans is compromised somewhat by their hypertrophied individualism and their resistance to any semblance of uniformity. Furthermore, ethnographic fieldwork is biased both by the anthropologist's selection of informants and by the information selected by the informant as worthy of being divulged. By supplementing my interviews and observations with simple statistical evaluations, I have tried to achieve a more objective representation. I distributed a questionnaire (see Appendix) designed to elicit a basic demographic profile of the Neopagans studied as well as to gather information concerning their beliefs about magic, healing, and the merits of their healing techniques as compared with those current in the mainstream health care system.

My first period of fieldwork, in 1983, involved four hundred to five hundred Neopagans camped at the Pagan Spirit Gathering (PSG) in the vicinity of Madison, Wisconsin. In 1984, the Rites of Spring gathering (ROS) attracted about two hundred participants, and swelled to accommodate seven hundred in 1989. This annual gathering services Neopagans in the northeast and is sponsored by the Earth Spirit Community based in the Boston area. The third gathering, Southern Pagan Regional Lunarfest (Spiral), takes place in Atlanta, Georgia. Earlier gatherings attracted one hundred to one hundred and fifty individuals; in more recent years about seventy-five participants have attended Spiral. The Tribe of the Phoenix (a group that I originally encountered at the Spiral gathering) is discussed in chapter eleven.[5]

For a week in 1985 I participated together with a group of about fifty Neopagans in an experience called, tongue-in-cheek, "witch camp," on a farm in Mendocino, California. It was organized and presented by a group called "Reclaiming," whose most prominent member is Starhawk, a psychotherapist, political activist, and educator. She presents workshops and lectures in various universities and other educational institutions around the United States and in Europe. Her books and political activism—which incorporate Wiccan rituals—have profoundly influenced the character of the Neopagan movement in the United States and other parts of the world. Starhawk, in fact, has come closer than anyone to being a guiding prophet.

My participant observation also took place in two covens: one on Long Island, New York, (which dissolved after about a year and a half) and another in Manhattan, into which I was initiated in 1986. The overwhelming majority of the members in both covens (each had eleven to thirteen members) are artists from various fields including acting, dance, and poetry.

In chapter two, we will look at the revival of the religion of Wicca (witchcraft) that took place in England, as revealed in the writings of the most celebrated English witch, Gerald Gardner. The importance of the creative process is explored in chapter three. Here we discover that the traditional Wiccan ritual may be interpreted as the template for the creative process. In the fourth chapter the reader will have the opportunity to explore the present-day witches' conception of themselves. The witch as a symbol is related to the historical studies of witch persecutions in Europe and the various images of the witch that emerged in ethnographic studies of witchcraft. In the fifth chapter, I discuss certain demographic characteristics of the group. The roots of the present movement in the Western occult tradition are traced in chapter six. Chapter seven is devoted to the Neopagans' approach to magic as it was revealed in the questionnaire, along with the descriptions and examples provided by some of the witches.

My first experience at a Neopagan gathering is the subject of chapter eight. In the ninth chapter, American Neopaganism is compared with the British Wiccan revival from which it emerged. Chapters ten and eleven concern the healing magic of the Neopagans and how they see themselves as healers in relation to physicians and the institution of professional medicine. In chapter twelve we learn how a shamanic witch used his magical skills and knowledge to transform himself. Chapter thirteen presents the Neopagan conception of healing as it is applied to social reform. The links connecting Neopaganism to other cultural radicalisms in the United States and with the Western occult tradition are explored. In the fourteenth chapter the forging of social bonds through collaboration in rites of passage (marriage, for instance) is explored along with the various social structures—from intimate covens to the loosely interwoven network of the national community—that coexist in the rapidly growing Neopagan movement. Concluding remarks appear in chapter fifteen along with some speculation on the contribution the movement makes to the evolution of culture and society while it struggles to contain or manage its own growth.

This book is a prelude to further research. Additional historical research into the periods of greater visibility of the occult might explain or predict the political and economic correlates which presage efforts toward cultural revitalization of a religious, spiritual, or idealistic sort.

I continue to investigate the efficacy of Neopagan alternative therapies and approaches to maintaining and restoring health. This is of particular interest because the emphasis on self-sufficiency might prove to be a valuable resource in a health care system where all possible adjustments fall short of reducing the cost of necessary services. A more open-minded evaluation of the possible benefits of the alternative therapies, which Neopagans and some people in the mainstream society are resorting to, is needed.

The art of the witches and Neopagans deserves deeper investigation. My continuing interest is rewarded by much valuable insight into the workings of the creative impulse in response to problems originating in the social sphere.

As a collection of highly individualistic and creative people, the Neopagans exhibit wide diversity in the interpretation of their fundamental beliefs as their many eloquent publications demonstrate. I have had to invent a hybrid anthropology to help me account for this. My task was made easier by the fact that I was able to explore the subtleties of magical thought in our shared language. Still, hybrid anthropology is fraught with many dangers. Many Neopagans will have reason to disagree with my interpretations and conclusions because, despite my research and experimentation under their tutelage, my grasp of the dense and obscure Western spiritual tradition which is our common language, limits me much as the struggle to master indigenous languages challenges my colleagues who conduct research away from home. Furthermore, although I have met hundreds of Neopagans, there are hundreds more that I have not met or read about, and inevitably their interpretations and practices will differ from what I have written here. I can only account for the narrow path I walked through this enormous and growing subculture.

My best defense is that as much as possible I allowed my subjects to speak for themselves and I have invited them as colleagues to evaluate my findings. This process reached a most satisfying level of collaboration in the exchange, between myself and Andras Corban Arthen, which resulted in the recounting of his efforts to transform himself by resort to his magic (see chapter twelve). Although I have carefully quoted my subjects from letters and audio recordings of interviews, some may feel I have misconceptions.

Another danger is that my colleagues may doubt my credibility more, perhaps, than that of other anthropologists who have emersed themselves in alien cultures. I have experienced disapproval of the very idea of studying peoples in my own country and for taking witches so seriously when anthropologists had established long ago that witches don't exist except as figments of the imaginations of the credulous. Although anthropologists have, for example, conducted participant observation among headhunters who are seldom suspected of murdering their neighbors, a look of suspicion passes over the faces of my colleagues when they realize that I have participated in the rituals and gatherings of witches and magicians. Can a social scientist who is an initiated witch be taken seriously?

A more pressing question, in my estimation, is the one relating to my ethical responsibility not to harm my subjects. In my own estimation, the success of this work will be measured by the extent to which it dissolves fear of a maligned aspect of Western culture, its own spiritual (occult) tradition, and opens the minds of the fearful and conservative minded who resist the kinds of shifts of awareness that the Neopagans are willing to make, not only to express themselves, but to explore broader undercurrents that are less explicit to others. I will be content if I can help my readers recognize the voices of many others in American society in the playful magic of the Neopagans whose gift, like that of the shamans in less complex societies, is to articulate what is diffuse and formless although deeply felt by many others in their society. Like the shamans, the Neopagans give a name and a face to emotional undercurrents of their societies. Anyone who does not recognize truth in the symbols they create is perfectly free to reject them. As we shall see in chapter thirteen, the willingness to harm those who hold a different vision, including witches—and those who call themselves witches—survives.

The Neopagans who have reviewed parts of the manuscript for this book have criticized it most frequently for not capitalizing witch or witchcraft and for using the term Neopagan. I hope that in these pages they will learn that the concepts witch and witchcraft are much larger and older even than their existence in Western culture and that they have not generally been used to denote a religion or a practitioner of a religion. Although paganism is indeed the oldest religion, I hope that this book will convince them that its revival in postmodern times is unique. Never before have pagans had the benefit of seeing a photograph of the entirety of their world as a planet set against the vastness of space. The postmodern pagans are the first to attempt to devise effective myths and symbols to articulate a global perspective that honors our planet as a deity. Inevitably, some Neopagans will have difficulty recognizing themselves in what I have written here, but I hope that most will find that my ethnographic portrait rings true.

Chapter Two

Gerald Gardner (1884–1964) and the Wiccan Revival

L ady Boadicea, who was ninety years old in the fall of 1987, told Geraldo Rivera she had been a witch for fifty years. With Halloween fast approaching, Geraldo Rivera devoted his television program that day[1] to witches. Lady Boadicea made an imposing figure, dressed in a purple and white ceremonial gown and the traditional crown of a high priestess of the religion of Wicca: a plain silver band with an upturned crescent moon. A witch's most essential tool, a ceremonial dagger, called an *athame*, hung from a belt at her waist.

She described her participation in witchcraft rituals that were undertaken to avert the threatened invasion of Hitler's forces in the 1940s.[2] During the second world war, Lady Boadicea said she and about two hundred witches gathered in London each Tuesday evening to "raise and direct energy to the most dreadful parts where the war was going on. We were just one section. Witches all over England were also working to put up a barrier to keep Hitler from landing in England. Days later, by the newspapers we saw that the terrible activity was lessening." Lady Boadicea was convinced that their magic had worked. "Hitler never did occupy England," was the smug conclusion to Lady Boadicea's story.

Also present at these rituals was Gerald Gardner, the British gentleman who was the originator of a popular movement in Great Britain that soon spread to the United States. Its devotees refer to themselves as witches. In 1939, just after the start of the second world war, Gardner was initiated into a coven of witches headed by "Old Dorothy" (Dorothy Clutterbuck). The coven into which Gardner was initiated was one of nine offshoots from one founded by George Pickingill (1816-1909) who traced his descent from Julia Brandon, a witch who died in 1071 (Valiente 1973).

Gardner wrote two novels in which he described his experiences with a "religion" of witchcraft that the participants also called Wicca. Gardner's contemporaries called themselves witches, Wiccan, or *the wise*, and their practice of enchantments *the craft of the wise*. They believed that theirs was the indigenous religion of Britain. For this reason they often referred to their magico-religion as the "Old Religion" or simply the craft.

The Old Religion, Wicca

The Saxons were criticized for bringing into Great Britain the traditions of worshipping nature and the practice of enchantments along with the veneration of sacred women who were tribal soothsayers (Crawford 1963). There are numerous instances of powerful priestesses—mediators between people and the divine—among continental Germanic tribes in the first seven centuries C.E. (L. Eckenstein 1896 in Crawford 1963, 99). Although there is no evidence in English documents that the powerful role for women was adopted in England (Crawford 1963, 99), these heathens from the forests of northern Germany were important members of tenth century English society.

This religion is called Wicca in the earliest laws against heathenism in English civil codes. Alfred's law of the ninth century was directed against the elaborate form of heathenism that the church fathers believed was seriously threatening the Christian church (Crawford 1963; Horsley 1979b). Alfred's law of the ninth century condemns the Wiccan (practitioners of Wicca) in this passage: "... *pa foemnan pe gewuniap anfon galdorcroeft 7 scinloecan 7 wiccan, ne loet pu pa abban*," that translates as "... women who are wont to practice enchantments, and magicians, and witches, do not allow them to live."[3]

It is significant that "7 Wiccan" occurs in this passage, in addition to other terms, because it indicates that it had a separate identity from the other forms of magic. Apparently it means "practitioner of witchcraft," because the cognate verb has the simple meaning "to practice witchcraft." In another passage in a tenth century English canon, we find the verb *wiccige*[4] associated with nature worship, thus linking witchcraft and nature worship. The code refers to lingering beliefs and superstitions about trees, stones, and wells, to divination "in sun and in moon and in the courses of stars, and to idol worship." Particular disapproval is directed against one who practiced "love enchantments" (Crawford 1963, 111).

Saxon wisemen and magicians were skilled in magical medicine (consisting largely of herbalism), and their knowledge was preserved in leechbooks that for a long time served as the only *pharmacopoeia* of the British Isles, except for the Britons of the west, who preserved much of the lore of the pre-Roman times (Maple 1962).

In a sermon delivered by Aelfric in the late tenth century, the Wiccan—who were by then clearly identified as women—were described as disciples of an elemental heathenism, teaching the worship of stones, trees, and wells. They dabbled in dream interpretation as well as brewing love philtres. The Wiccan possessed an occult knowledge that, although it was true, Aelfric warned, the Wiccan were dangerous because their knowledge came from the devil. This description is strongly reminiscent of what was said in the sixteenth century about the cunning-folk[5] who were later to be so numerous among the accused witches:

> The trade is thought to be impious. The effect and end thereof to be sometimes evill, as when thereby man or beast, grasse, trees or corne, etc.; is hurt; sometimes good, as whereby sicke folkes are healed, theeves bewraied and true men come to their goods. The matter and instruments, wherewith it is accomplished, are words, signes, images, characters.[6]

Aelfric's sermon provides an unusual, specifically Christian, way of conceptualizing witchcraft. Beneficial magic is condemned along with harmful magic as constituting witchcraft. Aelfric censures the Wiccans by saying that "It is for us to seek, if we are hard pressed, the cure from God, not from these grim women."[7]

The Saxons brought with them their northern gods of the German forest: Thor, Wotan, and the Valkyries (wild women who flew through the clouds on stormy nights). The tales of these fearsome women took their place among others that served as raw material out of which were created the witchcraft beliefs of more recent times (Maple 1962).[8] Magic, the natural philosophy of the Saxons, was also blended with the vestiges of pagan beliefs of classical times. Gardner's twentieth century revival contains the elements of the Wiccan religion: veneration of the old gods and nature; practical knowledge regarding medicine and herbalism; beneficial magic—enchantments for love, healing and divination. It is interesting that the preeminence of women in the role of priestess is revived in Gardner's Wicca.

An Overview of Gardner's Wicca

Gardner gathered a cult of practitioners who celebrated the old agricultural festivals, worshipped pagan gods, sought altered states of consciousness by dancing and other techniques, and raised and released vital energy from their bodies for beneficial magical ends. Gardner's books became the guidebooks for the creation of many witchcraft covens in Great Britain and other European countries as well as in the United States. Gardner was criticized for his efforts to "preserve" and publicize the Old Religion, mostly by those who claimed that they were preserving a different, older, and truer version of the pre-Christian religion. The dissenters generally called themselves "traditionalists" or "hereditary" witches. For the most part they agreed that witchcraft was once a universal religion and they hoped that researchers would one day piece together the fragments of the ancient tradition (Adler 1979).[9]

The Book of Shadows which contains the liturgy of Gardnerian witchcraft with the accompanying grimoire[10] serve as guidebooks for religious practice and magical workings. When I was initiated into the Minoan Sisterhood (a New York coven of witches based on a Gardnerian coven), I was permitted to copy the secret books. Because the initiation included a vow of secrecy, I cannot quote from the secret books.[11] However, I shall rely on them only to clarify or confirm information that is available in the published works of Gardner and other witches, in particular those of three English witches: *The Grimoire of Lady Sheba* by Jesse Wicker Bell (1974), *What Witches Do*, by Stewart Farrar (1983), and several works by Doreen Valiente, who was initiated by Gardner and helped to write many of his rituals.[12]

Gardner was an amateur anthropologist. His book *Keris and Other Malay Weapons* (1936) is evidence of his scholarly, if untrained, interest in the magico-religious culture of nonliterate societies. Gardner took up residence in Borneo in 1908 and came to know the Dyaks, whose tribal seances reminded him of those of the English spiritualists, and whose weapons—particularly the deadly blowpipes—fascinated him (Buckland in Gardner 1954, ii).

By far his most important, if controversial, work concerns what he believed was the surviving Wiccan religion in Great Britain. After gaining the permission of the coven into which he was initiated to write about the secret cult of Wicca, he lectured extensively on the survival of the witch religion and persuaded the English Ethnographical Society to recognize the witch faith under the title of "Contemporary Witchcraft in Britain, and the Survivals of Celtic Cults" (Buckland in Gardner 1954, v).

Gardner was greatly influenced by Margaret Murray's writings on the misunderstood horned god and the pagan cults of Europe.[13] In the preface that Murray wrote for Gardner's *Witchcraft Today* she compared Gardner's witchcraft to the "processional dances of the drunken Bacchantes," the "jumping dance" of the medieval witches, "the solemn zikr of Egyptian peasants, the whirling of the dervishes" (Gardner 1954, 16). In this, Murray is right on track: ecstatic dancing along with other techniques for raising energy are the heart of the magical practice in Gardner's witchcraft.

Legends of Wicca

Gardner believed, as Murray did, that the core elements of the Old Religion have been preserved from the Stone Age. Gardner (1954) and Murray (1933) use the term Wicca—which we first encounter in the documents of the ninth and tenth century referred to above—to describe the much older religion of the pre-Celtic aborigines who built the megalithic circles. There is no way of knowing if the word Wicca was used to refer to any such religion before it was written in the ninth century.

The neolithic peoples added agriculture to the older economies of fishing and hunting when they arrived in England. The religion would have combined veneration of the hunted animals along with the newer preeminence of the life-giving earth goddess and concern with the cycles of the sun and moon. These features are present in the German heathenism that the church fathers condemned under the name of Wicca as well as present-day Wicca. Still, it is hardly reasonable to suppose—as Murray and Gardner did—that even the "core elements" of any religion could be preserved intact from the Stone Age with the same name, Wicca. More probably the pre-Christian Old Religion was a collection of beliefs and practices deriving from the neolithic peoples, older indigenous ones combined with those of the Celts, Saxons and others who brought their culture to England. This multi-layered religion, which certainly sustained many transformations over time, is Gardner's Wicca.

It consists fundamentally of animistic nature worship, Gardner wrote, along with the reverence of two primary deities, the mother goddess and horned god. There is also a hierarchy of lesser spirits and a tradition of raising and releasing power from the witches' bodies with ecstatic dancing and other techniques (Gardner 1954).

Witches, according to Gardner, are people who have an inherent power in their bodies that they can release in various ways, the simplest being dancing around in a circle in groups, singing or shouting, to induce a frenzy. The power or energy that is released can be directed by the minds of the witches to effect magical intentions. The dancing and other techniques also produce a trance state, *extasis*, a Spanish word meaning "taking one out of oneself . . . into communion with the gods" (Gardner 1959, 151). Gardner used extasis to describe the ecstasy that is the defining characteristic of shamanism (Eliade 1964).

There have been witches in all ages and countries, Gardner wrote. He defined these witches as all-purpose magicians working to accomplish the practical needs of their communities with the aid of prominent ancestors (significant supernaturals whose status is just below that of deities) whom they call "the little gods" (Gardner 1954, 31).

After the Christians condemned the paganism of the Saxons—the most politically dangerous form of it—any other expressions of the Old Religion would have been driven along with it to out-of-the-way communities or to the Celtic fringes of Wales, Cornwall, and Brittany.

Gardner called the early Wiccans "the small people." The neolithic invaders were, in fact, small in stature, seldom more than five feet six inches tall (Atkinson 1979). Gardner theorized that after a few generations of scanty food, this small race probably intermarried with the Picts and "Pygmy tribes" and became even smaller in stature. Thus they came to be called "the little people" (1954).

These little people, also included fairies. For Gardner fairies were more than merely mythical. They had a natural aptitude for raising and releasing energy from their bodies and for achieving ecstatic visionary states. Their goddess was identified with Diana and Aphrodite. Some, though not all, of the small people were fairies, most of whom were exterminated by the Norman conquerors, although a few survived on the heaths as "heathens." In the obscurity of the wild heaths, the little people kept their magico-religion alive and gradually incorporated some Normans (1954).

Eventually, Gardner says, the Normans intermarried with the few remaining fairies and took over some of the priestly functions. The "hypernormal control of the body by simple auto-intoxication" did not come as naturally to the Normans as it did for their fairy ancestors. They had to condition their bodies with long arduous spiritual discipline and learn shortcuts to sublimate the body and isolate the spirit. These techniques constitute "the craft" of magic and the secrets of the cult (1954, 38).

Before the witch persecutions, when such large gatherings would have been dangerous, many covens would come together and hundreds of wild dancers shrieked wildly to raise and release power and to achieve the hyperaesthetic state. Later, the cult was kept alive in secret as family traditions. Gardner speculated that to prevent extinction of their lore, the Wiccans began to preserve in written records what had been conveyed in the rites (1954).

Gardner believed the cult was able to preserve its identity and teachings through the process of initiation. Initiates were informed, moved, and impressed by experiences that involve all of the senses, as they are presently in revived Wicca. Ineffable ideas are once again vividly portrayed in ritual dramas, music, and presentation of powerfully moving symbols. "It is not merely the religious legend which is preserved," Gardner wrote (1954, 38), "but also the rite, the conditioning and the effect that it produces. The religion may change, the race may change, the language may change, but the effect [of the rituals on the body] remains, and it is this which tends to keep the legend unchanged" (1954, 38).

The Wiccan Pantheon

As noted earlier, the principal deities of the witches are the mother goddess and the horned god, whose many secret names (derived from Greco-Roman, Celtic, and Northern European mythology, and other sources)—I was taught—should never be written and should be spoken only in sacred space. The little gods, referred to as the "mighty ones" or the "mighty dead," are prominent ancestors that resemble demigods or saints. As ancestors, the fairies would number among the "mighty ones" (Gardner 1954), but the butterfly-like creatures of folklore would take their places in a descending hierarchy of spirits, including sprites and elementals.

The mother goddess—who is incarnate love and the giver of life—rules the spring, pleasure, feasting, and all delights. She is associated with the moon. Gardner modified his position on the preeminence of the goddess over time. Earlier he wrote that the horned god and the mother goddess enjoyed equal importance (Valiente 1973). The indispensability of the high priestess and the goddess eventually became absolute in Gardner's Wicca. Although the high priestess might assume the part of the high priest, no man could substitute the vital role of the high priestess in cult practice (Adler 1979).

Gardner was probably influenced to make this shift in emphasis to the goddess by his collaborator, Doreen Valiente and by two literary works: Robert Graves' *The White Goddess* (1948) and the part-prose, part-verse, *Aradia, the Gospel of the Witches*, an account of Tuscan witch lore published in 1899 by American folklorist Charles Godfrey Leland.

A woman named Madalena, who claimed descent from an old witch family, permitted Leland to peruse the local witches' book—a mixture of myths and spells—that Leland described as a translation of an earlier Latin work. The myths concern the union of the queen of the witches, Diana (or Tana), with Lucifer, the sun. The daughter of these two deities, Aradia, was to go to Earth as the messiah of witches and teach the arts of witchcraft to oppressed humanity. This, Leland wrote, was the sacred gospel of the Old Religion (*la Vecchia Religione*) that prevailed in those areas in Italy influenced by the culture of the gypsies (Adler 1979).

Gardner agrees with Murray's thesis (1933) that the adoration of the horned god of the hunt survived in some stratum of the population and that he was honored as a great deity. After the Christians named him the devil, Murray implied, the worshippers adopted the Christian name for their god, thus calling him the devil. This was not the case, however, with the living witches with whom Gardner studied and worked (1954).

The mighty ones, or the mighty dead, whose cooperation the witches invoke to effect their practical magic, are by no means all-powerful, Gardner reported. They are uniformly benevolent toward humans, but the relationship is reciprocal, for these gods require the help of humans. The rites are celebratory because the witches believe that what gives pleasure to humans also gives joy and power (in the form of vital energy) to the gods, power that they can apply to their own uses as well as to the benefit of humans (Gardner 1984).

Love, Sex, and Death

The central idea or myth of the witches, Gardner (1954, 36) writes, is "The Myth of the Goddess."[14]

> Now G. had never loved, but she would solve all mysteries, even the mystery of Death, and so she journeyed to the nether lands. The guardians of the portals challenged her. "Strip off thy garments, lay aside thy jewels, for nought may ye bring with you into this our land." So she laid down her garments and her jewels and was bound as are all who enter the realms of Death, the mighty one.
> Such was her beauty that Death himself knelt and kissed her feet, saying: "Blessed be thy feet that have brought thee in these ways. Abide with me, but let me place my cold hand on thy heart." And she replied: "I love thee not. Why doest thou cause all things that I love and take delight in to fade and die?" "Lady," replied Death, "'tis age and fate, against which I am helpless. Age causes all things to wither; but when men die at the end of time, I give them rest and peace and strength so that they may return. But you, you are lovely. Return not; abide with me." But she answered: "I love thee not." Then said Death: "As you receive not my hand on your heart, you must receive Death's scourge." "It is fate, better so," she said, and she knelt. Death scourged her and she cried: "I know the pangs of love." And Death said: "Blessed be," and gave her the fivefold kiss,[15] saying "Thus only may you attain to joy and knowledge."
> And he taught her all the mysteries, and they loved and were one; and he taught her all the magics. "For there are three great events in the life of man—love, death and resurrection in the new body— and magic controls them all. To fulfill love you must return again at the same time and place as the loved one, and you must remember and love her or him again. But to be reborn you must die and be ready for a new body; to die you must be born; without love you may not be born, and this is all the magic."

The descent of the goddess to the underworld is clearly derived from the mystery religion that developed and flourished in the Graeco-Roman world in the third century before the common era (B.C.E.). These closed societies with initiatory rites, secret proceedings, and revelations appealed to the many people who were seeking spiritual enlightenment. The deities varied—Isis and Osiris in Egypt; Demeter and Persephone in Greece; Ishtar and Tammuz in Babylon; and Inanna and Damuzi in Sumeria—but they shared the death and rebirth theme based on myth cycles of the gods and goddesses of fertility and vegetation that gave agricultural peoples hope for survival after death. When these pagan themes reached the stage of philosophical (allegorical) interpretation, the confrontation with death became the model of spiritual rebirth for initiates of the mystery cults who sought to become like the gods, or to become one with them.

Gardner's myth of the goddess' descent especially resembles the descent of the Sumerian Inanna, who also was stripped naked to enter the underworld, and that undertaken by the Greek Persephone. The unusual ending—she remains in the underworld rather than returning—is a major deviation that may be due to Celtic influence. The Celtic otherworlds—the "land of youth" or "field of happiness,"—were places of supreme bliss, a land of magic, ruled over by dispossessed gods and inhabited by other supernatural beings (Corcoran 1984). It is understandable that a goddess would want to remain in such a place. A still more likely source for much of this myth is the Hermetic literature[16] that was important in Renaissance philosophy, a subject to which we will return in other chapters.

The mythology of witchcraft revolved around a concern with the afterlife, Gardner writes. This seems to involve an unending series of reincarnations, but it is Gardner's impression that witches believe that in time it is possible to become one of the "mighty ones."

The afterlife may be pleasant or unpleasant according to one's nature, but the god has a special place for those among his worshippers who have mastered "the craft," that is, conditioned their bodies and natures on Earth. The worthy dead could hope for a period of rest and refreshment in a sort of paradise called "summerland" among the mighty ones and the horned god, who is referred to in his death aspect as "the comforter and consoler" (Gardner 1959, 40).

The Old Religion contains a significant paradox: although it is earthy and celebratory, the ultimate boon of life-eternal among the mighty ones in summerland is reserved for those who progress through many births by learning, and learning entails the suffering, or hard work, of mastering the craft. Symbolizing this paradox is the witches' tool, the scourge (made of soft silk cords). Ritual flagellation with the scourge symbolizes both love and death and the tenet: "You must be willing to suffer to learn." Suffering in this sense means commitment to the long and arduous labor of spiritual growth, not the veneration of suffering as a worthy end in itself.[17]

The challenge of suffering is most clearly expressed in the mythology surrounding shamanism, which we will discuss in detail later. The idea that power, wisdom, novel insights—even a new self—may reward a well-managed crisis comparable to the breaking apart that shamans must survive to acquire their powers, is a major inspiration to present-day American witches.

Magic

The basic aim of the magical work in Gardnerian covens is the spiritual development of the individual witch through study and discipline— such as meditation—in order to refine the faculties of intuition, imagination, and will. Practical magic or spells are intended to benefit either the witch or his or her physical and social environments. Spiritual maturity *qualifies* the witch to perform sorcery. Although recipes for spells are readily available, experienced witches believe that it is immoral and dangerous to attempt to do magic before acquiring the spiritual refinement that provides some assurance that no harm will be done by it.

Eight ritual tools are significant in the work of spiritual evolution and craft (practical magic)—these being considered two sides of the same coin. The tools are revealed and their significances and uses explained to each new initiate.

Three of the tools are blades: a long sword, a black-handled dagger (athame), and a white-handled carving knife, (*boline*). The first two are used to draw symbols in the air, especially the circle that designates sacred space. It is also possible to "subdue rebellious spirits" with symbols drawn with blades. (I interpret this to mean—in a psychological sense—the removal of resistance to creativity.) The boline is used in the practical arts of sorcery for carving candles, cutting string or fabric, or harvesting herbs. The pentacle is a flat metal disc inscribed with symbols used to communicate with supernaturals. The censer for incense is used to encourage good spirits and banish evil ones. The scourge is a sign of power and domination—and, as mentioned above, a symbol of the axiom, "you must suffer to learn." The cords are used to bind spells with knots, to take measurements, and to restrict circulation of the blood to induce a trance state. The wooden wand is used to focus and direct the will (Farrar 1983; Bell 1974).

The Conduct of a Gardnerian Coven

Not only did Gardner publish books about witchcraft, he also became a master of the craft and claimed to have earned the right to initiate others into the mysteries and to reveal the secret lore and books to them. In this way, the craft is preserved and transmitted to individuals selected for their presumed inherent talents for psychic and craft work.

Gardner initiated many women and men into the craft, taught them to raise and release energy from their bodies, exposed them to the ritual dramas, revealed the secret lore and symbols (both oral and written), and gave them the opportunity to use the ritual tools. The cult secrets unfold in personal experiences that the initiate can transmit to others only by creating the identical conditions that would later enable another to have a similar experience. The craft is transmitted in these two ways: access to secret books, and personal experience with mind- and body-altering ritual acts.

Gardnerian covens generally meet once each month on the full moon (Esbat) and celebrate eight Sabbaths, or festivals, each year. Four of the eight Sabbath festivals mark the key points of the annual cycle of the planting and herd-raising year; the other four are the astronomical occasions: the solstices and equinoxes. The Christians established their religious holidays on or near these potent turning points in the pagan year. For example, All Saints' Day replaced Sawain, when the dead and the end of the harvest are mourned; the Christian purification of the Virgin falls on the pagan mid-winter torch festival, when the mother goddess' recovery from the birth of the sun god is celebrated; the Annunciation is celebrated near Beltane, when the pagans impregnate the Earth with their may poles and dance to awaken spring. Christmas falls close to the pagan Yule on the winter solstice. Often several covens come together on these occasions to celebrate elaborate rituals from the Book of Shadows and to feast.

Covens are ideally comprised of thirteen members: six male and female couples and a leader, who is generally the high priestess. They meet and worship naked in a consecrated circle nine feet in diameter. The reason for ritual nudity, Valiente (1978) writes—confirming and embellishing Gardner's own explanation—is related to the belief in the energy fields surrounding humans and animals: clothing interferes with the generation and discharge of that energy.

Witches pass through three levels of initiation to achieve the right to lead ceremonies and to start a new coven and initiate others into the craft. The narrative and actions of the rituals are highly structured. Ideally, they are recited and performed from memory; more often, they are read from the Book of Shadows. Two interesting rituals characterize Gardnerian ceremonies: "drawing down the moon"—in which the high priestess invites possession by the moon, or the goddess, (who embodies the qualities of the moon), and the "great rite," a sacred sexual union. A fuller discussion of these rituals will appear in later chapters.

The Ingredients of Gardner's Wicca

Gardner's Wicca is a collage, although he would have us believe that present-day Wicca is a survival of Stone Age cult practices of the aboriginal fairy race combined with traditions, such as Tantra,[18] imported from the East. After analyzing several revisions of the Book of Shadows, a Neopagan scholar, Aidan Kelly (1991) concluded that Gardner fashioned a new religion based mostly on the writings of Murray and Leland. After reviewing Gardner's Book of Shadows and grimoire, I conclude that his Wicca is the product of eclectic sources.

There is much that seems to be genuine folk culture: herbcraft, charms, rhymed incantations, and pagan lore. However, the Myth of the Goddess, the communal rites of worship and magic, the yearly round of eight Sabbaths, and the concern with survival after death in a communal paradise with the ancestors are clearly derived from agricultural myths and folk customs that might have originated with neolithic peoples, but not the hunting rites of paleolithic peoples. There is evidence of the existence of witches by whom these traditions might have been preserved, no doubt in fragmentary form.

Sybil Leek claimed to have joined one of four covens in the New Forest area in England that traces its history to the Middle Ages (Melton 1982). Such a claim would be difficult to verify, but Doreen Valiente documents the existence of a set of covens that were headed by the witch, George Pickingill, in the late 1800s.

One of these was Old Dorothy's coven into which Gardner was initiated.

Individual white witches[19] and wizards who probably did not belong to covens performed the valuable role of preserving the medical lore of the Saxon leeches and medieval magicians. Eric Maple (1962) provides evidence of another notorious British cunning man, James Murrell, who died in 1860 in the witch country of southeast Essex. In 1748, *Gentleman's Magazine* reported on a white witch, Bridget Bostock, who had a following of hundreds of clients. Her cures (with spittle and handstroking) so effectively lured patients from orthodox medicine that physicians hated her very name.

During the first world war there was a slight revival of witchcraft and magic and a reemergence of cunning men, who were often gypsies. In times of war, many individuals reverted to the old faith in the power of charms and talismans. The North of England, in particular the Vale of Pickering in Yorkshire, is the most renowned legendary land of witches. Well into the 1930s white witches openly sold love charms and magic medicines. A white witch from Lancashire named Nutter dispensed simples and prescribed magical cures in Victorian times (Maple 1962).

The west country, particularly Devon and Cornwall, preserved the legends and myths of pre-Christian England the longest. A cunning woman practiced in Bristol as recently as 1930. Another white witch of West Kent continued to do herbal cures and weather magic in 1962 (Maple 1962).

There is also much in the grimoire and even more in the Book of Shadows, wherein lore, philosophy and liturgy are contained, that indicates the strong influence of the occult philosophies of Neoplatonism and other intellectual, esoteric traditions that we will explore in chapter six. It is not surprising that many people criticized Gardner for inventing—synthesizing is a better word—his witchcraft rather than preserving a Stone Age religion.

Gardner's Wicca, a Nativistic Cult?

When present-day Westerners resort to pagan beliefs and rites in times of crisis,[20] we are reminded of the efforts of members of nonindustrialized societies to resist the impact of European culture, "nativistic movements," as they are described by Ralph Linton (1943). These movements involve efforts to restore an endangered society by reviving or perpetuating religious or magical traditions that embody the central values of a culture. The Plains Indians revived the Ghost Dance in the 1890s, for example (Kehoe 1936), and in this century Melanesians devised "cargo cults" to reinstate indigenous concepts of status and power (Cochrane 1970; Worsely 1968).

The revival of Wicca that became a broader revivification of paganism in the United States resembles these movements only in a limited sense. To put it differently, my experiences with Wicca suggest that efforts at cultural innovation or revitalization of this sort operate differently in present-day Western society.

While Lady Boadicea and the other witches who attempted to keep Hitler out of England with their rituals evidently believed that such an approach held more promise than that of the prevailing religion, they intended only to rescue the culture of England, not to revitalize it. The British witches changed their own behavior; they intended to change the outcome of a specific problem, not the beliefs or the behavior of others in their society. As we shall see, Gardner's Wicca provided the basis for a movement in the United States that more clearly attempts culture change.

Revitalization movements such as Wallace (1954) described are characteristically abrupt responses to crises or stress rather than a chain-reaction or gradual drift of the continually changing social order described by Firth (1954) and Leach (1967). Although Lady Boadicea and her covens of witches were responding to a crisis that threatened the homeostasis of their society, it is likely that these covens existed before the crisis and were not a reaction to it.

As is true of nativistic movements, the witches tried to eliminate an alien people and culture (Hitler's army) from their own (Kehoe 1936) by reviving customs, values, and aspects of nature from the past (Mooney 1896). Like revitalization movements (Wallace 1954), the Wiccan revival was initiated by a single individual. Gardner influenced a large number of people in England and the United States within a few years, and the Wiccan revival has grown and continues to grow at an amazing rate.

Gardner as a Prophet
of a Revitalization Movement

Gardner's Wicca is a resort to an older religion by individuals who are hoping to create a more satisfying approach to a crisis. The belief that humans are able to work magic collectively in small groups offers hope and provides the satisfaction of engaging in some purposeful effort to remedy troublesome situations. The myth of the goddess' descent must have provided hope for immortality and reunion with loved ones, should death come to them after all. World war II served as "suffering" to be overcome by "learning" by Lady Boadicea and other Neopagans. They gained spiritual maturity and took some action to transform a problem (raising energy to keep England safe from the advance of Hitler's troops). The goddess' promise, which is stated in "the charge" that Gardnerian priestesses recite in ritual (derived from Leland's story of the goddess), states that she will teach all the arts of sorcery so that those who seek her may be free of slavery.

Wallace (1954) writes that with few exceptions religious revitalization movements are conceived in hallucinatory visions by an individual who then feels a sense of messianic obligation to tell others of his or her experience. He or she becomes a prophet, preaching the revelation, enlisting disciples, and enlightening converts. Gardner's inspiration to preserve the Old Religion came during his initiation by Dorothy Clutterbuck, according to Bracelin. "When the word 'Wicca' was first mentioned . . . then I knew that which I had thought burnt out hundreds of years ago still survived" (1960, 165 cited in Adler 1979, 61). Following the repeal of the law against witchcraft, Gardner decided that the time was right to publicize the religion into which he was initiated (Valiente 1973). No supernatural being appeared to explain the society's troubled condition and to provide a utopian solution.

While Gardner enthusiastically preserved the cult, he was selective about those he initiated into it. His Wicca was, after all, a secret society—not a religion of converts. We may conclude that Gardner was not a prophet in the sense that originators of revitalization movements are.

Wicca, the Carrier
of the Western Occult Tradition

Although superficially a revival of folk magic, contemporary witchcraft is the most recent expression of the Western occult tradition that has its roots in Egyptian religion and the earliest science of Sumer: astronomy, geometry, and mathematics. The combination of Sumerian science and Egyptian religion serves equally well as a worldview supporting folk magic and intellectual magic. I believe it can best be described as a tradition whose purposes are to foster, guide, and contain the creative process within a moral framework.

The promotion of creativity on the part of individual magicians, and the fear of that creativity, revolve around the same issue: "Who shall have the right to create, revitalize, or introduce change?" During the witch hunts, the persecutors of the legendary female witch—the culture-heroine of present-day witchcraft—accused her of possessing and using power that belonged rightly only to the Christian God. Her creativity was unauthorized.

Present-day witches identify most strongly with this aspect of the historical witch: her or his daring to persist in self-sufficiency where the individual's authority is being eroded, even when that self-sufficiency is deemed superstitious by more powerful representatives of another worldview. In the historical witch, today's witches see an example of an extinct tradition of authority over one's own life arising from the influence of personality.

The historical witch is the prototypical victim of an advancing civilization that diminishes personal autonomy in favor of reliance on socially endorsed authorities. The folk traditions that were instruments of self-sufficiency were discredited as superstition and rendered illegal and heretical in the witch craze. Reliance on and deference to professional services of the state-endorsed religious and medical professionals became mandatory. The historical witch is the symbol of the courageous, skilled individual stripped of authority and credibility (except within a limited parochial sphere) by an encroaching bureaucracy.

Gardner's Wicca needs to be viewed as part of a long tradition of personal and cultural self-sufficiency. The Western occult tradition fosters spiritual maturity and creativity in those who are empowered by it to attempt cultural innovation. For major episodes in Western history, the resources of the occult tradition have been suppressed and hidden. Revived Wicca is evidence of its reemergence.

Chapter Three

Wicca, a Way of Working

Many witches say witchcraft is "a way of working" with the flexible nature of the world. Although it is etymologically incorrect, many of them believe that the word "witch" is derived from *weik*, meaning willow. Nonetheless, the witches make the word the basis for an apt metaphor: the craft is one of bending and shaping reality like a flexible branch of willow. Like the early Wiccans, present-day witches try to effect enchantments and healings by the use of a technology (magic) that is founded in the premises of nature religion.

The Book of Shadows prescribes a ritual for creating sacred space, "a fit abode for the gods to enter in"; however, I have seen that there is an unstated purpose: creation of a sacred *work space*. In fact, the basic ritual serves as template for the creative process, as we shall see in my interpretation of the Minoan Sisterhood's Yule celebration in which I participated on the winter solstice of 1986, about two months after I had been initiated into the first of three "degrees," or levels of expertise.

The Minoan Sisterhood

The Minoan Sisterhood is one of a cluster of covens that practice various modifications of Gardner's Wicca. All of the covens were descended from one that was formed by individuals—whose identities I prefer not to disclose—who brought Gardner's Wicca to America after being initiated in England by one of Gardner's high priestesses.

Carol Bulzone, the high priestess who initiated me, and a young man named Ed Buczynski organized two covens, the Minoan Sisterhood and Brotherhood, that deviated somewhat from Gardner's Wicca.[1] Carol and Eddie wanted to create a coven exclusively for female witches, and another exclusively for males. They believe that the male/female polarity exists in every individual and can be activated in rituals performed in covens consisting of members who are all of the same gender. Thirteen-member-covens are ideal, but the Minoan covens and most others in America operate effectively with fewer members. Although the Minoan Sisterhood coven was created for lesbian women, all but two or three of the eleven members were heterosexual at the time I was an active member. Creativity was a common thread in the lives of these women. Three of the members are actresses, three are dancers, one is a photographer, another is an artist's model. I never learned the occupations of two of the women. As we will see later, my artworks served as proof of my aptitude for the craft of witchcraft. Largely because of that, I was accepted in the role of anthropologist.

The exclusive female membership necessitates modifications of Gardner's two rituals, drawing down the moon and the great rite, a ceremonial *hieros gamos*[2], that I shall presently describe. There are various other ways in which the Minoan Sisterhood differs from Gardner's witchcraft. The Sisterhood has its own Book of Shadows that deviates from Gardner's in its reliance on a myth motif derived from Crete (Gardner's is eclectic, as we have seen). After I was initiated, I was given two Books of Shadows, one supposedly a copy of copies of Gardner's original, the other a copy of the one created by Carol and Eddie for the Minoan Sisterhood and Brotherhood.

Yule Celebration in a Minoan-Gardnerian Coven

On the evening of the solstice in the winter of 1986, the Minoan Sisterhood gathered in the back room of the occult supply store, Enchantments, in the East Village in New York City to celebrate Yule. This was one of the rare occasions when a male witch was present at a meeting of the sisterhood. The young man, whom I shall call Raven to protect his true identity, was invited to represent the sun god whose rebirth is celebrated at Yule.

As soon as the last customer left the shop and the iron gates were pulled closed and locked, the preparations for the ceremony began. The witches emptied the back room of its few pieces of furniture. Lexa, the kore[3] of the coven—second in command to the high priestess—mopped the floor with a cinnamon-scented concoction called "Yule" that was created according to a recipe in the grimoire. With this humble "purification," the coven members transformed a tiny room that ordinarily served as an office and consultation room for psychic readings into a temple.

The coven members built an altar in the center of the floor out of several crates of merchandise covered with a satin cloth. Magical implements, including an iron caldron and all of the tools of the craft mentioned in chapter two, were arranged on the altar. A wooden wheel, with eight spokes—one for each sabbath—represented the turning wheel of the year. It was placed among the usual altar furnishings that include small statues of the goddess and the god.[4]

On this occasion the image of the god was wrapped in a black cloth to symbolize his invisibility following the sacrifice or harvest that had been reenacted on the autumnal equinox. Candles were lit in each cardinal direction to mark the boundaries of a circle, nine feet in diameter, within which the ceremony would take place.

Generally the witches prepare themselves to enter sacred space by bathing in salt-water. In the shop the witches made do with a symbolic purification of anointing each of their pulse points with the musky "Minoan" oil. Most, but not all of the witches, removed their clothing. Many of them sang along with recorded music while they made their preparations and drifted into place in the circle around the altar. Then silence.

Creating Sacred Space

Everyone stood around the altar at the center of the circle when the high priestess took her athame between her palms to begin to create and consecrate a sacred space. Making magical signs with the athame and speaking blessings, the high priestess purified and blessed the substances on the altar representing the four "elements": salt for earth; incense for air; candle flame for fire; and water. Taking up the long sword from the altar she "cast," or drew, a circle approximately nine feet in diameter, and inside of it she placed a candle at the four cardinal directions, pointing the sword down while walking clockwise (*deosil*) around the circumference of the circle. All movement in the circle must be clockwise to be in harmony with the sun's apparent path. Deosil motion creates; anti-clockwise (*widdershins*) movement is used to banish or destroy.

After drawing the circle, the priestess purified and reinforced the circle with each of the elements by walking its perimeter four times: once with the candle, then sprinkling salt, then water, and finally creating a trail of incense smoke. As she distributed the elements, Carol "consecrated" the circle. She forcefully declared, while visualizing, that the circle she had drawn would serve as a boundary and as a container for the energy that the witches would raise and release from their bodies to imbue their magic with power.[5]

This operation is called the creation and consecration of the circle.

The sacred space is more accurately conceived of as a completely enclosed sphere; the circle merely marks the place where it intersects the ground.

The circle is said to exist "between the worlds," that is, between the world of humans and that of the gods, and between the realms of form and idea. It marks a boundary, or *limen*, between structures of time and space, between ordinary reality and the sacred time (infinity). The sacred space serves as both a work space for magic and a temple for worship and symbolizes the relationship between microcosm and macrocosm that merge inside the circle.

In a ceremony deriving from alchemy, the existing form of matter was reduced to the elements air, fire, water and earth (solid matter). In the course of the ritual, these raw materials of earthly existence would be reassembled in a new form, according to the design of the witches. Between the worlds, form is thought to be fluid and susceptible to refashioning when new relationships among its fundamental building blocks, the four elements, are established.

Humans also constitute a synthesis of the four elements. The more balanced the synthesis, the more highly developed the individual. Reaching such a balance is an important goal of the "work" of witchcraft. The most significant product of the craft is the physical, mental and spiritual self.

The creation of the circle serves as a psychological cue that informs the witches that a former state of being has been broken apart; the world of ideas and matter awaits restructuring by the witches' magic.

Invocation of Divinities and Elementals

After the sacred work space was prepared, the high priestess called out to the "guardians of the watchtowers" of the four directions, the "mighty ones," and the "lords" of the spirits of the elements (elementals) to alert them that magic was to be worked and invite them to protect the space and witness the rite.

"Elementals," generally thought by the witches to be invisible spirits of the elements, take their place at the low end of the Wiccan hierarchy of sentient entities believed to populate the supernatural universe. The elementals animate fundamental categories of existence: salamanders/fire, ondines/water, sylphs/air, and gnomes/earth.[6] Each of these is associated with a cardinal direction: air with the east; fire with the south; water with the west; earth with the north.

The ultimate manifestation of divinity is generally conceptualized by the Neopagans as the life force or energy that permeates and sustains the universe. As it manifests itself through matter, this divine force

Selena Fox invoking the spirits of the cardinal directions. She is wearing a ceremonial vestment made by the author.

polarizes as the opposites represented by the masculine and feminine principles symbolized by the goddess and god.

Each attribute of divinity is symbolized as an archetypal image of gods, or spirits, clothed in mythic form and reflecting spiritual reality. Each conveys to the worshipper that aspect of divinity that she or he is trying to access during a particular religious ritual, magical working, or mystical experience: Venus for love, perhaps, or Mercury for ease of communication.

The elemental forces of the natural world, although symbolized as creatures of the "Land of Faerie"[7]—sylphs, salamanders, ondines, and gnomes—are also imagined as psychic potentials: air as intellect; fire representing passion; waters, the emotions; and Earth, solid physical matter. In a theological sense, they represent a four-part subdivision of the cosmos.

When the witches invoke the divinities and elementals they ask for the permission, approval, and assistance of the universe and the spiritual beings inhabiting—or symbolizing—it. The "threefold law" expresses the awareness of adverse repercussions of creating badly: whatever one puts out into the universe is believed to return three-fold in kind to the creator. Magic, like art, is successful to the extent that it expresses something greater or more universal than the individual artist. The witches attempt to ensure that their creations will be beneficial not only for themselves in their limited sphere of existence but in the broadest possible sense for the universe—all time and space—within which they locate themselves as eternal beings.

Raising Energy

Next, the witches "raised" energy from their bodies to fill the circle by dancing and chanting the names of the goddess of the Earth and the dying and resurrecting god: "Isis, Astarte, Diana, Hecate . . . Pan, Woden, Baphomet, Osiris . . . ," after which—flushed and slightly breathless—everyone sat around the altar.

Energy is, to the witches, a valuable resource, a concrete substance that can be molded, directed, and projected over long distances. Human vitality—which the witches possess and the gods, mighty ones, and spirits do not—is the force of life that witches see as moving and changing the physical as well as emotional contours of reality.

Generally the next part of the ritual is the "drawing down of the moon," in which the priest draws the essence of the goddess and/or the moon into the high priestess to induce a mild possession state.

Drawing Down

As I have come to understand it, the drawing down ceremony bridges the gap between form (human) and idea (divinity); it is an invitation for inspiration. The witches assume the role of Demiurge in their rituals. They strive to "be as the gods" so that they can assume the prerogative of the gods: creation. Like artists seeking inspiration from the "muses," witches "draw down" divine inspiration from their gods, and like artists, they offer their bodies as vehicles of expression for these sacred influences. In other words, the witch as creator attempts to transcend the individual ego in order to express a sacred or more universal force.

The yielding of an artist, priestess, or priest to such an inspiration resembles collaboration more than the submission of a worshipper to the care of a protecting deity. The celebrant *invites* the influence of divine force. No matter how compelling the vision, one who has mastered the craft remains in control. In this reciprocal relationship the human may—or may not—give voice or substance to the inspiration, and in that way, serve the deity.

In the Minoan Sisterhood, the high priestess generally "draws down" the mother goddess and the supernatural powers associated with the moon into the kore. But this evening the sun god's rebirth was being accomplished, and his influence would be drawn down. She oriented the coveners by retelling the story: At this point on the turning wheel of the year, the great goddess, queen of the moon and Earth and sea, gives birth to the golden-haired son who illuminates the world. The son/sun will increase in strength and influence—the cause of joy and celebration—until his manhood and the sun's peak of influence is reached on the midsummer solstice.

The coveners are thus reminded of their religious beliefs and the supernaturals are honored by this recitation from the Book of Shadows:

> Queen of the Moon, Queen of the Sun
> Queen of the Heavens, Queen of the Stars,
> Queen of the Waters, Queen of the Earth,
> Bring to us the Child of Promise!
> It is the Great Mother who giveth birth to Him;
> It is the Lord of Life who is born again;
> Darkness and tears are set aside when the Sun shall come up early.
> Golden sun of the mountains, illuminate the land,
> Light up the world, illumine the seas and the rivers;
> Sorrows be laid aside, joy to the world!
> Blessed be the Great Goddess, without beginning,
> Without end,
> Everlasting to eternity, Io Evo He! Blessed be! (Farrar 1983, 91)

Following this act of worship, magic (a transformation) was attempted. The spirit of the male divine force was brought into the presence of the coven members through the body of the priest. Raven prepared himself to receive it by assuming the prescribed Egyptian "god position"; he crossed his arms over his chest with ritual tools in each hand. The high priestess touched Raven with a wooden wand. Raven's body relaxed, he uncrossed his arms and held them out to each side with elbows slightly bent. He entered a trance and began to speak.

There was a cryptic message (that required research in a book of Egyptian mythology later in the evening) and a prediction of abundance and peace. With a ritual gesture the high priestess woke him from his trance, and the coven "scribe" read to him the words he had spoken—or, according to theory, the god had spoken through him.

To acknowledge that the sun/son god was reborn, Carol removed the silk shroud that covered the image of the god that rested on the altar.

More generally when the moon is drawn down into the high priestess, she delivers a free-form "inspiration" as Raven did. As an alternative she may recite the "Charge of the Goddess," a statement of the goddess' covenant with her people. It includes the promise that the goddess will teach the arts of sorcery so that "ye shall be free from slavery" (Farrar 1983, 172). Freedom from slavery in this passage implied freedom, through magic, to create the conditions of one's own life.

The goddess—who represents eternal life—occupies a position of complementary opposition to the sun god, whose life cycle is one of endless births, deaths, and resurrections. The goddess represents the Earth and the moon; persistence of substance fluctuating through endless cycles of transformation. The yearly birth and death of the god might, I think, be described as analogous to the repeating cycles of respiration that support the eternal life of the goddess of the Earth. Together, they represent the rhythm of life: permanence consisting in a pattern of changes.

This abstract thought is expressed in the concrete symbol of a wooden wheel that spins, as the year does, in unending circles through periods of increase and decrease of light. Each of the eight spokes represents one of the major Sabbaths that mark the most significant turning points of the solar and agricultural seasons. The spinning Yule wheel wordlessly tells the witches that what seems to be darkness and death is merely the gestation of the goddess.

After some speculation on the meaning of Raven's speech, the witches prepared to play a magical game, by spinning the Yule wheel.

The Magical Work, or Play

Generally, "magic is worked"—that is, collective spell-working for some practical purpose—on the new and full moons; while Sabbaths, such as Yule, are reserved for worship, games, and celebration. The spinning Yule wheel is an exception, or combination. Each person developed in her or his mind a clear image of something they wished to accomplish, or help to accomplish, with magic. They carved words or symbols of that wish on a white candle with a boline. Each witch lit and fixed her or his carved candle onto the hub of the Yule with melted wax. When all the candles were positioned, the high priestess set the wheel spinning on the altar. As it spun faster and faster, the candle flames blurred together into a ring of fire, the visible circuit of a vortex of energy.

All the while, each witch concentrated on her or his wish, visualizing it accomplished. The witches generated more vital energy adding it to the vortex, by running and dancing around the altar singing the chant, "Listen to the Lord and Lady, in the Moonlight . . ." The singing speeded up until I could no longer sustain the vision of my wish without jumbling the words of the chant or stumbling over my own feet. The witches continued to laugh and sing while the wheel spun faster and faster, weaving energy into their visualizations. Soon everyone collapsed in laughter.

After a few minutes of rest, the witches rose and danced around the circle to "raise the cone of power" (generate more energy). As the dancers sang and spun around the circle, they visualized energy flowing from their bodies to the center of the circle, where it theoretically spirals upward into a cone. When the high priestess sensed that the group's collective energy had reached its climax, she gave the signal for everyone to release the cone of power. With that image in their minds, and with the force of their wills, the witches projected the cone of power into the world beyond the sacred space of the circle to accomplish the purposes they had visualized and inscribed on the candles. Having released energy from their bodies in loud, howling screams the witches dropped exhausted to the floor.

The Ceremony of Cakes and Wine

In Gardnerian covens the high priest and priestess perform "the great rite," a hieros gamos. In this sacred sexual union opposites are combined—male and female; sky and earth; gods and humans; eternity and periodicity, to name a few—for the purpose of generating energy and a state of grace, the witches say. The great rite is seldom performed in the ritual circle, and on the few occasions that it is done, the coven members generally leave the priestess and priest to enact the rite in private (Farrar 1983).

In the Minoan Sisterhood's Yule celebration, the more common symbolic great rite, "the ceremony of cakes and wine," was enacted: Raven held the chalice filled with homemade wassail. Into this vessel, that represented the receptive womb and the formative forces operative in the universe, Carol plunged the blade of her athame, that represented the phallus and projectile forces. While doing so she spoke of the blessings that result from the conjunction of the male and female polarities. Following that, cakes were blessed by touching them with the moistened dagger. The wine and cakes consecrated in this ritual are shared by coven members and the gods, who receive portions as libations.

As is the case in the alchemists' operations of purification, the witches' ritual divides the world first into four parts or elements that must later be distilled into one pair of opposites. In the great rite, actual or symbolic, the opposing terms of this opposition are conjoined to create a new synthesis, an idea that was expressed particularly clearly by an American witch in this poem:

> Blessed be the darkness, the vast expansion the all encompassing, all surrounding womb of space.
> Blessed be the light, the penetrating point the all focusing, all aligning core of creation.
> Blessed be the blade that divided the darkness from light, thus generating duality, And from duality is all substance formed.
> Blessed be the vessel, wherein the divided may unite.[8]

Several strata of mythic motifs are evident in the great rite. The literal hieros gamos is an obvious example of agricultural rites of sympathetic magic intended to induce fertility of crops and herds. Superimposed on the plant model is that of the hieros gamos practiced in the hieratic city-state.[9] In these societies a priestess who represented the Earth entered into sexual union with a king or his substitute who represented the sky. The sexual conjunction brought together the worlds of gods and humans.

The symbolic great rite, the ceremony of cakes and wine, is also reminiscent of the quest for the Holy Grail. The witches' chalice has associations with the Celtic caldron of rebirth, a distinctly feminine symbol. The dagger serves the witches as a representative of the sword that the knight, Galahad, of King Arthur's Round Table withdrew from a stone in a more recent version of the Myth of the Caldron in which it becomes the Holy Grail filled with Christ's blood. The more universal impulse to bring human society into life-generating harmony with the cosmos is expressed in the ceremony of cakes and wine through the more "local"—in terms of time and space—idea of the Arthurian grail legend.

The great rite, symbolic or actual, is the heart of the creative act. The phallus conjoined with the womb may bring human birth; the intellect—symbolized by the dagger—stirs, carves, and shapes the four elements contained in the chalice, cauldron, or other vessel. All opposites are brought into conjunction. Inspiration of the gods is combined with the will and talent of the craftsperson to give new form to the vital energy raised and released from the witches' bodies. The elements that were torn asunder and scattered in the consecration of the circle are forged into new relationships in the chalice that symbolizes the womb. The great rite or the symbolic ceremony of cakes and wine is the moment of creation, the *magic*.

The Feast

The wassail and cakes that had been consecrated in the ceremony of cakes and wine were passed so that each person might make a libation to the gods and taste the cakes and wine. Offerings were put into the libation bowl, whose contents would later nourish the garden behind the shop.

In the traditional feast of cakes and wine, a multitude of complementary opposites are brought into conjunction: cakes nourish the physical body and wine quickens the spirit. Liquid wine symbolizes the fluidity of energy, the probabilities and possibilities of the future, the—as yet—uncreated world.

Michael Thorne, a Gardnerian high priest, explained the magic of manipulating energy by resorting to the analogy of a lemon cake: it is easier to influence physical manifestation of the future while it is in the process of developing just as it is easier to introduce lemon flavoring into a cake while it is still in the form of batter, rather than after it is already baked.[10] The "batter" in the chalice is whipped with the athame. The wine represents the fluidity of sacred time and space; the more solid cake symbolizes the apparent solidity of physical form and the concrete structure of ordinary reality that is about to be reentered. The celebrants were theoretically transformed by the magic; the world and the self were recreated.

Following the ceremony of cakes and wine, the high priestess gave thanks and said farewell to the spirits, the mighty ones and the guardians of the watchtowers in the four cardinal directions. The threshold of sacred and ordinary time and space was considered dissolved when the high priestess declared that the circle was "opened." The festive mood intensified as the secular feast began in earnest: more food was spread out and gifts were exchanged.

"Magic is hungry work," the witches say. According to neurophysiologist Barbara Lex (1977), rituals (that involve chanting, dancing, and inhalation of incense) stimulate both the sympathetic and parasympathetic autonomic nervous system. During periods of sympathetic activation accompanied by heightened activity, such as ecstatic dancing, circulation is diverted away from the internal organs to the skeletal muscles and the appetite is suppressed. The rebound parasympathetic response is restorative. Circulation is returned to the viscera, and a relaxed mood is accompanied by an increased appetite.

One of the purposes of the feast that concludes all Wiccan ceremonies is "grounding." After the exertion of creativity—physical, mental, and spiritual—the body requires replenishment. Nourishment gives the body weight and substance. After a period of communion with the sacred realm, food reorients awareness to the mundane world. Feasting brings one back "down to earth."

Chapter Four

What Is a Witch?

L exa was asked by a co-worker, "What are you, a witch or some-thing?" Lexa had been reading Tarot cards for a friend. "Yes," she responded. To the next question, "What does that mean, to be a witch?" she offered an answer that is quite the opposite of a description of a "witch" that one would have offered in medieval times: "I am into healing the Earth. And I'm trained in the arts of healing and divination."

Anthropologists have established that the belief in witches' inherent ability to harm others through supernatural means is among the most widespread of all beliefs. Yet, self-proclaimed witches profess themselves innocent of the definitive characteristic of witchcraft.

In this chapter we address this paradox. A common ground is sought where the witch of legend, history, and ethnography bears some resemblance to this novel interpretation of the idea of the witch. We may summarize by describing a witch—from all of these perspectives—as the opposite of the prevalent conceptions of proper or "right" society. From the inside-out perspective of the self-proclaimed witches, the opposite of what a majority or powerful elite in any society regards as right, is not necessarily wrong, evil, or harmful.

Neopaganism

In America, Wicca is overlapped by a slightly broader category of magico-religion: Neopaganism. The revival of beliefs and customs associated with European paganism—including witchcraft—was labelled Neopaganism by Tim (Otter) Zell, one of the earliest formulators of a distinctly American paganism. In the United States, European customs and beliefs blended with broader interests in pagan (non-Judeo-Christian)

41

belief systems including various magico-religious systems, predominantly AmerIndian, but also including Egyptian, Celtic, Norse, Hebrew Cabala, Voodoo, Hawaiian Huna, and, even science fiction.[1]

The quartered circle format of orientation in sacred space provides a universal link among these diverse paganisms. Practitioners of non-Western pagan traditions such as Voodoo, Huna, or AmerIndian who identify themselves as Neopagans are less likely to consider themselves witches, although they readily join in rituals based on Wiccan traditions when they attend gatherings. Some, but not all, practitioners of more purely intellectual Western mysticisms such as Cabala or Hermeticism also consider themselves Neopagans, but they think of themselves as magicians rather than witches.

While I refer interchangeably to the subjects of my study either as witches or Neopagans, the reader should be aware of the distinctions described here. When I use Neopagan I am generally referring to a slightly broader category than witches. Even those who do not identify themselves as witches, however, are involved in a religious movement that takes its language of symbols ultimately from Gardner's revival of European Wicca.

In America, witchcraft and Neopaganism merge into the New Age movement, a movement so heterogenous as to defy clear definition. Broadly speaking, it is comprised of a collection of cultural radicalisms of a mystical sort and takes its name from the idea that a new astrological age is imminent, an age in which "global culture"[2] is expected to be transformed into a more humane and nature-oriented one.

The New Age movement embodies numerous self-help interests and a concern for both planetary and personal health. We will return to the place of the new witchcraft among other cultural radicalisms in other chapters. Most Neopagans distinguish themselves from the New Agers, whom they describe as more materialistic and exploitive of native cultures than themselves. On several occasions I have heard the distinction described in this way: a week-long pagan gathering costs $200, while a New Age workshop given by a white person masquerading as a Native American costs $500. Neopagans are skeptical of mixing spirituality and money exchange, and they resist even more vehemently following teachers or emulating gurus.

Neopagans, however, do share many beliefs with the New Age movement: a concern for mental, physical, and spiritual health in an increasingly hazardous world and a deep concern about the Earth's survival of nuclear and toxic threats. Both groups express these concerns in medical language: personal, social, and global "sickness" that requires "healing." Skepticism regarding institutionalized religion (especially Christianity) and professional medicine, it must be noted, is a shared and prevalent theme.

Universality of Witchcraft Motifs

Harmful magic, including witchcraft, is at least as ancient as the writing that enabled people to record their thoughts about it. Early Mesopotamian cuneiform tablets of Hammurabi's era prescribed remedies for the baleful effects of the evil eye.[3]

In the first known persecution for witchcraft that occurred in Egypt about 1300 B.C.E., a man named Penhaiben was condemned to death for performing harmful sorcery. Penhaiben was alleged to have broken into the royal palace and secured a book of secret and dangerous magic formulae belonging to his master, Rameses III. Mastering their use, he was able to perform all the feats of the "doctors of mysteries." He composed charms that effected all manner of misfortune and torment in the pharaoh's court, and as the report of the tribunal states, "He sought and found the real way to execute off the abomination and all wickedness that the heart conceived, and he performed them, with other great crimes, to the horror of every great god and goddess. Consequently he has endured the great punishment, even unto death, which the divine writings say that he merited."[4]

These early records present two essential features of the Western conception of witchcraft. In the case of the "evil eye," harm is effected with a mere gaze, with no weapon other than an *inherent human power* turned to harmful ends. In the case of Penhaiben, his crime was the *unauthorized* use of magical power.

There is no implication of impropriety about the use of these powers *per se*; had the doctors of the mysteries done precisely what Penhaiben did, there would have been no wrongdoing. The doctors of the mysteries were privileged in the use of the secret formulae. The accused was, in short, a magician without a license. The same prohibition on the *improper* use of magical powers seems to underlie the Exodus edict "Thou shalt not suffer a witch to live" (Exodus 22:18), since the Old Testament is full of instances of proper alliances with spiritual powers for human purposes. Moses produced water from a rock (Exodus 17:6), and Joshua commanded the sun and moon to stand still (Joshua 10:12,13), to mention a few.[5]

During the European witch persecutions many were accused of witchcraft because they were engaging in practice—this time medical— that put them into unlawful competition with the physicians and clergy who took healing to be their exclusive domain.

The collection of traits recognized as defining the witch enjoys global distribution. Witches everywhere, according to Rodney Needham (1979), represent the very opposite of the proper values of the societies in which they live. The acts that the witch is imagined to perpetrate are conceived as the most vile of all possible offenses. Witchcraft is an excellent example of conceptual opposition. The simplest and most efficacious means of classification is to organize concepts into pairs of opposites such as up/down; male/female; good/evil. The witch—who is in all societies aligned with the polarity of evil—is consistently believed to practice cannibalism, commit incest, and otherwise act in a vile and malevolent manner as only the proper-minded (who align themselves with the opposite polarity) might imagine (Needham 1979).

Besides opposition, other characteristics constituting the image of the witch are: inversion, association with darkness and the night, flight and the emission of light as they fly through the sky accompanied by animals, and bringing malign powers into action rapidly and over great distances. The witch's inversion is often more than a metaphor; among the Kagaru of Africa, for example, witches are believed to walk on their hands or backwards (Middleton 1963, in Needham 1979). Inversion, Needham contends, is an elementary mode of marking a contrast or boundary, especially a moral boundary. He offers the interesting fact that the Icelandic word for witch, tunrioa, means a female fence rider (Needham 1979).

The witch image is ubiquitous, Needham explains, because it is one of several "primordial characters." Such "primary collective representations" are spontaneous manifestations of properties of the brain. Their constancy and global distribution suggest that they are the product of genetically inherited predispositions (Needham 1979).

This may be so, but the present-day witches have put this primordial character in a new, transforming light. Many of the terrifying associations of witchcraft are turned to symbols of virtuous power. The self-proclaimed witches feel an affinity with the dark and the night; covens generally meet and celebrate after dark, and magic is generally believed to work better at night. Darkness has acquired the psychological connotations of the unconscious and chaos, the fruitful domain of the artists' imagination. Flight is a prominent symbol of the new craft of Wicca. As Needham indicated, flight is a widely exploited symbol for the transcendent power of the imagination. Witches will say they fly (tongue in cheek), knowing only the hopelessly literal-minded or credulous would imagine that they ride broomsticks.

Witches say they emit light (as, they claim, does everyone else). They acknowledge that the energy fields surrounding all living things are accessible to certain kinds of photography and the refined senses of some individuals who perceive them as light. Witches believe they are more skilled than others at manipulating this energy.

Witches honor the powers and qualities of animals. They shelter some unpopular animals. For instance, Lexa has iguanas and snakes for pets. In trance work, witches often invite possession by animal spirits. Many witches claim to have established special relationships with animals who lend them their powers (courage, cunning, or night vision, for example) and serve as their "familiars," or "guardians." They tend to refer to their pets as familiars (helping spirits). For witches, the animal nature that humans domesticate with culture is the source of magical potency. Furthermore, the new witches agree that they represent the opposite and the inversion of the values of the larger society in which they live, and this they offer as a condemnation of that society. Whether the witches found their heroine the witch in fairy tales, history books, or, as Needham would have it, in the spontaneous manifestations of their own brains, he or she is a complex character who does not yield to facile interpretation.

Anthropology of Witchcraft

Edward Evans-Pritchard provided an anthropological definition of witchcraft when he decided to translate the African Zande word *mangu* with the English word *witchcraft*. He chose to do so despite his comment that "When a Zande speaks of witchcraft he does not speak of it as we speak of the weird witchcraft of our own history" (Evans-Pritchard 1937, 64).

In fact, witchcraft for the Zande was a common, normal factor of life regarded with annoyance, not awe nor terror, while "to us witchcraft is something which haunted and disgusted our credulous forefathers" (1937, 64). Despite this discrepancy, Evans-Pritchard used the English word *witch* to translate *bora (ira) mangu*, meaning a person whose body contains *mangu*, witchcraft-substance, a material discoverable by autopsy.

Mangu has the further connotation of a psychic emanation from witchcraft-substance that is believed to harm health and property by nonphysical means. Witchcraft could be mobilized, "become hot," without the intent or even knowledge of the witch.

In Zandeland, witchcraft is though to be an objective physiological condition: the presence of mangu in the witches' bodies. Yet the qualities attributed to it are mystical. Witches "sail through the air emitting bright light," writes Evans-Pritchard, when they send their souls to do their evil deeds. "Witchcraft is like fire; it lights a light" (1937, 33). Of course, to the rational minded, "Witches, as the Azande conceive of them, cannot exist" (1937, 69). The same could be said of historical European witches. The Azande witches bear other resemblances to their Western counterparts in that "witches are those whose behavior is least in accord with social demand" (1937, 112).

Kluckhohn (1944) found that the witch was the imaginary person whom it is "proper to fear and hate," among the Navahos. Monica Wilson (1952), writing about the Nyakusa of Africa, discussed the witch stereotype as the person one would neither wish to resemble nor offend. In this way, the witch served to reinforce the accepted code of behavior.

Wilson's comparative study of African societies demonstrates the varying relations between witchcraft and social structure. In the kinship-based villages of the Pondo, where incest avoidance is an issue, accusations expressed the tensions between mothers-in-law and daughters-in-law and focused on sexual elements of witchcraft. In the Nyakusa villages—which are organized on the basis of age sets rather than kinship, and where hungry neighbors are a nuisance—accusations were among village neighbors and expressed an obsession with food rather than sex (Wilson 1952). In a similar comparative study, Nadel found that witch accusations were related to tensions caused by gaps in physical and social age within tribes (Nadel 1951).

In ethnographies of the witchcraft of pre-industrial societies it becomes clear that belief in witchcraft is a form of social control: harmonious relationships are promoted through the fear of being bewitched as well as the fear of being accused of witchcraft.

Evolution of the Western Image of the Witch

In industrial societies, including those of early Europe, the concept of harmful magic was regarded as distinct from its counterpart: the idea of beneficial magic—divination and healing. This distinction between harmful and beneficial magic was recognized in Roman law and dominated dealings with those accused of witchcraft in Europe until we see the Wiccans maligned in ninth and tenth century church canons. They were condemned for attempting to be *helpful* by resorting to powers now thought to belong only to the Christian 'god.

Magical practice was officially blended with heresy by the theology faculty at the University of Paris in 1398. The practice of occult arts and pacts with Satan were deemed a denial of faith (Fox 1968). A unique Christian concept of witchcraft was devised in which even beneficial magic, such as healing, was included with destructive magic as a variety of witchcraft that was both harmful and illegal. This Christian idea of witchcraft, then, is specific to advanced society, or "civilization."[6]

The most influential book to inform witch beliefs was the *Malleus Malificarum* (1487–1489) written on the authority of Pope Innocent VIII by the two German inquisitors, Kraemer and Sprenger. The authors provided procedures and criteria for identifying witchcraft and legal forms for examining and sentencing witches. With the aid of the new printing press, this document established the whole system of witch beliefs firmly in the minds of the inquisitors and society in general.

Kraemer and Sprenger presented a theory of a secret society that was in league with the devil to destroy Christian society. In his introduction to the translation of the *Malleus*, Montague Summers (1928) claimed that heretical witches intended to abolish monarchy, private property, marriage, inheritance, order, and all religion. Furthermore, religious groups, including the Waldensians, Albigenses, Henricians, Poor Men of Lyons, Cathari, Vaudois, Bogomiles, Manichees—all of whom suffered persecution for practicing witchcraft—were all part of the same dark fraternity that Summers compared to diverse types of communists in our own era (the opposite of right society). The *Malleus* confirmed most of the characteristics associated with a long tradition of witch theory: witches fly, in the company of their familiars, to orgies where they commit incest. Kraemer and Sprenger linked these notions with the crime of heresy—witchcraft is the most evil of crimes because it is direct treason against God. This use of witchcraft accusations as a political weapon started the process that gathered momentum and became the witch "craze" (Fox 1968; Larner 1984).

Believing himself to have been the target of black magic, James I of England became a scholar of witchcraft and published the book, *Daemonologie* (1603), that became a textbook for officials in England on a par with *Malleus Malificarum* on the continent. James I believed that witches were essentially female versions of the Faust figure. They flew to orgies to celebrate and have sex with the devil, and they entered into pacts with him in which they were granted magical powers (Larner 1984).

On the village level, people continued to worry about *maleficium* (the harm that witches might do), while the church and state officials, to whom they eventually brought complaints, were interested in the act of rebellion that the witch was deemed to have committed in order to have obtained her evil power—an act of apostasy. Individuals who attempted to help and heal their fellows were regarded as criminals as much as those who were accused of evil intent (Thomas 1971).

Eventually the common people were persuaded to adopt the demonologists' version of witchcraft and came to believe their troublesome neighbors were in league with the devil (Kieckhefer 1976). The probable scenario by which this change of mind came about was reconstructed by Christine Larner. Peasants brought their complaints to the courts because that system of repression was more powerful than countersorcery or any other defense against maleficent magic they had at their disposal. In the ecclesiastical and secular courts "lawyer and peasant confronted each other and finally emerged, through accusation, boasting, torture and confession with an agreed story acceptable to both'' (1984, 54).

In the twentieth century in England, Gardner invented another version of witchcraft. Individuals sought the formerly insulting epithet "witch" as a title of honor and power. The distinction between benevolent and harmful magics was redrawn. Maleficent satanic witchcraft contrasted with beneficent Wiccan witchcraft.

In honor of those who were persecuted as witches for practicing benevolent magic, the subjects of this study call themselves witches and speak of their magical work as the "positive path" to differentiate themselves from Satanists. They define their witchcraft as a pre-Christian nature religion and a tradition of beneficial or white magic (the classic combination of divination and healing). Regarding Christians as the villains in the persecution of witches and as destroyers of a former, more "life-oriented" nature religion, they embrace the names of the victims, "witch," "pagan," and "heathen," with pride.

Who Were the Historical Witches?

When Lady Cybele, a contemporary Wisconsin witch, told me that she and her European ancestors had been witches for several generations, I asked "What exactly is a witch?" She replied that a witch is "a person who has a generalized notion of the divinity of nature and techniques of practical magic." Then she offered the example of her Swedish grandfather, who had unusual rapport with nature, at least with bees.[7] He talked to bees and with his naked hand would plunge a tablespoon into a beehive, scoop out the queen, walk around carrying her with the swarm of bees on his unprotected arm, and then, without any harm to himself, put the queen back into the hive with the spoon.

Lady Cybele's grandfather left Sweden because he was haunted by the spirit of a man his father cheated in a business deal, she said. "In his village everyone saw ghosts," she said. "Ghosts were an accepted part of life where he came from in rural Sweden." Following a Swedish folk belief that the way to escape haunting was to cross salt water and change one's name, Lady Cybele's grandfather came to America, changed his name, and became a lumberjack in northern Wisconsin in the 1880s.

I wondered if Lady Cybele thought that the victims of the witch persecutions corresponded with the magicians, healers, and nature worshippers that present-day witches think of as their forebears. "The 'real witches'—what we think of as witches now," she said, "were the people who used the power that comes from within them for 'hands-on,' everyday things such as making the crops grow, making the rain come or go away, and healing.''

Lady Cybele told me she learned her weather magic—for which she is well respected in the witchcraft community—from her northern European grandmother. Others of her ancestors were persecuted as witches and driven off their farms by neighbors who objected to their weather-magic.

Who were the victims of the witch hunts? Were they people like her ancestors who tried to live in harmony with nature and who practiced practical magic? According to the stories that were passed on to Lady Cybele by her grandparents, for the most part the people who were persecuted were simple, elderly women who had no close male relatives to protect them. They were healers and herbalists who lived alone. They were a little eccentric and had a little property. "The main motive was not so much a religious fervor; it was a great way to grab some property. If your neighbors had three cows and you accused them of witchcraft and the charge was sustained, the church or state got two cows and the accuser got one, too. It had to do with preying on helpless people who had a little something—enough to make it worthwhile to go after them but not enough to buy off judges or persecutors.''

The Social History of the European Witch Hunts

With the turning of scholarly interest away from repression of witchcraft toward a better understanding of the social dynamics of witchcraft accusation, some confirmation is available for Lady Cybele's view of who the witches were, and what they believed and tried to do. Historians ask the kinds of questions I asked Lady Cybele: Who were the individuals drawn into the witch hunts—both witches and their accusers—and what might the motivations and dynamics have been? This line of inquiry reflects a social science perspective that has largely been inspired by anthropological studies of witchcraft elsewhere in the world.

Because the witch hunts were far too complex to be explained by a single cause, or, for that matter, by any single approach, scholars began to examine court records and other archives. They were able to produce focused, regional studies that describe the variations in beliefs and behaviors among social classes and regions and chart their change over time. Delcambre (1952) focussed on Lorraine; Macfarlane (1970) on Essex, England; Monter (1971; 1976) on Switzerland and France; Midelfort (1971; 1972) on southwest Germany; Boyer and Nissenbaum (1974) on Salem, Massachusetts; Sebald (1980) on Franconian

Switzerland; Larner (1981) on Scotland; Muchembled (1978) on Flanders and Artois; Demos (1982) on New England; and Hoffman-Krayer (1899) on Lucerne.

From these and other studies emerges the following picture of the witch hunts. In a period when new ruling classes demanded that official ideologies should receive assent from the populace, saving souls became more important than "common justice" (Fox 1968). The local harrying of individuals accused of harmful magic became a crusade against the enemies of the Christian church in the late fifteenth century in Italy and southern Germany. It spread through the continent in the following century, and eventually it came to the American colonies. It remained the most violent in Italy, Germany, and France. In England and the colonies the concern with harmful magic remained more significant than the idea of Satanic pacts, and the persecutions were less severe.

With political, economic, and religious changes increasing tensions in village life, the defenseless tried to defend and avenge themselves by resort to magic as a substitute for impotence and as a remedy for anxiety and despair (Thomas 1979). The decline in the manorial system resulted in poverty for many who were displaced from the land. The trend toward a cash economy and the shift from a neighborly to a commercial ethic caused social tensions to be expressed in witch accusations. The classic example, first described by Notestein in 1911, was confirmed by Macfarlane's research into the Essex county documents. Accusation of witchcraft followed the refusal of charity to the newly pauperized. Uncharitable householders who suspected the rejected beggars of cursing them were able to justify their stinginess by resort to the new Calvinist ethic and by accusing the beggar of witchcraft (1970).

Local tensions were also created by the attacks on the animistic mentality of the partly Christianized peasants (Larner 1981), and by the imposition of urban values on the inhabitants of the countryside (Muchembled 1978). New concepts of sin and personal responsibility for one's salvation created considerable anxiety. When famines and diseases were interpreted as punishment from a just God, responsibility for sin came to be seen to lie with witches (Delumeau 1977).

The scapegoats were not randomly selected; those who had a reputation for performing sorcery—for benevolent as well as malevolent purposes—were prime candidates for witch accusations. The demonologists' teachings that witches who could lift spells could also impose them lent support to peasants' hostilities toward their local healers, cunning folk, or wise men and women. Many quarrels, failed magics, and conflict over fees ripened into accusations (Larner 1984).

In Lucerne the most frequent accusation of witchcraft was against those believed to have the unusual power to predict and cause storms. Many others appear to have been diviners or healers who taught women enchantments to make their husbands love them and stop beating them, and other protective and healing magics (Hoffman-Krayer 1899). In Austria many of the accused were also healers and herbalists (Byloff 1929); likewise in northern Germany (Heberling 1915; Schwartzwälder 1958). Some wise women who fell victims to witch-hunts were also midwives. Throughout those parts of Europe for which adequate evidence is available, a large proportion of the accused were wise women and men, folk-healers, and diviners of peasant society (Horsley 1979a).

It seems that in Europe and New England the vast majority of those persecuted as witches were, in fact, poor, elderly, defenseless women. The economic motivation for the witch hunts, of which Lady Cybele speaks, is also in accord with the historical accounts. Although confiscation of property was not allowed in England, many witch hunters, torturers, and executioners on the continent grew powerful and wealthy, particularly in Germany (Sebald 1978).

Macfarlane's studies showed that the Essex witches were old, poor, and female, just as Lady Cybele conjectured. For the most part, too, they were older and poorer than their accusers. However, true to Lady Cybele's impression, it was usually the moderately poor, not the utterly destitute who were accused (1970).

Witches as Healers, Then and Now

When I asked Lady Cybele what it meant to be a witch now, she responded that a witch is "anyone who has the courage to stand up and call themselves one; anyone who lives in harmony with the Earth and follows the belief that you should harm none—including yourself—could qualify."

In this chapter we have seen that the idea of the witch is the opposite of right society—whatever a particular society might regard "right" to be. The witch in ethnographic literature is generally an exemplar of what one should not be or do. The perversity of which the historical witches in Europe were guilty, it turns out, was persistent self-sufficiency. Like Penhaiben, they were guilty of the unauthorized use of magical power. The victims of the witch persecutions dared to try to heal people, when by rights they should have relied on the professional physicians who gave expert counsel to identify them as witches. The victims of persecutions practiced enchantments to try to remedy practical problems, when they should have sought the expertise of the professionals who tried and condemned them, namely, state authorized law officials or ordained clergymen.

Victims of the European witch hunts would seem unlikely candidates for the position of culture-heroines. Yet many of the Neopagans idealize them, even believe that they are the same people, reborn. Many of the present-day witches claim to "remember" being tortured or burned as a witch in a former life. The idea is expressed in one of their most popular chants:

> We are the old people,
> We are the new people,
> We are the same people,
> Stronger than before.

What draws the sympathies of the self-identified witches so powerfully to the accused witches of other times? I think it is their respect for a source of power—inherent human potential—that the state is hard pressed to regulate or even detect. Attempts to protect pre-modern society from this invisible threat resulted in one of the most shameful episodes of Western history—the witch hunts. Identifying the legendary victims of these persecutions as culture-heroines suggests that the new witches feel themselves similarly empowered and similarly restrained by an encroaching bureaucracy, the "right" society. For that reason they make a promise to one another, and to all rebellious and creative people, with the rallying cry, "Never again the burning times!"

Chapter Five

What Kinds of Individuals Become Witches and Neopagans?

I n this chapter we discover what the Neopagans have in common that might account for their shared interest in reviving paganism. We will discover such things as where they live, how they earn their living, and what their political affiliations are in order to gain some idea of what distinguishes them from others in American society.

To begin with, any belief system, even one that includes magic, must seem plausible to those who embrace it. Of course there is always the option to select among criteria of plausibility, such as standards of reason or scientifically established probability. T. M. Luhrmann (1989), an American anthropologist, explored the process by which Londoners became committed to magical ideas. She concluded that whether the new belief system is radical or traditional, people bypass rational thinking in the process of adopting ideologies and ways of thinking and succumb to "interpretive drift." We are attracted first, Luhrmann contends, and compose ideologies to justify the persuasion afterwards. To a limited extent this is true of the Neopagans. Although for them the predisposing factor is personal experience, such as an unusual rapport with nature, or being subject to prophetic insights or a deep uneasiness about truths that are self-evident to others. In this case, persuasion is of the nature of confirmation, or explanation, rather than conversion to a new belief. In fact, confirmation by those whom they do not respect often has the opposite effect of causing them to doubt their experiences or to regard them as shameful or pathological.

Some Common Beliefs about the Kind of People Who Engage in Occult Practices

Robert Galbreath crystallized popular notions of the occult into the following useful definition. It pertains to matters that are "hidden" or "secret" in one or more of the following senses: (1) extraordinary matters, that by contrast with the mundane world are thought to possess unusual significance (such as omens, portents, apparitions, prophetic dreams); (2) matters, such as the teachings of mystery schools, that are kept hidden from the uninitiated and the unworthy; and (3) matters that are intrinsically hidden from ordinary perceptions, although they are accessible through the awakening of latent faculties of sensitivity (1983, 18).

Sociologists, Howard Kerr and Charles Crow (1983), found that the term occult generally refers to esoteric belief systems such as those based on Hermetic or Eastern lore. The recent occult "explosion" includes Satanism, Neopagan witchcraft, flying saucer cults, belief in survival-after-death phenomena, renewed interest in Oriental mysteries (Tarot and I Ching), and poltergeist. The Neopagans express interest and belief in the full range of these occult phenomena, except Satanism.

For some individuals, interest in the occult is superstitious. For others occult beliefs constitute an aspect of religion as we have defined it. Occult is another way of describing the "sacred" domain of religion, that is, things set apart from mundane experience that are intrinsically hidden from ordinary perceptions. Many people find the occult a reservoir of symbols that are more powerful, pervasive, and motivating than those associated with the belief systems we more readily dignify as religion. In some cases the omens, apparitions, and other experiences associated with the occult move believers just as conventional religious experiences do, and they are as hard to verify. Occult experiences call for special treatment appropriate to the sacred. If we are to approach these beliefs and the people who hold them without prejudice, we must investigate them as we would any other alien belief system. We should ask how they relate to social, historical, political, and economic forces in society; what behaviors do the beliefs motivate? We should search for the internal consistency that distinguishes religious beliefs from superstition.

Belief in the occult inspires such practices as astrology, "dousing," magical healing, ritual magic, university investigations of psi, predictions by psychics, claims by spiritualists that they transmit messages from "the other side," claims by others to be channels (vehicles for communication) for supernatural personalities, and experiences of supernatural and paranormal "phenomena" such as ghosts, ESP, and UFOs (Kerr and Crow 1983).

Believers in the occult and peripheral spiritual or religious traditions are generally considered gullible, somewhat pathetic, and perverse for their assumed rejection of perfectly sound rational scientific thinking in favor of such interests.

Irrationalism, as the word is generally used in relation to the occult, often implies the sense of being wild, unreasonable, incoherent, emotional, or in favor of abandoning reason (Galbreath 1983). Neopagans are not satisfied that reason is, in itself, sufficient to grasp the whole of reality. Nor is reality rational, they protest, and reason is a limited tool, after all. Who would deny that thought and behavior are affected by non-rational factors or that excessive rationality gets in the way of full awareness of reality?

Without discounting the achievements of science, occultists have argued that what they see as the positivist deification of quantity and objectivity ignores physical realities that are ultimately knowable if only approached correctly. Poll research suggests that on the popular level, there is little correlation between occult beliefs and antagonism toward science.[1]

The most immediate explanation for acceptance of these unusual beliefs is that those who criticize and wish to transform culture are the disinherited (Anderson 1979; Lewis 1971). A very important distinction must be made between those who respond to disinheritance by *inventing* a religious revival and those who *follow*. The Neopagans share the potency of imagination with the prophets of crisis cults and revitalization movements as well as with poets, artists, and other visionaries. However they vehemently refuse to *follow* anything other than their own convictions.

Rather than disinherited, Margot Adler described them as "those few strong enough and fortunate enough in education, upbringing, or luck to be able to disown by word, lifestyle, and philosophy the totalistic religions and political views that dominate our society" (1979, 38).

How is it that the majority of Americans retain their conventional faith and continue to act on optimistic premises despite the fact that the world has grown more hazardous? The plausibility of both optimism and pessimism are equally valid and interesting questions in these circumstances.

One impediment to concern over the future lies in the conventional omnipotence attributed to science, technology, and professionalism in American society. Although there is growing skepticism, most people continue to hope that professionals, particularly scientists, will be able solve all problems with their impressive technology and superior knowledge. If not, at the very least, these authorities will tell us when to begin to worry. Experts who present bad news can generally be discredited by other more optimistic experts. Neopagans, along with many other postmodern thinkers, have lost confidence in such authorities, preferring to interpret "reality" themselves.

Contempt is typically combined with an ill-defined fear of individuals who are involved in the occult. People see these "weird" individuals as a threat to society. It may be that they feel challenged on a very fundamental level—their understanding of the nature of reality. As John Huizinga (1950) pointed out in his classic study of the play element in culture, cheating is far more tolerable than forsaking rules of the game. Magicians and mystics commit that offense. In doing so, they inspire fear and hostility in the more conservative minded, the supporters of the right society for which the witch is the symbolic opposite.

Having dispensed with some preconceptions about believers in the occult, I will tell how I met and gained the acceptance of the Neopagans, how I studied them, and then we will see what they taught me about themselves.

Meeting and Studying the Neopagans

I came to meet the Neopagans and witches at a large gathering—the theme of which was art and music—for the purpose of performing for them.[2] Because they approved of my art work, I was automatically and immediately regarded as a witch, or magician, which surprised me; and the acceptance pleased me.

Prior to that time, all I knew about Neopagan witches was what I had read in three books by American feminist witches: *The Holy Book of Women's Mysteries* by Z. Budapest, *The Spiral Dance* by Starhawk, and *Positive Magic* by Marion Weinstein. I was surprised to discover that my performance art served as credentials in lieu of initiation or even very much knowledge about witchcraft. To be regarded as a witch by many American Neopagans—who are far less formal than British witches—one need not be initiated *per se*. As one American witch said in response to the question, how does one become a witch? "Say you are a witch three times, and you're a witch." In this way one may come to think of himself or herself as a witch. However, to convince other witches, I discovered, one must demonstrate possession of the qualities that comprise "talent" for originality and creativity.

I decided to make Neopagans the subject of an anthropological study about a year following my first encounter with them at the PSG gathering in 1983; they were pleased and honored. I had already established contact, trust, and mutual respect, and I had learned enough about their subculture to enable me to present my inquiry in their terms.

Neopagan gatherings are well suited for participant observation.

Everyone participates in rituals and in the labor of running the gathering. Each person is required to contribute two to six hours of work during the gatherings to help run the health care and child care facilities, to prepare and clean up after meals, to serve as lifeguards or security guardians at the entrance to the camp, and to fulfill many other responsibilities.

Health care was my favorite job, for which I wrongly felt well qualified, having practiced professional nursing for many years prior to becoming an anthropologist. My experience with hospital nursing had little relevance for their very different approach to healing, which we will explore in other chapters. It was, however, the perfect vantage point for observing the practice of nontraditional medicine.

Early in my acquaintance with the witches—particularly before I decided to conduct research—I was able to respond emotionally and physiologically to the rituals. After I began to study the dynamics of rituals, and became involved in planning and performing in them, I became less susceptible to physiological responses and more appreciative of rituals as an art form. I remember with considerable awe those early feelings of uncritical engagement. I continue to be moved and delighted by the impressive music and pageantry.

I conducted interviews, made audio recordings, photographed the rituals and other activities, and communicated with many of the Neopagans by mail. I read close to forty of the numerous books they have written about themselves, and I spent several days visiting Circle Farm, reviewing there the largest collection of Neopagan writings in the United States, including term papers, newsletters, and numerous published and unpublished books. I am indebted mostly to Debbie Ann Light, who afforded me access to her extensive library for my archival research and guided me to relevant primary sources.

In an effort to find common threads and the core of what these individualistic people believed, I created a questionnaire to which I received 189 responses (See Appendix). Except for five respondents who were members of the Minoan Sisterhood, all were participants in regional gatherings or were witches to whom the questionnaire was given by a coven member who brought it home from a gathering. I was pleased that many informants found the questionnaire interesting and wanted to share it with their coven members at home.

I introduced the questionnaire with an invitation to rephrase questions, to offer free-form answers, and to add as much paper as was needed to complete responses. The data was processed on the IBM mainframe computer at the State University of New York at Stony Brook with a program that I designed to accommodate the structured as well as the free-form responses. The program's format was the product of my preliminary review of approximately one-third of the responses.

I used the questionnaire as a tool for expanding my exposure to the population. I attempted only a very simple accounting of demographics, but I probed basic beliefs and practices regarding magic, psychic skills—particularly healing—as well as opinions regarding allopathic medicine. I distributed the questionnaire slightly more randomly than I selected subjects for interviews. At group meetings I announced that I wanted respondents to answer my questionnaire. I sought out a few individuals to interview whom I knew had had an experience with a medical problem, so I could learn how they coordinated their magical healing with conventional medicine. Generally they also agreed to complete the questionnaire.

The questionnaire became a valuable participant observation tool, often serving as the impetus for a detailed interview or as a stimulus to group dynamics. At some gatherings I set up a tent and served cookies and iced tea to attract respondents. Some of my most interesting field experiences took place in the tent when a group discussion on controversial issues would erupt spontaneously in response to a question on the questionnaire. On these occasions I turned on the tape recorder, listened, and watched.

On occasion I did make an effort at randomness. When people were waiting for group meetings to begin or for meals to be served, for instance, I distributed questionnaires to every third person in the crowd.

By the fall of 1985—after two years of fieldwork conducted mostly at gatherings—I recognized the need to observe the workings of the witches' magico-religion in their ordinary lives. Regional gatherings provide broad exposure to the national community, but these gatherings are unusual and very festive occasions. Thus, to compare the temporary community life of festivals with a local, stable coven of witches, I requested initiation into the Minoan Sisterhood. The role of the anthropologist—student of one's subjects—coincided with the role of "witch trainee."

I began to shop at Enchantments (see chapter three) and finally asked Carol, the owner of the shop and high priestess of the Minoan Sisterhood, how I might become a candidate for initiation. She invited me to join weekly discussion groups, conducted by Lexa, for uninitiated individuals who were interested in the craft. I experienced my first watered-down Minoan-Gardnerian rituals there.

A few months passed. I received no invitation to be initiated. Hoping I might earn an invitation the same way I gained acceptance at the first Neopagan gathering, I offered to do a performance art piece as part of Enchantments' summer program of lectures and celebrations. It worked. At the conclusion of the performance—which was enthusiastically received—Carol and Lexa invited me to join the coven and promised to notify me of the auspicious time. Within a few months, Lexa told me to appear on a Sunday evening in the fall of 1986 with a new double-edged dagger to serve as my athame.

The ceremony of initiation was moving and frightening, as any good rite of passage should be. Having earned the right, I received the "revelations of the mysteries." The "tools of the craft" (see chapter two) were presented and explained to me. By placing the chalice, blades, cords, and pentacle in my hands, the artists, dancers, and actresses who were my coven mates initiated me into the simple secret that witchcraft is the creative process.

Demographics[3] and Descriptions of the Neopagan Community

The Neopagan community is diverse, and immense. The boundaries of the group and of the beliefs they share are difficult to assess because there is agreement only on the most fundamental level among these highly individualistic witches. Witchcraft and Neopaganism merge into feminism, the occult, political liberalism, and the New Age phenomenon. Yet they remain in many ways quite distinct. In a society as complex as the United States, the incalculable social forces which contribute to such a subculture have long histories and are difficult, if not impossible, to isolate.

We cannot know how many Neopagans there are because most of the witches are secretive in self-defense against being misunderstood and persecuted. Occasionally individual Neopagans will speak publicly or submit to media coverage, but most cannot risk public exposure.

Because Neopagans mistrust the standardizing influence of formal organization there is no central agency to provide statistics on the movement. The most reliable source of information about the national movement is the networking resource at Circle Farm in Wisconsin. Circle is a private organization, not an administrative or regulating body.

Geographic Distribution

Fondness for nature religion must represent nostalgia, rather than direct experience with nature because the majority of the Neopagans live in the cities (51 percent); only 19 percent reside in rural settings. Thirty percent live in suburban areas.[4]

The population distribution of respondents to my questionnaire reveals the greatest concentration in the northeastern United States, followed by the north central region (including Wisconsin, Illinois and Ohio) and the southeastern states. The West Coast represents the next greatest density, with the plains states barely represented at all. This particular spread may well be accounted for by the fact that my fieldwork was conducted mostly at gatherings that took place in Massachusetts, Wisconsin, and Georgia.

To balance somewhat the effects of concentrating my fieldwork in these areas, I resorted to another criterion: the publication of Neopagan newsletters. At Circle Farm, I tallied the number of newsletters on file by state (and those few they had received from abroad) as an indicator of the location of Neopagan groups.

New York, California, and Wisconsin showed the highest numbers in both categories. The twelve states from which no one responded to the questionnaire and in which no newsletter is published (based on the archives at Circle) are Delaware, Idaho, Kentucky, Louisiana, Mississippi, Montana, Nevada, North Dakota, Oklahoma, South Dakota, Utah, and Wyoming. Although this data does not prove conclusively that there are no Neopagans in these states, we may infer that these regions are sparsely populated with them.

We would expect the density of population in New York and California where there are many colleges and universities. Also, in these states, there are many urban areas where novel ideas are more likely to arise and spread. The four areas of highest population concentration also

Location of Neopagan questionnaire respondents. One dot represents one person.

Location of groups publishing Neopagan newsletters. One dot represents one group.

coincide with those locations where British Wicca was originally imported to the United States.

Several Americans initiated into Gardnerian covens in England returned to the United States to set up covens at home: notably Rosemary and Raymond Buckland who created covens across the country, and Donna Cole, who started some in Chicago. On the West Coast, Victor Andersen, who had been a mystic since childhood, became a teacher of many Wiccans in California after reading Gardner's *Witchcraft Today*. In England, Alexander Saunders added some ritual magic material to Gardner's and created a variation called Alexandrian Wicca, which came to the United States principally via two groups, one in Boston headed by James Baker, and another in New York headed by Mary Nesnick. After abandoning the Alexandrian tradition, Nesnick founded another called Algard, which is a combination of her own and Alexander Saunder's approach (Melton 1982).

While the strongest influence on the growth and spread of American witchcraft is the published works of witches (especially Starhawk and Adler) and the cross-fertilization that occurs at gatherings, these data suggest that diffusion of the British tradition from the original four regions also influenced the pattern of distribution.

Political Affiliation

Twenty-four percent of the respondents who answered the question[5] declared that they had no political affiliation. The next highest percentage indicated that they are Democrats (24 percent); only 3 percent are Republicans. The remainder (46 percent) indicated affiliations with the following parties (in descending order): Liberal, Independent, Anarchist, other, Libertarian, Socialist, Green Radical, and 2 percent are affiliated with the Progressive party.

Gender, Sexual Preference, and Age

The San Diego study found their respondents to be equally divided between men and women. Thirty-eight percent of the respondents to my questionnaire[6] are male; 58 percent are female; 4 percent identified themselves as androgenous.[7] The data support my field observations; by rough count I consistently found twice as many women as men.

The larger number of male respondents to the California study may indicate a division along gender lines between those Neopagans who belong to groups and read periodicals and those—among whom there is a higher percentage of females—who are more interested in participating in gatherings. The San Diego study is based on some interviews, attendance at group rituals, and review of pagan publications. The study originated with editors of periodicals and leaders of groups listed in the resource guide published by Circle.

In response to the question regarding sexual preference, I discovered a high percentage of non-heterosexual Neopagans.[8] Sixty-one percent declared themselves heterosexual, and 11 percent declared themselves homosexual, 28 percent bisexual. A total of 38 percent, then, declared a sexual preference other than heterosexuality. This unusually high percentage may reflect a greater willingness to discuss unconventional sexual preferences in the uncritical environment of the gatherings, or even more likely, that individuals having an unusual sexual preference are drawn to this uncritical religion.

I regret that I neglected to ask respondents to register their ages. The San Diego study found the majority to be between twenty-five and fifty years of age, with the highest percentage falling between thirty-one and forty. While all age groups are represented at the gatherings—infants to adults in their eighties—the majority appear to be between twenty and thirty-five years of age. I suspect this is at least partially attributable to the fact that more young people attend gatherings, being more tolerant of the primitive camping conditions.

Religious Affiliations

The all-encompassing goddess provides a contrast to the father-god of Judeo-Christianity, the religious heritage many radical thinkers—not only the witches—connect with the ills of "patriarchal culture." By the late 1970s the goddess had become a significant cultural symbol associated with various holistic movements: feminist, ecological, anti-nuclear, holistic health, Third World, and various New Age groups. In the preface to the second edition of "The Great Goddess" issue of *Heresies: A Feminist Publication on Art and Politics* (1982), the editors wrote that the above-mentioned alliances and coalitions are drawing closer to forming an integrated, powerful, and comprehensive political/spiritual force against oppression in any form and for the common good of humanity. This has gained the title "feminist spirituality."

By creating a religion of devotion to her, Neopagans and witches distinguished themselves from other groups and movements that take the great goddess as one of their powerful symbols. Gardner's influence was only one among many of the resources—mythology, psychology, feminist art and literature—that inspired the creation of rituals and other art forms to express this form of feminist spirituality in the United States.

Very few were introduced to paganism as a child as Lady Cybele had been. A large number of respondents to my questionnaire (24 percent)[9] said that they were brought up in the Roman Catholic religion; if we add Greek Orthodox, a total of 26 percent of the respondents were raised as Catholics. Many of the former Catholics spoke of a fondness for elaborate rituals that was satisfied by both their childhood religion and their chosen one. While Catholicism is the most represented single denomination in which the Neopagans were raised, the majority of the Neopagans (60 percent) were Protestants as children. The Neopagans are above the national average for membership in the denominations of Judaism (9 percent compared to 4 percent) and the Unitarian Church (4.2 percent compared to .1 percent). Three percent follow "their own religious path." (See table 1 for a breakdown of childhood religious denominations.)

Kirkpatrick found that the majority of subjects (53 percent) consider witchcraft their primary religion. Only thirteen of my respondents reported that they continue to practice another religion along with Wicca or Neopaganism, and five of these are Unitarians.

The only thing common to both radically individualist religions and Christian Fundamentalism is their appreciation of the personal religious experience. Otherwise they are the opposite poles that organize much of recent American religious life. The Old Religion takes the position

Table 1
Childhood Religious Affiliation

Denomination	Number of Neopagans Affiliated*	Percentage Affiliated	Percentage of National Population Membership**
Protestant			
Bapitst	24		18.0
Methodist	21		10.7
Episcopal	10		2.3
Presbyterian	10		2.3
Lutheran	10		5.5
Congregationalist	4		0.1
Quaker	3		0.4
Evangelical	1		0.5
7th Day Adventist	1		0.45
Total	**84**	**59**	**39.4**
Catholic			
Roman Catholic	35		35.1
Greek Orthodox	2		1.4
Total	**37**	**26**	**36.5**
Other			
Jewish	13		4.0
Unitarian	6		0.1
"My Own Path"	3		
Total	**22**	**15**	**4.1**
Summary			
Protestant	84	59	39.4
Catholic	37	26	36.5
Other	22	15	4.1
Total	**143**	**100**	**80.0**

*Forty-six people did not respond.
**I have provided percentages of national population constituting membership only in religious groups mentioned by the Neopagans. Source: "Religious Bodies-Selected Bodies" (based on data reported for 1984 to 1986) in U.S. Bureau of the Census, Statistical Abstract for the U.S. 1988. Information provided represents latest information from religious bodies with memberships of 50,000 or more and excludes a few groups giving no data. Not all groups follow the same calendar year nor count membership in the same way.

that a god or goddess is immanent in the material world including within the self; Fundamentalism asserts that God controls humans from a distance. The Earth-healers emphasize inner freedom and personal interpretation. The Fundamentalists prefer authoritarian collective religion.

The two approaches to moral behavior differ drastically. Because Christian mythology asserts that the external God has preordained all of human destiny and that Christ's death redeemed all sinners who believe in him, Christians feel somewhat removed from responsibility for the workings of destiny. The Earth-healers see themselves as active, not passive, participants in the unfolding of history. A sense of personal responsibility informs the two simple laws of Wicca: "The Wiccan Rede: That ye harm none, do what ye will" and "The Three-Fold Law: The repercussions of every action return to the doer three-fold in kind."

These two very general rules regarding morality require personal and individual evaluations of each action. The rules of the Christian faith, especially Fundamentalism, are more specific and numerous, requiring uncritical obedience to externally derived rules. Neopagans, on the other hand, see themselves engaged in a personal dialogue with the natural and social world. These opposite approaches to moral behavior may result in guilt and fear of externally imposed punishment for disobedience for Christians and a constant—often anxious—vigilance on the part of the witches, who interpret both good and bad fortune as the repercussions of their own actions.

Whereas Neopagans and other Earth-healers feel a personal responsibility to prevent ecological and nuclear disaster, Fundamentalist Christians take the perspective that the trend cannot, should not, be reversed. It is God's plan, according to biblical prophecy, that the world will end in a violent cataclysm, Armageddon. Many Christians believe that the hostilities in the Middle East fulfill the prophecy and suggest that the end will be played out over the next few decades.

Christian Fundamentalists and Earth-healers (such as Neopagans, New Age enthusiasts, and the like) are one another's devils in this debate. The radical cultural evolution that the Earth-healers advocate is subversive, even blasphemous, in the estimations of Fundamentalists who regard Earth-healers as enemies of the church and, in a structural sense, the opposite of right society. To the Earth-healers, the Fundamentalists are witch-burners. This time the stakes are higher— all life forms on the planet.

Rejecting Christianity[10] and with it all historical religions, Neopagans seek inspiration in "primitive" religion. R. R. Marett wrote that "primitive religion is danced, not believed."[11] Dance implies rhythm, joy, and aesthetic enjoyment, and the taking of pleasure in the animal nature of the body; it implies a pattern of living as well as a ritual activity. Fundamentalist Christians regard much of this as sinful. They remember with disgust that the legendary predecessors of present-day witches danced (naked) and took pleasure in their animal natures in (improper) sex acts at wildly celebratory Sabbaths (orgies).

Education and Occupation

The Neopagans are well educated, and in their academic studies and occupations they reveal a pervasive interest in the arts and healing. Seventy percent have four or more years of education beyond high school, compared to only 19 percent of the population (twenty-five years old and over in 1984) of the United States.[12] The Kirkpatrick group found that sixty-six percent had college degrees. Combining Ph.D.s, Masters, Bachelors, and Associate degrees, my total, 65 percent, is close to that of the California study. (See table 2 for years of education completed and table 3 for highest levels of education completed.)

Thirty-six point five percent of those who attended college and responded to my question regarding their major area of study revealed an interest in the arts and humanities. Only 9 percent of college freshmen in the general population selected the arts and humanities as their probable field of study in the period of 1966 to 1986. For the students in the national community, business was the most highly represented of all areas of study (26 percent), whereas only two Neopagans selected business. In this regard the Neopagans contrast dramatically with the larger society. (See table 4, for a comparison of major fields of study selected by Neopagans and by college freshmen in the national community.)

The largest category of employment for Neopagans (22 percent) is "helping and healing." The next largest category of employment is "arts and entertainment."[13] With writers included in that category, the total rises to 20 percent. Following that, the next most significant category of occupation is "computer-related," 10 percent. (See table 5 for a breakdown of these and other occupations.)

Work, Income, and Lifestyle

Kirkpatrick's team found the witches to be "under-rewarded" while occupying high-status occupations and being more highly educated than the general population. My statistics bear this out, only if we are speaking of monetary reward. If we take as our criterion the Neopagans' own definition of reward, it is not true.

Kirkpatrick's team discovered that 80 percent earned less than the 1983 median income. Selecting the year 1986 somewhat arbitrarily as midway

Table 2
Years of Education Completed

Years of Education Beyond High School	Valid Percentage of Neopagans Having This Amount of Education*
18	.6
12	.6
11	1.1
10	.6
9	2.8
8	4.5
7	15.2
6	13.5
5	7.9
4	23.0
3	7.3
2	15.2
1	.6

*Eleven people did not respond

Table 3
Highest Level of Education Completed

	Valid Percentage of Neopagans Who Have Achieved These Levels of Education*
PHD	4.2
MD	1.1
Masters	22.8
Bachelors	31. 7
Associates	4.6
Trade or Technical School Diploma	6.9
High School Graduate	23.8
Not High School Graduate	1.1
Did not respond	3.7

*Seven people did not respond.

Table 4
Selection of College Major

Major Field of Study	Number of Neopagans Who Selected This Field*	Percentage of Neopagans Who Selected This Field	Percentage of College Freshmen Who Selected This Field, 1966–86**
Arts and Humanities	48	35	9.0
Social Sciences	25	18	8.0
Natural Sciences	18	13	—
Health Sciences	13	9	2.0
Other Subjects	35	24	49.0
Total	**139**	**100**	**68.0**

*Fifty Neopagans did not respond
**From "Summary Characteristics, College Freshmen: 1966 to 1986." Source: The Higher Education Research Institute, University of California, Los Angeles, California. *The American Freshman: National Norms*, annual. Based on sample survey and subject to sampling error.

in the collection of my questionnaire data, I found 79 percent of individuals' and 50 percent of household incomes fell below the median income for households ($24,900) and that 29 percent of my respondents (individuals, not households) earned less than $7,000 yearly. This figure reflects earnings, it must be noted, not necessarily income. Two questions on this issue sought to establish "salary," both personal and that for the household. The 29 percent of individuals earning less than $7,000 may have access to other income and support that makes it possible for them to survive reasonably well while earning very little from their own labor. Seventy-nine percent of individuals earn $25,000 or less. (See table 6 for yearly personal and household income of the Neopagans.)

My data for household income are handicapped by the fact that 43 percent did not answer the question; many respondents may have passed over it after having responded to the question probing personal income. The lack of household income may relate also to the fact that there are many individuals who live alone. Twenty-six percent of those who did respond reported a household income of $15–25,000 yearly; only 8 percent reported a household income of $7,000 or less.

Fifty-three percent of the respondents indicated that they were satisfied with their jobs;[14] 31 percent indicated that they were somewhat satisfied, and 16 percent reported that they were not satisfied.

Neopagans are not as materialistic as most members of the consumer

Table 5

Occupations of Neopagans Compared to Civilians in the United States

Occupation	Total Number of Respondents*	Percentage of Neopagans Employed in This Field	Percentage of Civilians Employed in This Field**
Helping and Healing			
Health care, non-professional	12	7.80	6.70
Health care, professional	11	7.20	4.70
Social workers	7	4.60	1.20
Physicians	3	2.00	***
Total	**33**	**21.60**	**12.60**
Arts and Entertainment			
Arts and Entertainment	21	13.70	***
Writers	9	5.90	***
Total	**30**	**19.60**	***
Other Occupations			
Computer-related	15	9.80	3.60
Business	10	6.50	14.50
Students	10	6.50	***
Office Work	9	5 .90	13.20
Manufacture, Industry, Trade	16	10.50	4.70
Retired and Unemployed	8	5.20	***
Education	7	4.60	5.10
Religious Practitioner	6	3.90	***
Ecological and Conservation	4	2.60	***
Service	2	1.30	23.00
Occult Retail	2	1.30	***
Retail Sales	1	.70	23.00
Total	**90**	**58.80**	**87.30**

*Thirty-six Neopagans did not respond.
**For occupations employing 100,000 or more in 1986. Includes wage and salary jobs, self-employed and unpaid family members. Estimates based on 1983–1985 Occupational Employments Statistics Surveys.
***Not mentioned.

Table 6
Yearly Personal and Household Incomes

Yearly Personal Income

Income Range	Percentage of Neopagans Within This Range	Number of Respondents*
$0–7,000	29	41
$7–15,000	24	34
$15–25,000	26	37
$25–35,000	12	17
$35–45,000	6	8
$45,000+	3	4

*Forty-eight did not respond.

Yearly Household Income

Income Range	Percentage of Neopagans Within This Range	Number of Respondents*
$0–7,000	8	8
$7–15,000	16	17
$15–25,000	26	28
$25–35,000	18	19
$35–45,000	16	17
$45,000+	17	18

*Eighty-two did not respond.

society; indeed, consumerism is regarded as one of the most sinister travesties of patriarchal culture. As one might expect of artists and visionaries, the Neopagans value free time to create and celebrate, and they are generally willing to sacrifice material rewards for this freedom.

Work is a significant spiritual issue. Neopagans' attitude regarding work finds precedent in the medieval craft guilds. Rather than the necessary means, creative work should be the aim of a satisfying life. The Neopagans bring as much of the necessary work in their lives into this kind of spiritual, expressive process, making their lives a work of art by integrating what in mainstream culture is now divided into

separate domains of activity: work, leisure, and religion. For most Neopagans this remains at best a partially attained, albeit worthy, aspiration.
As is generally true for creative people, the generation of income—a
necessary prostitution—becomes an activity separate from the truest
expression of their creativity. Writing, painting, spinning, weaving,
cultivating herbs, healing, and other such labors inspired by passion
rather than profit have a prominent place in the lives of nearly every
Neopagan I have met. Unfortunately, few are able to earn a living exclusively with their crafts. Phillip Moon, a nurse, described his work
as "about seventy percent calling, the rest is a job" (personal communication, 1993).

Neopagans have the challenge also of finding work that does not participate in the pollution and exploitation of the Earth. It is a balancing
act to avoid giving the most and the best of their creativity to the "mere"
pursuit of earning a living.

As a result of this preference, in any case, Neopagans are "under-
rewarded" in terms of the monetary values of the larger society. As is
characteristic of artists, the first priority is to communicate effectively,
to have one's art responded to. They are resigned, as artists must be, to
the fact that society does not reward most artistic creativity with wealth.

Prestige is another important reward for work. Competent creativity
is the very currency of prestige at gatherings and within covens. Those
individuals who create moving rituals, perform well at the talent show,
and make beautiful ceremonial tools, jewelry, robes, and other items
are admired and respected. However, the audience for this prestige is
small; the same individuals who are famous within the Neopagan
communities must struggle to defend the peculiar values and less than
opulent lifestyle in the mundane "material" world. Considerable conflict
is suffered as a result of this kind of status inconsistency, which under
these circumstances is better described as status relativity.

On the issue of work versus craft, and the rewards thereof, it was
interesting to talk with Ken-Ra —who calls himself a "magesmith," a
blacksmith who makes magical tools—when I attended my third Pagan
Spirit Gathering in the summer of 1986. He confided that his dream was
to be paid for the work he loves, and to improve his skills. He was content
to receive $8.00 an hour for his labor that he described in this way:

> You are covered head to foot with dust, dirt, grunge, and coal dust,
> and you're breathing smoke for long periods of time at the forge,
> you've got blisters and calluses on your hands and your arm is sore
> from about there [pointing to his forearm], all the way up the
> shoulder, over the shoulder, and down to the back. The small of your
> back aches, and your knees hurt. . . . It's hard on the body, noisy
> on the brain, and all of that. For computer people, "Poof!" it appears,
> fast and easy. I can't do that.

Each year Ken-Ra is inspired to create a ceremonial weapon that he presents as a gift to a person who is involved in magical work. Generally he is not aware of who is to be the recipient until after the project is well underway or completed. I was involved in the presentation of one of these gifts at the first PSG I attended in 1983. He asked me to confirm his choice of the recipient for the labrys he said the goddess had inspired him to make. It was a twin-bladed ax resembling the butterfly-shaped implements excavated at Crete.

Occasionally when the goddess "commissioned" him to create a ceremonial weapon, Ken-Ra requested a favor in return. The first time, he told me, he asked for "the love of Her people," meaning the Wiccan and others engaged in goddess-venerating traditions. The boon he requested for the weapon he made in 1986 was a job that he desperately wanted, working as a blacksmith for the city of St. Paul. He would make a good living, but the greatest appeal was that he would be, as he told me:

> doing what I want to do. And it will improve my skill beyond any measure of . . . There is a major difference between making an athame, a labrys, or a sword, and putting a new point on a jackhammer bit, but it's still steel; it's still learning the skills; and the shop has a lot of tools—like a power-hammer—that I'd love to get my hands on. . . . I would love to have one.
>
> Also I met some people recently who are busy making Damascus steel, as many a 15,000 layers of steel welded together. It is may be the strongest steel ever made, incredibly impressive, and rather beautiful. Being able to do that impresses me.
>
> I've also, in the last year, acquired an apprentice. There's a very good chance my skills will not die with me.[15]

Although the job didn't work out, Ken-Ra got his power-hammer. An unexpected windfall came his way three weeks after he had a vision of Hephaestus in a cloud pointing a hammer at him. He used it to buy a power-hammer.[16] Although the goddess still has a part in his work, in terms of gift-giving, Hephaestus has assumed a more prominent place as his muse. A copy of the letter that he presents with his gifts advises recipients that if they feel moved to reciprocate they might "do something for a friend of mine, the Grand Master also known as Hephaestus."[17]

Satisfaction with their home life was higher than the Neopagans' satisfaction with occupation. Sixty-one percent were satisfied with their home life; 25 percent were somewhat satisfied, and 14 percent reported that they are not satisfied. It is well to remember that for the majority of Neopagans home life includes the space and opportunity to perform their crafts and magical work.

Forty-nine point seven percent expressed satisfaction with the sexual aspect of their lives. Sexuality is a religious and magical activity for the

Ken-Ra, the blacksmith. He is holding a ceremonial weapon (labrys) he created.

Neopagans. Twenty-seven percent said they were somewhat satisfied,[18] and 23 percent were not. We have seen that a large percentage of the Neopagans are not heterosexual, a lifestyle that finds little support from the mainstream and is fraught with other challenges—such as difficulty in finding partners—that might interfere with satisfaction.

Power and Powerlessness

Kirkpatrick's group of sociologists hypothesized that Wiccans sought training in the craft to gain power and efficacy that they felt they lacked. My experience suggests that Neopagans believe that all peoples—not only themselves—feel powerless in the face of certain threats to individual freedoms, health, and the environment.

The Neopagans are distinctive in their belief that individuals can and should be powerful, but they do not define power in the sociological sense of the capacity to control others. Their goal is to "reclaim" powers of the mind, meaning not only the intellect, but also the imagination, will, intuition, and other mental faculties with which they may control their own lives, rather than submit to impersonal social forces. Furthermore, they believe that powers of the mind—on which the legendary witches were forced to rely—are especially useful in these critical times when, they feel, changes are required in both human consciousness and the socio-cultural conditions of life. The witches of the past lacked the technology and power structures of contemporary society (which now seem to be as much the sources of the problems as their remedies), yet they were able to influence, to help, and to terrify one another by resorting to powers inherent in the human condition. Neopagans have faith that anyone may relearn and use inherent powers. Most others in American society rely on other sources of power that are not equally accessible to all members in society, such as wealth, weapons, influence, and prestige.

Wiccan and Other Neopagan Traditions

Seventy-eight percent of the respondents to the Kirkpatrick study indicated that they considered themselves witches. Only 25 percent of them had been formally initiated into a coven. I regret that I did not ask, but I believe that at least that many, and probably most, of the Neopagans who attend gatherings think of themselves as witches. Others think of themselves as magicians or shamans,[19] but all are comfortable with the Wiccan style of worship except for some feminist separatists who exclude the god.

In my questionnaire I asked what traditions of magic respondents practiced. The highest percentage (19 percent) identified themselves as "eclectic," a term denoting an inventive and experimental approach to witchcraft that borrows from many different sources, primarily from the writings of Starhawk. Most eclectic witches only learned about Gardner second-hand by reading books, principally Starhawk's or Adler's. Initiation and secret books of shadows are generally not significant in these groups.

Combining Gardnerian, Alexandrian, and the Algard traditions as essentially British revivals, only 11 percent of my respondents fall within that category.

Almost 7 percent of the respondents participate in a strongly feminist style of Wicca. Many Dianic witches think of Wicca as exclusively women's religion.[20] Men are excluded from Dianic covens, as is worship of the god.

The most famous Dianic coven is the Susan B. Anthony Coven of Los Angeles, which was originated by Hungarian-born Z. Budapest, whose *Holy Book of Women's Mysteries (I & II)* serves as a Book of Shadows for many self-made witches. Like solitary practitioners, Dianic covens emphasize creativity, and they design and perform exercises to increase psychic skills of prophecy, divination, and visualization for effective spell-working. The eclectic covens gain much inspiration from the Dianic witches.

About twenty percent of respondents to the questionnaire are involved in a specific ethnic tradition: Celtic (10 percent), Native American (4 percent), Druid (3 percent), Minoan (3 percent), Norse (2 percent), and Lavecchia, an Italian tradition of which Leland wrote (.5 percent).[21] These groups cling to the idea of practicing an ancient tradition. In fact, most of these resemble Gardner's Wicca with pantheons and creation myths of other ethnic groups substituted for Gardner's. Most retain a similar ritual structure and celebrate the yearly round of eight Sabbaths. We will have the opportunity to discuss the operations of an eclectic, the most prevalent type of coven in the United States, in chapter fourteen.

Neopagans, the Opposite of Right Society

My analysis of the demographic characteristics of the Neopagans revealed that in all respects they differ from the larger population. Their childhood religious training and their sexual preferences are distinct. They are far more educated than the normal population yet they earn considerably less. In terms of four other criteria—political affiliation, selection of academic studies and occupation, and most conspicuously, the preference for pagan, rather than Christian religion—the Neopagans are the inverse of the larger population. We may summarize by saying that the Neopagans are among the minority in a democracy whose traditions and policies are shaped by the majority. They differ from the more compliant individuals who modify or adapt their opinions to accommodate the values accepted by the majority in society and from the secular radicals who are content to phrase their debates in the language and symbols of the larger society.

The Neopagans, who as a group are markedly more interested and involved in the arts and humanities than the larger population, create new symbols. Like shamans, artists, and visionaries, they are flexible, imaginative, and inventive.

Why some individuals are more imaginative than others is a question not easily answered. I noted earlier that the Neopagans deny having acquired their "unusual perspective" from any dramatic crisis or transformation traditionally characteristic of shamans, innovators, or followers of crisis cults and revitalization movements. I can say with confidence the Neopagans are poets, artists, and visionaries whose religious convictions cannot be understood unless this fact is taken into consideration.

The portrait that emerges from these statistics is that of the creative individual. Erich Neumann (1959), a Jungian psychologist, describes the attributes of the creative individual as distinct from his "normal" and neurotic fellows, in terms that resonate with our description of the Neopagans.[22] While it is often assumed that the creative individual—artist, poet, inventor, scientist, or religious mystic—is unbalanced mentally in favor of the unconscious, Neumann found them to be distinguished by a special alertness, or "intensity," that results from the ability to sustain considerable tension between the equally well developed ego and the unconscious source of novel visions (1959).

Although the creative individual may experience considerable psychic pain and confusion when transpersonal consciousness delivers a creative vision by bursting through normal consciousness, he or she is distinguished from the neurotic or psychotic in that strength of ego development affords the power to submit visions to the formative, interpretive functions of the conscious mind (1959).

The creative male, Neumann observed, remains open to the "feminine principle," and the unconscious source of transpersonal material. Achievement of maturity in other men involves repression of the "anima."[23] This openness to the source of creative insights makes the flooding of consciousness less traumatic for the creative individual than for others who must experience these insights as violent eruptions (1959).

The greater openness to the feminine is apparent in male Neopagans, who reject the one-sidedness that marks ego-identification with the purely masculine consciousness. Creative men remain more child-like, and to a large degree, bisexual (1959).

Neopagan men are at home in goddess worship. Neumann's observation that creative men think of themselves in terms of the archetypal son-hero of the virgin mother is a particularly apt description of Neopagan males. The agricultural myth cycle (see chapter two)—of the Mother Goddess and her son-consort god—that is significant in Neopaganism endorses the male identification of himself as son and hero. The important theme that spiritual maturity entails a balance between the male and female psychic gifts supports—as little else in Western culture does—the openness of males to feelings and behaviors generally defined as purely feminine, including receptivity to creative inspiration. The goddess religion gives vivid expression to these feelings and, therefore, supports and magnifies this quality of the creative psyche.

Ultimately the creative individuals are distinguished from others who experience psychic breakthroughs of transpersonal consciousness by their ability to produce an "achievement" rather than a neurosis as a product of the experience. We have seen that a high percentage of the Neopagans either studied or are employed in the arts, while nearly all of them engage in some art or craft. In chapter twelve, we will explore in detail how one Neopagan passed through the difficult psychic ordeal of the creative process and emerged with some important achievements.

Not every person who possesses the qualities of the creative individual described here, and in Neumann's essay, is capable of producing a work of art, i.e., an achievement that is of some significance to the larger community. All who are attracted to Neopaganism endorse the qualities of creativity as being valuable to society. Neopagans take the perspective that creativity can be taught and developed in the study of magic. Although creative talent is valued and may serve as qualification for admission into a coven, the ability to create is regarded as everyone's birthright. The Neopagans feel that in order to reach one's full potential as an individual and as a responsible contributor to society, a person must develop the qualities and skills of creativity.

Chapter Six

The Western
Spiritual Tradition

G ardner's Wicca is the most recent of several revivals of an enduring—although generally submerged—aspect of Western
culture. Each recurrence was marked by prominence of the imagination
and its application to creativity in magical practice. This subculture,
the Western occult tradition, consistently promotes revision of the self
and the conditions of one's life—including social reform—by resort to
imagination, will, and craft. This assertive approach to life is based on
religious beliefs that remain constant as do the philosophy and repertoire
of symbolic expressions. When Neopagans speak of the Old Religion,
they imagine the Stone Age traditions idealized in Gardner's myth of
the origin of Wicca. Perhaps the circle dance to raise and release energy
and achieve ecstacy is preserved from paleolithic cultures, and surely
initiation through reenactment of death and rebirth is ancient and
ubiquitous. In this chapter we will see that, as Gardner himself said,
Wicca derives its ancestry not only from fertility cults but from the
magico-religion of Egypt (1954). Finding the rituals in Old Dorothy's
Book of Shadows fragmentary, Gardner wanted to enhance them to make
them more workable (Valiente 1978). For this purpose, Gardner resorted
to the wealth of resources preserved in the Western occult tradition.

Because these traditions were committed to writing, reworked, and
transmitted over the centuries, they survived to provide Gardner with
an articulate philosophy and system of practice onto which he could
graft the remnants of northern European traditions that were preserved
in the more fragile memory and oral tradition of an obscure subculture.

The Western occult tradition is a systematic set of beliefs regarding
the place of humans in the cosmos; it has thus been called a philosophy.
Because the originators and preservers of the tradition recorded their

disciplined observations of the cosmos and experiments with nature, it has been called science—or more often, a pseudo-science. Some of the beliefs may not be accurate according to our present knowledge of the universe, yet they are systematic. Because these beliefs relate to sacred things and find expression in both worshipful and magical practices, we may think of the Western occult tradition as constituting a religion. We should cease to think of it in terms of the prejudice that caused it to be occult, that is to say, hidden. In fact, it no longer is. I will refer to it as the Neopagans have taught me, as the Western *spiritual* tradition. Following the example of one of its most venerable historians, Frances Yates, we could also think of it as the Religion of the World (1964).

The Deep Roots of Western Magic

The Western spiritual tradition is the product of the merging of the remains of pre-literate religions of the Mediterranean and the Middle East. The fusion of what was principally Egyptian and Greek thought took place in the Nile valley during the Ptolomaic and Roman periods. The primitive religions had by then been thinned out and modified by the friction of age, and the conscious elaboration of philosophers, priests, and healers. The final result contained a large measure of Greek philosophy; Plato's voice is particularly prominent. The product was a practical, spiritual "way"—an attempt to understand the self, the world, and the divine (Fowden 1986, xvi).

The oldest records of this religion are magical papyri compiled in Greco-Roman Egypt between the second century B.C.E. and the fifth century C.E., although they represent even earlier Egyptian beliefs and practices.[1] From the first to third century C.E., Egyptian and Gnostic scholars assembled another body of treatises which they attributed to the Greco-Egyptian patron god of magic, Hermes Trismegistus[2] and others in his circle including Asclepius, the divine physician (Fowden 1986). In late antiquity this syncretized religion reached Byzantium, and through Arab channels it arrived in the West in the twelfth century. All the while it maintained continuity of philosophy and practice, while its science of astrology improved. It flowed into Renaissance magic along with the endowment of such medieval magicians as Roger Bacon and Albert the Great, who had been influenced by Arab magic[3] (Couliano 1984).

The Greek magical papyri, discovered in the nineteenth century in Thebes, record magical spells, formulae, hymns, and rituals.[4] The authors of the papyri assimilated Egyptian, Greek, Babylonian and Jewish religions; however, very little of the religion of the Romans, who were in control of Egypt in the later period, was incorporated. Like Neopaganism, this religion was patched together from remnants of older ones and molded into a new set of unified attitudes and beliefs. Also like Neopaganism, it remained distinct from the religion of the dominant culture.

In this Old Religion we find the central myth of Gardner's Wicca (the goddess' descent to the netherworld) and the preoccupation with the underworld and the beings inhabiting it. Most often, practitioners invoked Hekate, whose fame persisted in pre-modern Europe where she became queen of the witches who flew with her at night. She remains prominent in Neopagan religion as goddess of the moon and death, and guardian of the crossroads, including the one into the netherworld.

Significant, too, was a fascination with the forces of the universe. Although Neopaganism is based on a more complete astronomical science, it is a more recent version of these religious concerns with the universe. While Neopagans focus on the Earth as powerful deity (although vulnerable planet), the people whose religion comes to us through the papyri were daunted by the capricious energies coming from the universe. They depended on magicians—either temple priests or wandering craftsmen—to negotiate on their behalf with the deities, demons, and spirits inhabiting the underworld to achieve the goals of human life (Betz 1986). Ironically, Neopagans now peruse artifacts of this unbroken tradition of Western magic that has survived through the coming and going of religions, the scientific and technological revolutions, and modern medicine to find resources to aid them in preserving the same natural forces from which the authors of the documents sought protection.

Gnostic Hermeticism

The Hermetic documents (those attributed to Hermes Trismegistus) contain smatterings of Platonism, Neoplatonism, Stoicism, and other Greek thought. Although Jewish and Persian influences are also apparent, the strongest influence is Greek Gnosticism. The heart of Gnosticism is the belief that certain individuals can achieve gnosis (the Greek word for knowledge), here meaning the achievement of an immediate glimpse of the inner workings of the cosmos and a transfiguration from human into a divine condition. This experience resembles shamans' ecstacy, except that in Gnosticism, individuals may learn techniques for initiation into the experience by reading privileged information rather than surviving profound suffering as shamans must do (Raschke 1980). The "privileged information" was contained in the Hermetic treatises. Religious practices that were originally communal, such as those of the mystery cults,[5] were diverted in Gnosticism to the *private* mystical experience (Raschke 1980; Yates 1964).

Festugière, a prominent translator of the Hermetic literature, identified two types of gnosis in the Hermetic writings. The "pessimist" gnosis expresses world-denying nihilism. For example, the early doctrine of the "vehicle of the soul" teaches that cosmic knowledge is impressed on the soul at birth and determines its destiny. Not until the second century C.E. does the doctrine merge with the idea that the soul assimilates planetary accretions that link it to the body and the world below as it descends to Earth. The soul must rid itself of the accretions it acquired from the material Earth and stars in the upward ascent toward god, because according to this theory (that is influenced by Judeo-Christian dualism), these connections are polluting (Couliano 1984). In "optimist gnosis," the life of the world of matter is divine; there is no taint of evil to be transcended (Yates 1964). Neopagans identify with the taproot of Gnosticism that circumvents Judeo-Christian world-denial and reaches back beyond Plato to the optimistic, animistic, worldview of the earliest civilizations.

An example of this world-loving paganism is the following myth, which, like Gardner's myth of the goddess, tells of the inescapability of death in a constantly dying and resurrecting world. The tone of the story tells that this is an acceptable, even elegant arrangement. Like Gardner's goddess, Tat, the son of Hermes Trismegistus, wondered why all things must die. Hermes responded to his son:

> . . . living beings do not die . . . being composite bodies they are dissolved: now this dissolution is not death but the dissolution of a mixture. And if they are dissolved, it is not to be destroyed but to be renewed. What in fact is the energy of life? Is it not movement? Or what is there in the world which is immobile? Nothing, my child.
>
> But the Earth, at least, does it not seem to be immobile, O father?
>
> No, child: on the contrary alone of all beings, it is both subject to a multitude of movements and stable. . . . Without movement, indeed, it is impossible for that which gives birth to give birth to anything. . . . Know then, child, that all that is in the world, without exception, is in movement, either diminishing or increasing. And that which is in movement is also in life, but there is no necessity that every living being should conserve its identity. For no doubt, considered in its totality the world is immobile, my child, but the parts of this world are all in motion yet nothing perishes or is destroyed.[6]

In Gardner's myth, the lord of death provides the same explanation. The idea that the world is constantly dying in one form and being born in another underlies the faith that humans may participate in these changes with magic. This idea is expressed in a chant that witches often sing to raise energy to empower their magic: "She changes everything she touches, and everything she touches changes."[7] "She," in this chant, is understood to be the goddess, personification of the ever changing world, and the magician as female witch.

Revival of Pre-Christian Mysticism in the Italian Renaissance[8]

The Christian church persecuted the Religion of the World into obscurity until refugees of Constantinople brought the Hermetic manuscripts to Florence in the late fifteenth century where they profoundly influenced Italian Renaissance culture. Marsilio Ficino (1433-1499), physician and scholar, translated the manuscripts for Cosimo de Medici and experimented with the magic he learned (in order to obtain medical benefits). At the same time, refugees of Spain brought the Hebrew Cabala.[9] It was eagerly received, most prominently by Pico della Mirandola (1463-1494), who blended it with Hermeticism, and with his mentor, Ficino, founded an Italian Renaissance Hermeticism (Yates 1964).

Because Renaissance scholars believed the ancient Egyptian, Hermes Trismegistus, personally composed the treatises, it was possible for Ficino and Pico to make the Hermetic literature acceptable to Christian culture by interpreting it as a prophecy of the coming of Christ. It was not until 1614 that Isaac Casaubon shattered that myth by establishing that the Hermetic documents were written after, not before, the birth of Christ. He attributed authorship to Gnostic writers of the late first to the late third century C.E.[10] Pico della Mirandola made the Cabala even better adapted to Christian culture by linking it with the Christian angels and by finding the name of Jesus in its sacred alphabet (Yates 1964).

In the Renaissance, Western magic was elevated to a fine art. For their spells, Renaissance magicians fashioned opulent combinations of plants, gems, metals, and Orphic hymns[11] to entice celestial influences, or they crafted invisible images in the mind to incorporate the powers associated with celestial and archetypal forces.

By contrast, a magician of antiquity, wishing to obtain foreknowledge and sound memory, for example, would tear out the heart of a hoopoe bird (*Upupa epops*), pierce it with a reed, grind it with honey while the moon rose, and drink the concoction during seven recitations of the formulae stating his desire.[12] Medieval magicians conjured with similar mechanical incantations, resorted to animal sacrifice, and used artifacts of the dead in their spells. To accomplish the same purpose, a Renaissance philosopher—preferring to think of his[13] conjurations as medicine or science rather than magic—would purify his spirit by taking the pleasant air in a garden, where he would absorb the beneficial rays of the sun, breathe the perfume of plants, and sip a potion of wine mixed with ground gold or precious stones. Renaissance magicians believed that when the soul was made pure and shone like a mirror, it received and transmitted clear and accurate images of things in the sensory and celestial realms to the intellect and deposited them in the memory. All of these magical technologies, from the piercing of the bird's heart to the ingestion of golden potions, derive from the same theory of the continuity between humans and the world that never changed—whether the world was perceived as geocentric and finite (Aristotle, Ptolemy, and St. Thomas); infinite with God at the center (Nicholas of Cusa); or, having the sun as its center (Copernicus and Bruno).

"Egyptian" Religion: The Mystery of Creation and Destruction in a Constantly Changing World

The Hermetic texts describe a religion in which the universe is seen as alive and divine. Humans, having descended into the Earth plane from their origins in the source of the divine universe are, by a sort of kinship, divine also. The divine source is not necessarily anthropomorphic; it is referred to instead as light or idea and sometimes metaphorically as father. Religious practice entails the quest of returning to the divine source after death and making contact with it while still alive.

For the Egyptians of that time, the constantly dying and resurrecting world was a continuous interwoven fabric. Having absorbed the Hermetic literature, Ficino was able to synthesize a theory of the substance and force of magic. All things in the universe are infused with *pneuma*, or spirit, which he described as

> a very thin body, almost nonbody and already almost soul; or almost nonsoul and almost body. In its composition there is a minimum of the terrestrial, a little more of an aquatic, and still more of an aerial nature. But most of it partakes of the nature of stellar fire. . . . It is altogether shiney, hot, humid, and invigorating.[14]

This common cosmic spirit (*spiritus mundi*) provides a channel of influence between heavenly bodies and the sublunar world. Neopagans speak of a similar unifying, all-pervading substance as energy, aether, or spirit. Wiccans include it as the fifth and finest element. Ficino explained that the soul, itself consisting of pneuma, is able to contemplate images communicated to it through that medium (Couliano 1984).

Love (eros) is the driving force of magic, Ficino explained. Parts of the world are drawn toward one another by an attraction born of their common nature. "The work of Magic is a certain drawing of one thing to another by natural similitude."[15] The universe, in this religion, is "in love with itself," held together by bonds of attraction or sympathy such as those lovers experience.[16]

To attract his desire, the magician must use his talents to gain control of the mind of the one he would draw to him. That is to say, he must influence the mechanism by which the imagination translates the data of the senses into images the soul mirrors to the reasoning part of the mind. Non-human entities, lacking the image-making capacity, must be approached by resort to more automatic responses by manipulating inherent "sympathies," or attractions among parts of the world that share a common nature. To cure an animal, for instance, the magician might bring it into contact with a plant or mineral substance known to have an astrological affinity in common with the affected organs.

By manipulating the substance of magic, which is pneuma, with the force of eros, Ficino believed a magician could either directly influence objects, individuals, and societies or invoke powerful invisible beings to aid him. To accomplish this, he must gain a thorough knowledge of the nets and baits that he must set out to gain the desired result (Couliano 1984).

Giordano Bruno's Psychology of Magic

Giordano Bruno, apostate monk and Renaissance philosopher, expanded Ficino's equation, eros = magic, into a psychology for manipulating the masses of people as well as individuals. The process is "to bind" (vincire), using as a tool the "chains" (vincula) of love. To gain the following of masses or the loyalty of an individual, the first crucial step in Bruno's magic is to learn the subject's desires and expectations. Bruno, who liked to think of himself as a philosophic painter whose canvas was the pneuma and whose colors were *phantasms* (phantasies), recommended as the second step that the magician create an effective phantasy and convey it through the subject's imagination to the cognitive faculty where it would determine her or his emotions[17] (Couliano 1984).

Semi-Divine Magus Man: Artist

The Hermetic text named for the physician, Asclepius, inspired the Renaissance idea that "magus man" has within him the power to marry heaven to Earth[18] (Yates 1964). Partaking of the divine spirit (pneuma) and the intelligence of the cosmos, humans have the potential of manipulating the world through their knowledge and consubstantiality with it. Just as psychic pneuma animates the human organism, so the cosmic pneuma pervades the world. The divine soul of a man might communicate via the medium of pneuma with a corresponding center, the heart of the world, located in the sun (Couliano 1984). In order to realize this potential, Ficino recommended purification of the soul with ascetic discipline, so it might communicate accurately.

For Bruno, development of the personality of the magus entailed nothing less than becoming like God.[19] By refining and enlarging the imagination and the will, Bruno believed a magician could incorporate within him the archetypal images of the universe, so he might reflect the whole universe of nature and of man in his mind and partake of their powers. For this purpose, he recommended his art of memory, which he adapted from ancient techniques practiced by orators. Rather than placing parts of a speech within spaces in an imagined architecture within the memory, Bruno recommended that a magician imbed in his memory the images or statues of the celestial gods and forces that he wished to incorporate into his personality (Yates 1964 & 1966; Couliano 1984). We will return to Bruno's art of memory later in this chapter.

Having made himself divine, Bruno claimed, the magician is qualified to influence the world. He wields the power to create phantasies of different kinds at will to inspire either attraction and joy or aversion and revulsion.[20] For most people, the realm of the imagination is controlled by external forces, either supernatural or human. The craft of poets and artists, however, demands that they be in control of the faculty of the imagination. Like them, Bruno warned, a magician must render himself immune to emotions prompted by external causes. To control others, the magician must be invulnerable to his own devices.[21]

Renaissance Magic Shared the Purpose of Art

In the Renaissance, magic operated through the imagination and became closely allied with artistic expression. Although she distinguished art from magic, Suzanne Langer's comprehensive theory of art (1953) helps us to understand the common ground where both artist and magician attempt to effect a change through the use of effective symbols. Langer believed that the art process consists of the application of the craftsperson's utmost technical skill and conceptual power (imagination) to creating a non-discursive but articulate symbol of sentience.[22] To achieve that purpose, the artist produces a work of art; the magician, who must be an effective artist, creates a spell.

Rather than restricting intelligence to discursive forms and relegating all other conceptions to some irrational realm of feeling and instinct, her theory of art distinguishes between two symbolic modes. Of the two mental activities, art is better suited to expressing feelings, many of which are particularly unsuited to discourse (Langer 1953).

Like artists, Renaissance magicians brought together arrangements of colors, sounds, images, and so forth. If it works, the ruling power and purpose of art (and I would add, magic) is served; something that is more than the sum of its parts, an effective symbol of sentience, emerges.

The Renaissance magician resorted to the doctrine of signatures to cause that "something" to emerge from his arrangement. According to this doctrine, the truly wise who could grasp the relationship of the parts of the universe might capture sensual qualities, even celestial presences, by means of their nets and lures, sounds, substances, and forms (Couliano 1984).

Art achieves its purpose of expression, Langer (1953) claimed, when it produces the exhilaration of a direct aesthetic experience; it formulates conceptions of feelings and visual and audible reality and impresses them upon the soul. We surrender and are changed by it.[23] We may say the same about the aim of Renaissance magic.

Like a painting, sculpture, or musical score, a Renaissance magical operation presented a complex *gestalten* to produce an intellectual excitement of a specific nature. For example, in the description of the spell that follows, we see that the Renaissance magus, Campanella, addressed the senses of sight, smell, taste, sound, and perhaps touch, all in the service of producing a desired change in the individuals who were present at the ritual. The aim of this particular spell was probably to protect against disease-bearing eclipses and the harmful influences of Mars and Saturn.

> First they sealed the room against the outside air, sprinkled it with rose-vinegar and other aromatic substances, and burnt laurel, myrtle, rosemary and cypress. They hung the room with white silken cloths and decorated it with branches. Then two candles and five torches were lit, representing the seven planets; since the heavens, owing to the eclipse, were defective, these were to provide an undefective substitute, as one lights a lamp when the sun sets. The signs of the Zodiac were perhaps also represented in the same way; for this is a philosophical procedure, not a superstitious one, as common people think. The other persons present had horoscopes immune to the evil eclipse. There was Jovial and Venereal music, which was to disburse the pernicious qualities of the eclipse-infected air and, by symbolizing good planets, to expel the influences of bad ones. For the same purpose they used stones, plants, colours and odours, belonging to good planets (that is Jupiter and Venus). They drank astrologically distilled liquors.[24]

Renaissance spells resembled, as do Neopagan rituals, the performance art of contemporary artists. Several media, such as visual theatrical props and music, are combined to convey a feeling that language alone is particularly unsuited to communicate.

According to Otto Baensch (1923, in Langer 1953), the aim of art (and, I would add, magic) is to embody a feeling so definitively that any person emphatically disposed toward the artistic medium experiences an apperception of the same sentiment that guided the artist.

The element of automatic efficacy generally associated with magicians appears in this description of art. Neopagan practitioners of magic taught me that the fulfillment of the function of magic, like art, is by no means guaranteed, because it depends on—among other things—the susceptibility of the subject. Bruno also acknowledged the importance of inspiring susceptibility in the subject.

Magic operates according to the principles of aesthetics, although that is not to say that magic is always the same as art. To a large extent, an artist strives to convey comprehension of feeling; a magician attempts to excite the experience of a specific feeling. Both use symbols to achieve it. Many artists are not interested in showing or performing their work; they are content that the art process is complete when they have solved the problem they set for themselves: arriving at an effective symbol. Magicians have a more practical aim. The effective symbol is a tool to aid her or him in creating a change. Furthermore, it must be adapted to the particular predisposition of each audience the magician attempts to affect. For example, to be "empathetically disposed" to Campanella's elaborate arrangement, it is likely that one would have to know about eclipses and the zodiac.

Artists of the Renaissance heightened creative perceptions with magical techniques. The allegorical images of planetary gods and mythic themes were intended to release a counterplay of imagination and thought (Wind 1958). The paintings and sculptures are provocative and explicit assemblages of numerical harmonies, colors, plants, gem stones, and so forth. Boticelli's "Venus" could serve as a statue for Bruno's art of memory or for a spell to draw the goddess down. When artists such as Raphael, Michelangelo, and Boticelli succeeded in causing that "something" to emerge, their purposes, methods, and the criteria of success greatly resembled those of their contemporaries, the Renaissance magii.

The Link between Bruno's Mysticism and Wicca

Giordano Bruno articulated a "new philosophy," as he called it, although it was more accurately a utopian religion with millennial aspirations.[25] Several themes that are recognizable in Gardner's Wicca appear in Bruno's writings. The goddess Diana is important, as is the idea that one must suffer to learn. A trinity of concepts that is central to Gardner's Wicca (love, death, and magic) and the idea of the witch as midwife to social reform are significant in Bruno's writings. Perhaps the title of the witches' Book of Shadows, derives from Bruno's treatises on the art of memory, *On the Shadow of Ideas.*

Bruno's rhetoric was patently pagan. He boldly abandoned the precaution of justifying the Hermetic literature by Christianizing it, claiming that the Egyptian religion it related was superior to Christianity. In the witch persecutions, he paid for this audacity with his life.

Bruno declared that Christianity, and all other beliefs of the masses, were set up by magical processes requiring faith, the strongest bond, the "chain of chains."[26] He recommended the use of the same technology to introduce an alternative religious perspective (Couliano 1984), which we will explore in more detail in chapter thirteen.

Diana

Gardner's ceremony of drawing down the moon was almost certainly inspired by Leland's *The Gospel of the Witches* (1899). In it, the goddess, Diana, gave birth to Aradia (Herodias) whom she sent to Earth to teach the people sorcery. The father of the child was Diana's brother, Lucifer, the god of light or splendor (Leland 1899).

Bruno wrote a book of love poems about Diana, *Heroic Furors.*[27] The poems were not about sexual love; they describe "heroic" or mystic attraction to the deity. In Bruno's poems, Diana is still the moon goddess; however, the splendor of the sun that she reflects is Amphitrite, who is also female. Amphitrite is divinity, the universal soul, the one that includes all things. It is not possible to see the Amphitrite, in her best and highest form. It is possible, however, to see her shadow, Diana. For Bruno, Diana is the manifest essence of Amphitrite, reflecting her in nature, as the moon reflects the sun. Bruno's Diana is simultaneously nature, the moon, truth that is also beauty, and the object of the mystic's quest.

Ordinarily, human eyes cannot see Diana, Bruno writes. Yet, in his love poems, as in Leland's *The Gospel of the Witches,* she is accessible. Diana and Aradia promised to come to Earth on the full moons, whenever the people gathered in some secluded place and called them. In Bruno's love poems, she is naked. Yet, to see her, Bruno wrote, one must die to the human condition (Yates 1964).

You Must Suffer to Learn

Bruno envisioned the possibility that a human being might glimpse the essential truth of existence (Diana) by resort to the intellective process he described in the *Heroic Furors* and other works. He created a phantasy to convey how one might accomplish this, using the characters in the myth of Actaeon as "statues" to be placed in the gallery of the memory.

In Bruno's interpretation of this well-known myth, the game that Actaeon, the hunter, pursues is occult knowledge. As the hunter advances he comes upon Diana, bathing naked in a spring. It is only the limits of intellect that prevent the hunter from embracing the splendor he sees. When Diana discovers the hunter, she changes him into a stag, and his own dogs devour him. The dismemberment transforms the hunter. The dogs release him from his former life in the world of sense and illusion. Dead to his former commonplace, civilized, and social self, he becomes wild as the stag far from the contamination of ordinary desires. He begins to live intellectually, like a god.[28]

Actaeon, seeing Diana naked, falls so much in love with the beauty of the body of nature that he is changed into the object of the hunt. Bypassing the faculty of phantasy and the spiritual mediation between the body and soul, he opens the heart (soul) so wide to the divine vision that he is absorbed by it. With his soul—not his eyes—he drinks in Amphitrite, the true essence of all being reflected in nature, Diana.

Having achieved initiation into direct knowledge of the world (gnosis), Actaeon became a paradoxical being. Bruno believed he, too, was such a being, a "dead man alive," liberated from the confines of the human species, qualified to be a religious leader because he had been transformed by the virgin goddess, the unattainable Diana (Couliano 1984; Yates 1964).

Love and Magic in Wicca

In Wicca, as in the Hermetic writings, there is a continuity between the operative love of the magus and the divine love circulating in the universe. Erotic love both resembles the mystical experience of gnosis and is itself one of the procedures by which the magician achieves it. Agrippa, on whose writings Bruno relied heavily for his discussion of eros, merged the two kinds of love, erotic and heroic, as do the Neopagans. Agrippa had the following to say about love that comes under the influence of Venus: "it turns and transmutes the spirit of man into a god by the ardor of love . . . The soul thus changed receives . . . so great a perfection that it knows all things . . . it can sometimes do work greater and more marvelous than nature itself, and such works are called miracles . . ."[29] We recognize this as gnosis and the empowering inspiration that motivates artists and craftspersons to create.

For Ficino and Bruno sexual love was entirely other than the love that draws one towards divinity. Experiences of gnosis belong to the intellectual part of the soul, Bruno wrote, although the experience that makes the soul "divine and heroic" can be likened to the trance or the *fulgor* of passionate love. Bruno issued the warning that the magician must render himself impervious to the love lest he fall victim to his own lures. In this trance, the immortal mind forsakes the body and gains the experience which gives it miraculous or magical powers.[30]

In Gardner's myth, the goddess "was bound as are all who enter the realms of Death" (Gardner 1954, 41). The witches' red cord is used both for measuring and for binding the body to modify circulation and produce trance. While the mind ascends to other realms, the body experiences a symbolic death. "The body . . . asleep in the ligature of the senses" symbolizes death or transcendence of the material body (Yates 1964).[31]

In Wicca, the stimulation of erotic energy figures among the techniques for raising energy for effecting magical transformations, or "miracles," as Agrippa would have it. For contemporary witches, eros and the sexual embrace merge in the great rite, which is both magic and worship.

The Hermetic Trinity

In a collection of Bruno's writings, *The Shadow of Ideas (de umbris idearum)*, there appears a set of three concepts, and their symbols, that are also significant in Gardner's Wicca.[32] The three figures appear in Bruno's discussion of the practices of Egyptian priests who drew down parts of the soul of the universe to animate, or "make gods" of, their statues. Bruno adapted this drawing down to his art of memory. Yates called it the "Hermetic Trinity" (1964). It expresses a significant theme in Hermetic literature, the three-part hierarchy: god, world, and humans, and also love, death, and magic. In the present context, Bruno said the first concept, *figura mentis* (☉), represents divine universal force (pneuma) and is the source of the others. *Intellectus* (☽) is "the word" or "expression" that communicates divine force. The letters, "magic" appearing in counter-clockwise order on the third, spell out its significance. Bruno named it "figure of love" (★). The human mind, being the vehicle of *intellectus*, receives the divine pneuma and

(a) "Figura Mentis."

(b) "Figura Intellectus."

(c) "Figura Amoris."

Figures from Giordano Bruno.

communicates it to the world of nature.[33] Magic, as we have already seen, is the circulation and transformation of universal pneuma by the force of love. Bruno recommended these concepts as being the most "fecund" for all the sciences and for operating magically, particularly for the art of memory that he was expounding in those treatises.

The magician might draw down parts of the universe into himself as the Egyptian priests had drawn them into their statues, he claimed. This is also the purpose of the Wiccan ritual, drawing down the moon. The high priestess who receives the lunar influence, wears a crescent moon crown, on the inner surface of which all three symbols are carved.

We have already encountered this three-part hierarchy in the allegory of Actaeon. There, the essence is called Amphitrite; her brilliance (the sun) is reflected in Diana, as the sun is reflected in the moon. The encounter results in the *magic* of Actaeon's transfiguration.

The five-pointed star (pentagram) is the most important of all symbols of the craft, comparable to the star of David as a symbol of Judaism or the cross of Christianity. For witches the five-pointed star, which is to be drawn in one continuous inter-woven stroke, is called "the endless knot." It symbolizes the unity of the three-part hierarchy of divine source, the interconnected pneuma-infused world and humans. Humans strive upwards toward the celestial divinity, draw down it's force, and circulate it along the currents of sympathies by which the parts of nature are attracted. Another of the significances of the pentagram is the human form: it has five points, one for each limb and the head.

The endless knot, a pentacle carved in wood by Herb Eldridge.

In the ceremony of drawing down, the high priestess assumes postures characteristic of Egyptian statues. She serves as a reflection of the divine universal force, which for the witch has a dual nature as goddess and god. In the Yule ritual described earlier, Raven served as a reflection of the god or sun. Either priestess or priest reflects or creates a shadow of the source, or idea, and they communicate it to the other coven members.

The traditional charge that the high priestess speaks when the moon is drawn down into her expresses the goddess' love (*amour*) for the coveners. This has two interpretations. First, is the affection the goddess feels for humans which is expressed in her promise to teach them sorcery with which they might protect themselves. Also, the priestess is the conduit for love as a divine force (*eros*) that Ficino said moves pneuma, the substance of magic.

When the priestess recites the charge, in the first person, she uses words that humans would imagine a divine and ineffable source to speak, if it were to use language. Let us return for a moment to the story of Actaeon's transmutation. When he discovered nature exposed and naked and was absorbed into it in love, it would not be too far fetched to imagine that if he heard Diana speak (and surely she would not because such an experience is ineffable), he would hear a speech that resembles in essence the Wiccan charge of the goddess:

> I am the beauty of the green Earth,
> and the white moon among the stars,
> the mystery of the waters,
> and the passion of human hearts.

> Call unto your soul; arise, and come unto me,
> for I am the soul of nature, who gives life to the universe.
> From me all things proceed, and unto me all things must return.

> Before my face, beloved of All,
> let your divine, inmost spirit be
> enfolded in the rapture of the infinite.
> And let my worship be in the heart that rejoices.

> For behold, all acts of love and pleasure are my rituals.
> Therefore, let there be beauty and strength,
> power and compassion, honor and humility,
> mirth and reverence within you.

> And, you who think to seek for me,
> know that your seeking and yearning
> shall avail you not, unless you know the mystery:
> If you find not what you seek within you,
> you will never find it without.

> For behold, I have been with you from the beginning.
> And I am that which is attained at the end of desire.[34]

Love, Death and Sympathetic Magic

Like the story of Actaeon, the Hermetic *Pimander* and Gardner's myth of the goddess tell of the fundamental connection of a three-part world: the high realm of gods, nature (Earth or goddess) and the realm of death, or the underworld. The half-divine being (the magus) of the *Pimander* descended to Earth from the higher realm of the gods because he fell in love with the image of himself that he saw reflected there. Nature embraced him and they "burned with love" (Yates 1964). The magus of the *Pimander* tale entered lovingly into the sympathies that bind Earth to heaven, and this emotional relationship was one of the chief sources of his power.

In the myth of the goddess, she and death "loved and were one." The goddess also gained power in her descent when death taught her "all the magics." To be born you must die, he told her (Gardner 1954, 41). To create, the magician must destroy existing bonds of attraction. Here is a paradox: love as creative magical force is the same as death. Creativity is destructive—the cause of joy as well as suffering. The witches' scourge symbolizes the necessity of suffering in the service of learning (being transformed by knowledge).

Neopagans are concerned that those who would work magic not only acquire the knowledge and skill of breaking and forging bonds of sympathy, they must acquire expertise in matters of ethics to qualify them to decide which bonds may be broken and which forged in the service of beneficial magic. "Love is the Law [according to which the universe operates]; Love under Will [of the magic user]" is the "golden rule" of Neopagan magic. Theoretically, the magician who is motivated by love, would not harm the object of that love. It is impossible to know if Renaissance magicians' conception of love included the beneficent affection that the Neopagans attribute to it;[35] they were working within the moral imperative that no magic except Christian magic could be beneficial.

Neopagans and their Renaissance predecessors knew that the magician must be in control of a refined and powerful will. To participate deliberately in the evolution of form is to behave like a Demiurge; about that, the Renaissance philosophers were explicit. Those who experimented with Hermetic magic practiced spiritual disciplines to purify their souls and thereby their motives. The Hermetic imperative, one must "fall in love" with nature, may have meant to the Gnostic writers and Renaissance translators no more than that the magician must engage the forces of eros. However for the Neopagans, nature serves as example, and the imperative to love nature inspires the good rather than harmful use of magic in the service of the universe, not merely the self or society.

The Witch as the Midwife to Social Reform

While in England, Bruno provided the earliest reference to a witch or sorcerer as heroine in his political message, *Spaccio della bestia trionfanta* (1584), which was written in England following a visit to Paris where Bruno had received some encouragement from Henry III. Bruno proposed that France and England join together in friendship against the menace of the Catholic reaction to the Reformation, particularly against Spain. Bruno wrote of an "illumination" that arrives in the British Isles. He exhorted seekers of illumination to summon the

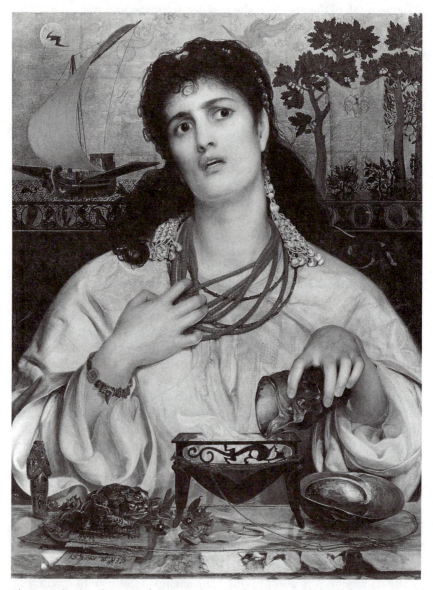

Photograph of Anthony Frederick Sandys' *Meda*, 1868. Published by permission of the Birmingham Museum and Art Gallery.

daughter of the sun, Circe (typically an evil enchantress). Here presented as a good magician, Circe "with plants and minerals working her incantations, would be able to curb nature."[36] In answer, Circe, daughter of the Sun, appeared. The one in whose presence the mystic truth unveils itself is the unique Diana, the Amphitrite. In this context the Amphitrite is the English queen, the "diva Elizabetta," the ruler Bruno expects to bring in his new dispensation. Bruno expressed unbounded admiration for Queen Elizabeth I, and his writings contributed to the creation of an Elizabethan chivalric cult (Yates 1979).

Circe appears again in Bruno's *Cantus Circaeus*,[37] one of his many works on the preparation of the mind of the magus. Again relieved of her customary evil associations, Circe ushers in the hoped-for moral reforms. Circe calls on the gods to restore virtue, and with her own magic she sets about restoring order where Christians have made a mess of things by worshipping dead things, setting men against one another, and "breaking the laws of love."[38]

Circe's sorcery is very familiar. With incantations and arrangements of plants and stones (reminiscent of the magic of the Wiccans), Circe makes magical gestures in the air, just as Carol, the high priestess of the Minoan Sisterhood, did in the Yule ritual. Circe holds out a plate on which "writings of the sacred gods" are written. We have seen that such a plate, the pentacle (generally made of engraved copper), is also used by Gardnerian witches for the same purpose: communicating with the gods.[39]

Here in Bruno's writings we find early precedent for the tools and ritual occupations of the present-day witches, and for their view of themselves as midwives to a new age of restoration after the disastrous centuries of Christian culture. Despite the religious reformers' attempts to purge all forms of the social progress (especially science) of occult associations, the positive image of the witch survived in art and literature.

Centuries later, in "The Witch of Atlas," Percy Bysshe Shelley presented the character of a lady witch as a benevolent savior, as Bruno had presented Circe. In Shelley's poem, furthermore, the witch heals nature with the mystical energy of "love," which is so important in the Western spiritual tradition. In the poem we recognize love as a cosmic impulse to creativity.

> A lady-witch there lived on Atlas' mountain
> Within a cavern, by a secret fountain. . . .
>
> . . . And others say, that, when but three hours old,
> The first-born Love out of his cradle lept,
> And clove dun Chaos with his wings of gold . . .
>
> . . . Then by strange art she kneaded fire and snow
> Together, tempering the repugnant mass
> With liquid love—all things together grow
> Through which the harmony of love can pass . . .[40]

Photograph of John Williams Waterhouse's *The Magic Circle*, 1886. Published by permission of the the Tate Gallery, London.

The Pre-Raphaelites, both painters and poets, also portrayed female witches in a sensuous and sympathetic way as Bruno and Shelley had done. In many of the paintings of Edward Burne-Jones, in particular, one sees images of lady sorcerers performing the same ritual acts using the same ritual tools used by witches today.

Tempting though it may be, it would be unjustified without further historical research to suggest that Bruno did found the cult of nature he advocated as an alternative to the Christians' worship of dead things or that Wicca is its progeny—although Yates strongly suspects that the cult, called the Giordanisti,[41] actually did exist (1964; 1972). However, it would be equally unwarranted to dismiss the similarities between the magico-religion that Bruno described in his copious publications and that practiced by present-day witches.

Undeniably, both embrace a religious experience of the gnostic type, an elaborate tradition of pneumatic sympathetic magic, and religious practice that begins with the perfection of the magician and ends in aspirations for social reform. More specifically, they both idealize the female magician as their heroine and celebrate the same mysteries involving love, death, and magic.

Bruno's magic, which works on the manipulation of relationships between things, "attraction," "bonds of love," or "sympathy," is the foundation of the same idea that is articulated by the witches—that it is possible to manipulate "energy," an invisible force surrounding and infusing solid objects for magical purposes. They also have in common at least one magical tool, an inscribed plate, and the idea of binding the body to liberate the soul. At the very least, we can be sure that Bruno's writings were influential and that his influence persisted and is apparent in Gardner's witchcraft.

The lore of the cult of Queen Elizabeth I, to which Bruno contributed his ideas while he was in England, must have been a resource available to Gardner. I expect that the Wiccans borrowed from it long before Gardner encountered Old Dorothy because elements of chivalry are well imbedded in its lore and traditions. Often the high priestess and priest are called lady and lord, for example, and a popular legend tells that the royal Order of the Garter was founded by King Edward III in the fourteenth century after he defended the honor of an unidentified lady of elevated royal rank. The lady exposed her involvement in Wicca when she dropped the buckled garter that served as an insignia of a witch's rank and level of accomplishment. To salvage the lady's honor, the king is said to have placed her garter around his own leg and spoke the slogan that became the motto of the order, *Honi soit qui mal y pense* (Shamed is he who thinks badly of this). Many contemporary Wiccans believe that many of the noble-born, including members of the English royal family, have been involved in Wicca.[42]

Folk Magic Absorbed Renaissance Magic

Literacy must have been an important dividing line between simple sorcery and the intellectual magic that descended from the Renaissance. As more people became literate, the magical books—and perhaps some of the learned treatises—became accessible to more people. By the time Gardner encountered Wicca, in Old Dorothy's coven, intellectual and folk magic had thoroughly merged.

Bruno's bold ideas influenced the ideological movements of the early seventeenth century, most significantly, the Rosicrucian movement that presented itself as an alternative to both the Protestant and Catholic reformations. To remedy the destructive influence of Christianity he recommended founding a "cult of nature" (Yates 1972). We can only wonder what he would think of Neopagan Wicca.

After Bruno's martyrdom, liberal Protestant thinkers, including Fludd, Kepler, Descartes, and Bacon, continued to seek inspiration in the culture of the Renaissance while founding the new science. Modern science is both a continuation of Renaissance ideas and a negation of its glorification of the imagination.

Liberal and utopian movements, including the Rosicrucian Brotherhood, discussed later in the book, gained an enormous underground influence in the form of secret societies. In 1888 the Hermetic Order of the Golden Dawn was founded by a coterie of leading Hermeticists, Masons, and Rosicrucians (Yates 1972). Gardner was a Freemason, and he met Old Dorothy through his membership in a Rosicrucian theatre company.

The hybridization of folk traditions and the Western spiritual tradition had already been accomplished by the 1850s, according to Doreen Valiente's recounting of the meeting of the witch, George Pickingill, with two eminent master Masons, Hargrave Jennings and W. J. Hughan. Pickingill was the founder of several covens, including Old Dorothy's. Valiente tells that "Old George" awed these Masonic "Rosicrucians" with his expertise and knowledge of "the inner secrets of Masonry" (1978, 18).

A British cunning-man, James Murrell, who died in 1860 in the "witch country" of Southeast Essex, was also acquainted with the learned variety of magic. There is ample evidence that the magician attempted to cure people and animals with herbal remedies, incantations, and the laying-on of hands; traced lost and stolen property by gazing into his magic mirror; identified and rebuffed witches with his iron "witch bottles"; practiced astrology; and summoned forces from the other world to help with the more difficult cases. In the wizard's trunk of magical implements were books on astrology, astronomy, herbalism, and geomancy.[43] The Christian version of the Hebrew Cabala had apparently found its way into Murrell's folk magic because in his books of magic and conjurations the "good angels" were named and described (Maple 1962, 163–171).

The Fluctuating History of the Western Spiritual Tradition

Together the Catholic and Protestant religious reformers destroyed a common enemy—the pagan culture of the Renaissance. By censorship of the imaginary, and asserting the idolatrous and impious nature of phantasms, the Reformation discredited the ideas that the natural and social world is a spiritual organism in which perpetual exchanges of phantasmic messages occurred. Out of fear of being accused of demonic witchcraft, people abandoned magic, astrology, alchemy, and the art of memory. Ironically, the Catholic counterreformation handed the Inquisition over to the Jesuits, whose spiritual practice included the education of the imagination, a sort of art of memory in which the tortures of hell and the suffering of humanity rather than celestial influences were impressed on the memory. Together the Protestant and Catholic reformers built a common edifice: modern Western culture (Couliano 1984).

The reformers established lessons we henceforth took for granted: (1) the imaginary and the real are two separate and distinct realms; (2) magic is a form of absorption in phantasy as an escape from reality; (3) the reality principle is set over and against the pleasure principle (Couliano 1984, 222).

The Renaissance held forth the possibility of reading the book of nature. For the thinkers of the Reformation, nature was a sinner, a seductress, a place of exile. The witch was imagined as the opposite of lawful Christian culture whose laws protect people from natural destruction.

Try as we might, it is difficult to see the past without prejudice born of present circumstances. The "selective will," or *interpretive grille*, in any given era is interposed between content and our treatment of it (Couliano 1984, 11). Historian Couliano pointed out the distorting influence of the interpretive grille: it imposes emphasis and suppresses certain ideological contents, even inverts ideas. For instance, Yates' assessment that Renaissance Hermeticism helped to prepare for the Scientific Revolution as a kind of first phase represents an interpretive grille that was, until recently, unquestioned, except by those scholars who dismissed Hermeticism as completely without merit. The intensive training of the imagination in relation to the religion of the world may well have contributed to the discovery of the mechanical universe, Yates thought. Her assessment reveals the beginnings of a disenchantment with modernism that is characteristic of a more recent interpretive grille, however. She wrote that great changes in social relationships followed the shift of allegiance to a view of the world as mechanism. As it turned out, science was allowed to develop in isolation from a concept of utopia and apart from the idea of a reformed society educated to receive it. The comparative disregard of the social and educational possibilities of the movement was "surely unfortunate for the future" (1972, 232).

Defining modernism as those social changes that accompanied the Industrial Revolution, many contemporary philosophers, scientists, and artists declare themselves postmodern. They mistrust the notion that modernity is progress; it failed, after all, to liberate humankind from ignorance and irrationality. They point out the world wars, the inequalities of wealth, and the destruction of many of the world's cultures that have resulted from the mechanization of human life. Impersonal social relationships and the blind efficiency of the nation-state have robbed life of its meaning and joy, they claim (Rosenau 1992).

Much like the founders of revitalization movements, postmodern thinkers wonder how the world got to be in the present state of disaster. When they look back to find a past golden age that preceded these problems, the postmodern thinkers and the Neopagans settle at the same point: the wrong turn taken into modernism, for which the burning times of the witch hunts cleared a gruesome path. To postmodern thinkers (especially Neopagans), Renaissance culture which came to an end in the burning times represents the last vestige of a truly civilized age. Efforts on the part of the Neopagans to establish a more satisfying personal and social order begin with a resort to premodern culture for inspiration.

Postmodern thinkers have in common with the Gnostic authors of the Hermetic texts and their Renaissance devotées (whom Yates [1964] claimed also felt a disenchantment with the prevalent approach to knowledge in their own time[44]), a desire for a more religious approach to knowledge. The authors of the Hermetica were disappointed with early Christian rationalism and Greek philosophy. Rather than an intellectual exercise, as it had been in Greece, philosophy was to serve as a way of reaching an intuitive knowledge of the divine. Gnosis was to be prepared for by ascetic discipline and a religious way of life.[45] The Hermetic treatises provided guidance for such a quest.

In those times when Gnosticism was free of Judeo-Christian dualism and associated with paganism, Yates called it the Religion of the World, and the Neopagans include it in their concept of the Old Religion. In these periods it emerged from obscurity, as it has presently, in parts of Europe and America.

Modification and Survival
of the Magical Philosophy

After Francis Bacon discredited individual brilliance or special illumination in science in favor of the long arduous method that "goes far to
level men's wits"[46] the use of the imagination was diverted into the arts,
literature, religious cults, and secret societies. The magus man became
the creative genius or inspired intellectual. The questing of a spiritual
elite after personal illumination and self-perfection became a symbolic
protest against the revolutionary social and cultural changes that had
taken place since the Reformation (Yates 1972).

The Religion of the World survived in the Romantics' idealization of
nature and the pagan past. The Renaissance concept of magus man
survived in mature Romanticism in the idealization of the power of the
imagination and the creative self. As an agent of transformation, the
Romantics believed they could actually reconstitute ordinary reality with
images and symbols. For the Romantic poet, god "comes into being"
via the imagination, in which the Romantics invested all hope of self-
transcendence. The Romantics were confident that the advancement of
humankind was effected through the masterful strokes of great
individuals (Carlyle 1795–1881); Nietzsche's Ubermensch (overman or
superman); and the idea that powerful individuals can will their
destinies. They placed their faith in the will and power of individuals
over and against the modern notion of collective progress.
Revolutionaries of the Romantic movement expressed their hopes for
social reform in personal revelations and persuasiveness of artistic
expression rather than in political reform (Raschke 1980).

Conjuring was taken over by poets, such as Arthur Rimbaud and
William Butler Yeats, who spoke of "the alchemy of the word," referring
to its powerful effect on consciousness rather than its logic or grammar.
Yeats, as is well known, was an occultist of this persuasion, an adept
of the Hermetic Order of the Golden Dawn.

One Neopagan writer acknowledged the link between Romantic
philosophy and Neopaganism—including Wicca—by remarking the
common "emphasis on individual, subjective transformation." The
present-day witch, like the Romantic poet, is "the artist-magician"
whose "magic is an artform" (Runyon 1978, 22–23).

Present-day witchcraft, therefore, did not spring fully formed from
the head of Gerald Gardner; it represents a resort to a magical philosophy
that is quite ancient and has been significant in various historical periods
of ideological transition in Western history. Even in the obscurity the
Western spiritual tradition suffered following the witch persecutions,
the magicians' ideas were nurtured and expressed in the works of artists
and poets.

Chapter Seven

Contemporary Western Magic

One afternoon at a PSG gathering, I was distracted from a discussion about magic by a child playing at the border of the woods. My companion remarked that it is possible to effect dramatic changes in the world if one is truly motivated. For example, she continued, if a mother noticed a tree limb falling dangerously near her child, she could divert its fall to protect him or her—even if she were as far away as we are from that little boy. "How is that possible?" I wondered.

In this chapter, we will see how she and other Neopagans answered my question. We will explore certain key ideas, technologies and assumptions regarding their magic and compare them to the older tradition of Western magic and the magics that anthropologists have observed elsewhere in the world.

Magic, as we are defining it, is a religious activity. Most of us in Western society have abandoned the belief that action undertaken may cause a desired effect by magic. Discussion of any magic must be prefaced with an orientation to the religious worldview within which it operates.

The Neopagans believe that the world is organized according to the following "Seven Hermetic Principles," that are summarized by "Three [anonymous] Initiates."[1]

1. The principle of mentalism: The All is Mind; the universe is mental. (I interpret this to mean everything is to some extent sentient or aware.)

2. The principle of correspondence: As above, so below; as below, so above. (Just as sacred forces [above] affect humans [below],

so might human actions affect the larger universe in a like manner.)

3. The principle of vibration: Nothing rests; everything moves; everything vibrates. (Subtle forces are transmitted in a vibratory manner.)

4. The principle of polarity: Everything has its pair of opposites; opposites are identical in nature but different in degree.

5. The principle of rhythm: Everything flows out and in; everything has its tides; All things rise and fall; the pendulum swing manifests in everything. (Magical actions must be in harmony with natural rhythms, like the seasons or cycles of planetary movements.)

6. The principle of cause and effect: Every cause has its effect; every effect has its cause; everything happens according to law; chance is but the name for Law not recognized; there are many planes of causation but nothing escapes the Law (The universe operates in an orderly and consistent way.)

7. The principle of gender: Everything has its masculine and feminine principles; gender manifests (itself) on All planes.

I would add to these principles the following axiomatic beliefs regarding the nature of energy: Energy is limitless, indestructible, flexible, and it follows thought. Oriented within these religious beliefs regarding the nature of the universe—both natural and supernatural— we may begin to explore the Neopagans' beliefs about magic.

On the questionnaire I asked informants to "describe your idea of Magick."[2] After a preliminary review of about one-third of the 189 free-form responses, I coded the results by creating twenty-eight variables to accommodate the most significant issues or elements offered in the definitions.

Since most of the definitions incorporated several issues each, many respondents will appear in more than one category. For example, one respondent provided the following definition of magic: "to cause change in conformity with will through normal action as well as ritual." This respondent contributed to the three variables: "causing change," "will," and "use of ritual." Had I asked specifically about each of the twenty-eight variables, I expect larger percentages of the population would have responded to them. As it is, the percentages indicate the number of individuals to whom the issue was significant enough for them to volunteer it. In the following discussion percentages of the total population are provided.

The highest percentage, 42 percent, mentioned the directing, focusing, or channelling of energy in their definitions of magic. Another 2 percent mentioned the involvement of light, a related concept. Energy is one of the two most significant elements in the Neopagan conception of magic; the other is change of consciousness. First, we will turn our attention to energy. In terms of anthropological discussions of magic, this is the least understood aspect.

Energy

People everywhere think witches emit light from their bodies (Needham 1978). Gardner wrote that witches are those people who are capable of releasing energy from their bodies (see chapter two). Energy, light, and movement are related concepts that describe the force or power of magic. In the dance and the sexual embrace of the great rite, energy is released as a result of a *biological* activity; in the symbolic conjoining of opposites—when the priestess plunges the athame into the chalice (see chapter three)—energy is released as a result of a *mental* activity, a communication.

When it comes to explaining energy, most Neopagans, as well as others in our society, resort to words from other languages or explanations deriving from science. Starhawk, for instance, wrote:

> Ironically as estranged science and technology advance, they have begun to bring us back to a consciousness of immanence. Modern physics no longer speaks of separate, discrete atoms of dead matter, but of waves of energy, probabilities, patterns that change as they are observed; it recognizes what Shamans and Witches have always known: that matter and energy are not separate forces, but different forms of the same thing. (1982, 10)

As Selena Fox pointed out, there is more prestige in aligning one's beliefs with science. For the well educated, it is important that their beliefs not be in absolute conflict with their understanding of the nature of the world in scientific terms, such as the theory of conservation of energy, for instance (personal communication, 1987). Neopagans understand the dynamics of energy on diverse levels that are not necessarily uniform in their details, but none would be in conflict with the seven principles.

The Western Conception of Energy

The American Heritage Dictionary provides the following definition of energy:

> 1.a. Vigor or power in action. b. Vitality and intensity of expression.
> 2. The capacity for action or accomplishment. 3. Power expressed with vigor and determination . . .[3]

When I visited Circle Farm in 1987, I asked Selena Fox to define energy. In her ministrations as healer and priestess, Selena works primarily with energy. Her techniques include some which resemble therapeutic touch, guided visualization, as well as others. Energy, Selena claimed, is the life force that exists within all things throughout the universe. It resembles and is somewhat connected with spirit, (personal communication, 1987). *Spirit*, incorporates other elusive concepts such as movement, light, will, soul, and essence ("that which constitutes one's unseen, intangible being"). In English usage, spirit means "that which is traditionally believed to be the vital principle or animating force within living beings" (*American Heritage Dictionary*, 1993).

Energy has an electromagnetic component, but it is more than that, according to Selena. All things, including rocks, are alive with vibratory energy, Selena believes. Each species has a distinct physical configuration and a unique essence or vibratory rate of the life force, but within each species there are variations. Fluctuations within the vibratory range reflect the state of vitality and are perceptible to some people as light or auras (personal communication, 1987).

Dolores Krieger (1979), originator of "therapeutic touch," a healing modality in nursing, relies on Hindu *prana* to describe energy. Related to the Sanskrit *vayu*, which is concerned with air, prana is more importantly related with motion, she writes. The literature of the East says that prana derives from the sun. This statement is not at variance with our current recognition that the life process in humans is dependent upon sunlight, she continues, for the photons coming from the sun set off the process of photosynthesis of organic matter that contributes to biological processes in humans. Considering that the process begins with inorganic matter, "the statement sounds more like a miracle than do the ancient texts of the East" (Krieger 1979, 12).

For Neopagans, the energy that infuses, creates, and sustains the physical body moves in emotions, feelings, and thoughts and is the underlying fabric of the material world. Each human being is an energy pattern that many people can literally see and feel. This pattern is generally described as having branches that extend down the arms and out through the hands and sweep up from the top of the head, down and around the body, and back to Earth, creating a surrounding energy field, or aura, which is a protective yet permeable filter.

Starhawk commented that there is no English word that adequately describes the witches' idea of energy. Like Krieger, she needed to borrow exotic concepts: the Hindu prana, Chinese C'hi, and Polynesian mana. We have seen that in the Renaissance these concepts were described by a perfectly good set of terms that originated closer to home—in the Western spiritual tradition: *fulgor*, Bruno's energy flow; *spiritus*, which means an airy luminous substance or breath; *eros* or *mens*, the energy/light/love that derives from the sun. However, to the Western mind these terms, which are part of its own cultural heritage, are more alien than those borrowed from foreign cultures because they have been, to use a psychoanalytic term, "repressed."

The occult is a repository of rejected knowledge; it evokes feelings of ill-defined fear, revulsion, shame, guilt, and disdain. In that fearsome darkness the witch character lurks, along with the male magician (personified by Dr. Faustus). All of this is associated in our minds with the underworld that had been the treasury of "the measures" belonging to the earliest science of the Sumerian astronomer-priests. In myths, heroes journeyed there to retrieve valuable information regarding the operations of the universe. Following the witch hunts and the victory of the Enlightenment, the underworld became the domain of evil and suffering, the Christian hell.

From this "skeleton closet" of Western society, Frances Yates and a few other historians have carefully dredged up "the measures" of Renaissance magic, the Hermetic texts, and Bruno's formulae. Within this cache are perfectly explicit terms for concepts of energy, the force behind magic, and the light witches are believed to emit from their bodies.

Hermes Trismegistus explained to his son Tat that the energy of life is in constant movement and transmutation. Bruno wrote of energy (fulgor) as the divine love (amour) of the magician that is continuous with the energy, or movement, of the universe. Fulgor is released in the experiences of erotic love, ecstacy, or gnoses. Echoing Bruno's Hermetic trinity: love, sex, and magic, Starhawk writes:

> Energy is ecstasy . . . No drug can take us so high; no thrill pierce us so deep because we have felt the essence of all delight, the heart of joy, the end of desire. Energy is love, and love is magic. (1979, 129)

Some respondents to the questionnaire (15 percent) indicated that magic operates with an energy source that is external to the self. This view is consistent with the idea that energy in the universe is continuous. Because of this, the witch I was talking with at PSG explained, a mother's passionate imperative can divert the trajectory of a falling limb away from her child. The power of the will here can have an effect there because all space is filled with energy that is continuous and susceptible to manipulation.

Neopagans find this belief empowering. Energy is one of the multiple levels of physical reality that is susceptible to manipulation without complicated technology or socially conferred authorization. They believe energy can be (a) raised by groups or individuals, (b) drawn down from the sky, (c) raised from the Earth, and (d) "channeled" for the purpose of healing individuals both near and distant, all in accord with notions of the properties of energy that are consistent with those expressed in the literature of the Western spiritual tradition deriving principally from the Hermetic texts. Ironically, because the Western spiritual tradition has been off limits to intellectuals since its eclipse into the underworld at the end of the witch hunts and the birth of the Enlightenment, these home-grown concepts are often believed to derive from Eastern mysticism that arrived in the West in the nineteenth century.

Pagan Notions of Mana

Primitive people have a feeling, Marett wrote, that there is an occult power in certain persons and things. This feeling, for which Marett (1909) used the Polynesian term, *mana*, is the emotion of awe, which is a compound of fear, wonder, admiration, interest, respect, and perhaps even love. The presence of mana distinguishes sacred things and separates them from the secular realm. Whatever evokes this emotion is treated as religion.

Magic is essentially a cathartic expression of emotional tension that requires release, Marett added. Ordinary situations in social life generate states of emotional intensity, and ideally they are vented in useful activities such as hunting, fighting (if we may think of fighting as practical), and lovemaking. When a person is overcome by hate, love, or by some other strong emotion, and there is nothing of a practical nature that can be done about it, he or she may resort to magic as an outlet for the superfluous energy. That may be "make-believe" activities—such as destroying an image of the person who inspired the unwelcome feelings—or substitute activities, such as dancing (Marett 1909).

Marett thought of energy—as few scholars did[4]—in terms of tension or actual substance that may accumulate and require release by moving or expressing it in some way. This idea is in agreement with Bruno's notion of fulgor as well as those ideas underlying the Neopagans' conception of energy manipulation. Magical acts are not make-believe for present-day Western magicians and witches, nor are they merely cathartic. In fact, the magicians would say that Marett had it backwards. Dancing is not an outlet for superfluous energy. Like the inevitable situations in social life that generate emotional intensity, dancing is an effective technique for raising energy. The source of the energy is less important than the way the energy is transformed, focused, and released in magical expression. The transformative aspect of magic is accomplished in symbolic communication that witches call changing consciousness or awareness.

Rather than the residue of an unpleasant emotion that must be gotten rid of, Neopagans regard energy as a valuable resource. Not only certain malevolent witches but all humans have the inherent ability to generate this valuable resource from their bodies. If energy is the residue of frustration, rage, or even illness, it must be transformed before it is directed to accomplish any beneficial purpose. The magic of raising, transforming, and releasing energy was demonstrated to me in a ritual performed by American witches in Wisconsin at the 1983 PSG gathering. In this ritual—to which we turn our attention now—the belief that the energy in the universe is interwoven into a continuous fabric with "knots of love," was dramatized in a communal building of a web.

The Web-Building Ritual

While the three hundred witches and other Neopagans gathered in Wisconsin during the summer solstice of 1983, Starhawk was engaged in one of her magico-religious-political demonstrations on the grounds of the Livermoor nuclear power plant in California. She led a Wiccan ritual with other witches and Neopagans in an effort to halt the construction of the nuclear power plant located on a vulnerable fault line. In sympathy and support of the demonstration, about one hundred witches gathered in Wisconsin to "send energy" to Starhawk and her collaborators.

Following a very simple creation of a circle—by inviting the spirits in the cardinal directions—the priestess spoke about Starhawk's project and the many problems that require such courageous efforts. "What would you wish to remedy?" she asked the participants. Quietly at first a few individuals named such things as pollution of the waters. Gradually, as the priestess urged the circle of standing participants to walk as they spoke, the statements grew more impassioned. The wheel of celebrants spun a little faster. Outcries interrupted and overlapped as the participants inflamed one another. The movement became a resolute march. Anger, fear, and other emotions were voiced, often tearfully, as individuals named, in increasingly impassioned shouts, the abuses that they wished to end: pollution, domestic violence, animal experimentation, violations of religious rights, and so on. When the priestess sensed that the group's catharsis had reached a peak, she stopped in her tracks, and the group fell silent to hear her advance the theory, "The Earth does not need more negative energy."

The passion aroused by concern for the Earth is a valuable resource, she said, if we transform and direct it with our will. "What will each of you do to remedy these problems?" she asked. With the intent of the magic thus clarified the participants resumed their dance around the circle and, this time, the outcries told of commitments to correct the many problems they had named. In this way they transformed the meaning they attributed to the reservoir of energy. Rather than the residue of desperation, it became, in their minds, a power source for hopeful, creative action. The priestess threw balls of yarn to people around the circle and told them to hold the thread and pitch the balls of yarn back and forth across the circle as they shouted out their intentions. Some vowed to volunteer for environmental changes, social services (such as shelter for battered women and children), or personal tasks such as feeding stray animals. As they spoke, marched, and criss-crossed the circle with balls of yarn, they began to see a web taking shape in their midst. Suspended within the hoop of dancers, the web thickened and emotions rose. They began to sing while the promises were called out. Soon the singing turned to laughter and tears when the group achieved a collective peak of emotional intensity.

Generally the energy is visualized as spinning into a cone shape that is projected beyond the circle to effect its purpose (as in the Yule ritual of the Minoan Sisterhood). In this ritual, the energy infused the web instead. By a process resembling Hermetic pneumatic magic, the group's energy was invested in the fibers of the web—much as the spirit of gods had been drawn into Egyptian statues and magical amulets (according to the Hermetic texts). Passion and intent were woven with yarn into a visual, energy-filled representation wrought of rage, fear, and sadness metamorphosed by potent magic that is both work and play.

The participants congratulated themselves for creating a beautiful work of art (the web), and for the healing magic they accomplished. They healed themselves, by releasing and transforming maladaptive emotional states, and the Earth, by converting feelings of helplessness into creativity on its behalf. The participants cut the web into pieces to take home. They decided to deliver or mail the fragments to a location that needed healing energy.[5]

The two aspects of magic as the Neopagans understand it—energy manipulation and communication—worked together. Energy, the residue of normal vitality, was generated deliberately, although many participants probably brought tension and anxiety with them to the ritual. With their will and intent, the magicians directed, channeled, and focused it into a tangible artifact while clarifying feelings to themselves.

Both a symbol and a container for the transformed energy, the web served the function of art as well as magic. As a model of the inter-connected universe, the web communicated the hope that action in Wisconsin could be helpful in California.

There is no clear distinction between symbolic and empirical action in the Neopagans' conception of magic. No magical act is a mere make-believe release of tension. The symbols are dynamic; they contain, mold, and move energy—the bonds of love, attraction, or sympathy that hold the world together in its present form. In this reflexive magic, the symbol also impresses the mind, including that of the magician, its creator.

How Magic Operates

In the free-form responses to the questionnaire, informants provided the following faculties through which magic operates a) one's own power or will, 12 percent; (b) imagination, 5 percent; (c) psychic powers or skills, 5 percent; and (d) creativity, 4 percent. More important than all of these, change of consciousness, was offered by 19 percent of the respondents. Energy is the power source for magical operations; changing consciousness describes a collection of methods magicians use to give form, purpose, and meaning to energy.

Changing Consciousness in Regard to the Idea of the Witch

Magic is, among other things, a way of transforming expectations and shifting consensus by resort to powerful symbols, including archetypes and myths. Take the image of the witch, for example. In the Western mind, the witch, as personified evil and darkness, emitter of light and malice, is further burdened with repressed shame and horror associated with memories of the witch hunts. At the dawn of the Enlightenment, Francis Hutchinson was moved to explain a gentleman's distaste for the whole subject:

> As the very nature of the Subject carries both Horror and Difficulty, polite Men and great Lovers of Ease, will turn away their Thoughts from it with Disdain.[6]

Like all repressed memories, the symbol of the witch as a victim of this shameful episode in the "advance" of Western civilization is distorted and confused. Is the witch the possessor of malign powers, or is she an impotent cartoon? Was she a threat to Christendom, or were the Christian persecutors a threat to individual freedoms? Who is really guilty of perverse crimes and sexual perversions, the witches or the learned clergy and officials who tormented them?

Today's witches are attempting to change consensus in regard to the meaning of the witch as a symbol. To assume the witch as a personal identity provokes all the powerful emotions associated with it. The energy embodied in these emotions can be manipulated, rechanneled, and transformed by the skillful magician for his or her own purposes.

Witches and Neopagans would inspire less opposition if they called themselves "nature lovers" or "cunning-folk healers"—as their persecuted predecessors were called—anything but witches and pagans. However, they use these energy-releasing names intentionally. Psychotherapists often use the very words and images that evoke powerful responses to challenge patients who expend so much life force to avoid the ugly truth that they have made themselves sick. For witches and therapists alike, the idea is (1) to confront the fearsome symbol, (2) to discover its true content, and (3) to divert the power that lies hidden within it to some useful (magical) purpose.

I asked the "green witch" (herbalist) Susun Weed why she calls herself a witch. "It was only one of many derogatory female archetypes that I deliberately became," she explained. Susun's former husband told her every day how helpless and dependent she was on his protection. She believed him and felt safe within his care until he was sent to prison, leaving her unemployed, unprepared to be employed, and the single parent of a daughter.[7]

Part of her recovery from these disastrous circumstances was her decision to empower herself by becoming all the derogatory feminine archetypes: dyke, whore, bitch, and witch. As she expected, she found that her socially conditioned beliefs about these epithets were as misleading as the lie her husband had told her about her helplessness and dependency. "There is pleasure and power for women in each one of these," she said. "In a male-dominated society these ugly symbols are used to frighten women into repressing potential powers" (Weed 1989).

On the most fundamental level, a witch is a person believed to possess inherent and unauthorized power, the kind of power that escapes social control because it resists detection. For those who are excluded from the privileges and the benefits of any social system, this power to do magic—or the ability to inspire in others the fear of it—is a potent weapon of self-defense. In addition, their skills—herbcraft, midwifery, enchantments—afford witches some measure of self-sufficiency in matters of healing and the satisfaction of other practical needs when rights and privileges available to others are withheld. This is the power contained in the witch archetype that contemporary witches are attempting to release and harness. It is, in essence, self-sufficiency.

When a Neopagan witch refers to herself or himself as one, energy in the form of fear, revulsion, derision, surprise, or puzzlement is inspired in the hearer, but a feeling of power is evoked in the witch. Present-day witches claim that energy and transform it for their magical purposes. On meeting a living, breathing, self-identified witch, a person is given the opportunity to reconcile expectation with reality. Little by little, light is shed on a repressed, distorted symbol.

Susun Weed, green witch (herbalist). Photograph included with the permission of Susun Weed.

So far these efforts to change the idea of the witch and the pagan in the popular imagination have resulted in more confusion than consciousness-raising among unbelievers. However, the movement is growing fast as many individuals have changed their conception of the witch figure sufficiently to adopt the role for themselves. Following change in perception come changes in actions, and the responses of others to new behaviors.

The deeper one delves into the forbidden powers of the witch, the more one questions the willingness to condemn and scapegoat others. The issue of who shall be authorized to wield power demands more careful scrutiny as does the possibility of developing inherent human potentials such as those attributed to witches. In the process, the symbol of the witch unfolds and turns itself inside out. It serves those who identify with it as a tool to change their relationship to the world. For Neopagans, this kind of willed change is magic.

Changing Consciousness in Regard to the Sacred/Secular Dichotomy

The idea of changing consciousness is fundamental to the distinction (or lack thereof) between sacred and profane domains. We have seen that Marett (1909) explained the distinction between the sacred domain (that of religion) and the secular by the presence of mana in the former and its absence in the latter.

According to Durkheim, the quality of sacredness (which resembles Marett's mana) is superimposed onto an object or a person's character (1915). In contrast, the vital principle—energy, or spirit—is understood by Neopagans to be intrinsic to the person, animal, plant, or thing—not superimposed on it. Energy, as Selena Fox explained, is the vibratory rate that is unique to each species or genus of thing. According to this way of thinking, a symbol, such as a totem, is merely a convenient way to refer to intrinsic, sacred, unique qualities.

As Bruno wrote, the magician's imagination may be trained to mobilize, attract, or evoke within the self qualities or powers by the use of magical techniques. Often these techniques included the utterance of a word or sound whose vibration "draws down" or attracts the spiritus of the desired sacred power (generally referred to as a deity). This idea that sacredness corresponds to vibratory rate is appealing to the educated Western person because such an idea is not in conflict with scientific explanations of the nature of matter. On the subatomic level, matter, as most individuals educated at the high school level in the last two decades are aware, is vibratory, and variances in vibratory rates are legitimate ways to differentiate the unique qualities of matter. The absence of these energetic vibrations constitutes death; presence indicates life. This perspective on the nature of reality affords the opportunity to associate mystical concepts such as spirit, energy, and life force with respectable and easily understandable scientific ideas (especially when they are presented by the numerous popularizers of science). Religious perspectives and factual scientific ones no longer require compartmentalization.

This is not the only way that Neopagans think of energy, spirit, and sacredness. Many do not know or care to think of gods and mysterious forces on a level of scientific reality. Many prefer to think of the goddess as a big woman in the sky, or, as Merlin Stone, a feminist scholar and author of *When God Was a Woman* (1976) said, "I used to think of Her as a little lady sitting behind my sternum."[8]

The merging of magico-religious and scientific ideas regarding the nature of reality is a recent phenomenon that has changed the way Western-educated people think about issues of religion, sacredness, and magic. It also changes our understanding of the potency of symbols. Symbols are both abstract representations of an ineffable idea and also substantive materials such as herbs, minerals, and the effluvia of animals. These living plants and animals—even rocks—possess qualities of motion, vibration, and unique characteristics that may be experienced as sacred or mundane, or both at once.

Evans-Pritchard wrote that the Azande used plants and other substances that were believed to possess inherent powers (1937). When Neopagans say this same thing about their magic, we have some understanding of what that power is. It is the life force, energy or vibratory rate, or inherent qualities of the materials that may be employed for beneficial (or harmful) ends. It resembles the Renaissance idea of pneuma.

In this way of thinking, the natural world is experienced on its own terms, not merely in terms of its relationship to, or utility for, humans. Each species and genus of things is recognized to possess unique qualities beyond its outward appearance through which it affects humans as a visual symbol. The visual and symbolic impression it makes on the human mind is a human phenomenon; its inherent qualities exist independently of the use humans may make of them.

For Durkheim, the soul is society individualized, the social personality as distinct from the individual organism. It is the society within each of its members, its culture and social order, that makes one a social being instead of a mere animal (1915). The Neopagans turn this conception inside out. The soul or essence of a person is the animal nature. Rather than ennobling, social forces pervert and obscure the vital force or soul. The social personality must be transcended to know a person's soul or divine part. Divinity for the Neopagans is linked to the life force— immanent in every atom of the individual organism—that connects them to other animals and natural phenomena. Sacredness is not a social attribute; it is an inherent quality of the animal, vegetable, or mineral nature of the thing itself. Sacredness comes to humans by identification with other species via their common vibratory nature. Contrast this with the predominant notion of sacredness wherein humans are ennobled by it to the extent that they differentiate themselves from the rest of nature.

The Neopagans view this distinction between sacred and profane as a matter of shifting consciousness, attitudes, or awareness within the perceiver rather than a criterion for sorting out discrete categories of phenomena, people, or activities. The Old Religion attributes divinity to all things by virtue of their participation in a divine, living, moving, changing universe. From this perspective, magic and worship both begin by shifting awareness to the divine or moving quality in all things.

Dolores Krieger's discussion of prana provides us with an example of the process of shifting consciousness. As described earlier, we can view prana merely as a process of photosynthesis in plant matter. In the Yule celebration described in chapter three, the same phenomenon was celebrated as a religious mystery, the return of revivifying light of the sun on the winter solstice. This phenomenon can be construed a secular reality (scientific fact) or a miracle, depending on the attitude or position of the individual contemplating it. Nothing is added, subtracted, or superimposed. The subjective experience of the phenomenon may be transformed by "changing the mind" of the perceiver.

All religious and magical operations begin by establishing a sacred location (between the worlds of gods and humans) within which time and space operate differently than they do in the profane world. Everything becomes a miracle within the circle, it being more a perspective on reality than a location in space. In sacred space, the sun becomes a god, and photosynthesis its numinous life force.

There is very little rigid segregation of "sacred" objects. Many Neopagans preserve a separate room or area as a temple in their homes. Traditionally the witches' tools—sword, athame, boline, inscribed metal pentacle—are kept inviolate. The more Americanized witches (and other Neopagans) take pleasure in using simple kitchen tools as ceremonial ones.[9] Common paring knives are the best tools for the witch who truly believes in immanence: the goddess (divinity) is in all things (even kitchen tools) and all acts, including peeling a potato, may be sacred acts depending on one's focus.

For magical operations, shifting awareness between the conceptual categories of solid/fluid, and matter/energy are essential. Energy is fluid and flexible and, to the magician's way of thinking, susceptible to manipulation.

The beginning of any creative act, for a plumber as well as a magician, is the identification of the level at which the object of their craft is flexible and susceptible to transformation by the means and tools available. The difference is between adding flavoring to the batter or to the cake as we noted in chapter three. The level at which witches are best equipped to effect transformations is that of moving energy or changing mental attitudes and emotions by symbolic communication. Others who possess institutionalized authority or elaborate technology—guns, for instance— are not limited to the level of manipulation that uses inherent human potentials. The resort to this basic human potential differentiates the craft of witchcraft from other acts that effect change.

A magical operation begins by directing attention to the sacred quality of the world. The bonds of attraction (or sympathy) that hold together form, and the barely perceptible vibratory qualities of matter that the magicians seek to modify are more comfortably placed in the sacred rather than the secular realm of experience.

From the perspective of science, the quantum leap is an especially inspiring phenomenon for witches. By shifting one's focus to the subatomic level, magicians imagine drastic transformations of configurations in space to be within the realm of possibility. According to the Heisenberg principle, those unpredictable and abrupt transformations are subject to human intervention. All of this constitutes a shift of consciousness to a position from which the magician feels potent and becomes more likely to act with confidence, authority, and power.

In terms of healing an illness, magicians must shift their awareness to a level at which the situation is flexible and susceptible to the available influence and tools. Surgeons tend to intervene on the level of solid tissue by removing or rearranging it. Lacking these specialized skills and access to elaborate technology, witches approach healing at the level of consciousness and energy. The magical healer begins by focusing attention on the patient's energy level and psychological condition, which are more susceptible to change by the means available to the healer. Even those witches and Neopagans who believe it is possible to dissolve solid tumors would begin by focusing their attention on the level of greatest flexibility—energy, rather than the solid properties of matter.

Change of consciousness may be the *process* by which magicians prepare themselves and perform magic, and it may be the *aim* of magic. In order to cause healing, for example, the magician would change the patients' attitudes and beliefs, which in turn, influence the quality and meaning attributed to vital energy and the willingness to mobilize it to heal themselves. Changing the consciousness of others, shifting consensus, or influencing others by resort to the sacred are acts of magic.

Energy, we have seen, may be generated by various means: gratuitously as in illness, for example, or deliberately by dancing or singing, in the sexual embrace, or by stimulating feelings of revulsion, rage, or sadness. Energy is the raw material. *Changing* the energy, its vibratory rate, its location, or one's subjective experience of it, is where the transformation (magic) occurs. Applied to healing, magic means attributing a useful meaning to accumulated energies (both the patient's own and those generated by others to give to the patient). This attribution is a cognitive function that relies on the effective use of symbols. The human faculties through which the transformations of consciousness that constitute magic are achieved, the Neopagans say in their responses to the questionnaire, are personal power or will, the imagination, psychic powers, and creativity.

The Magician's Will

In magic, personal power, or will, operates in ways similar to those used in ordinary persuasiveness, except that magicians follow ritual procedures to enhance that quality, and spell-working (craft) is the technology for focusing the will to achieve the desired ends. The will also implies focused intent, passion, and desire, and can therefore be seen as an energy source. Fire is the element associated with the will; a wooden wand is the magician's tool for focusing and directing it.

Aleister Crowley (1926) clarified the role of will in the magician's operations by using the Greek word *thelema*. His thelemic magic effects transformation by the deliberate use and focus of the disciplined will, or thelema. This kind of magic involves a great deal of manipulation of symbols (as was described in the Hermetic texts) to establish or activate connections or attractions (sympathies) among parts of the universe or to draw spiritus (energy) into talismans. It relies, also, on the use of images, plants, minerals, music, and invocations.

It is Crowley (1926) who formulated a well-used version of the Wiccan Rede: Do What Thou Will is the Whole of the Law and Love is the Law, Love Under Will. The dual aspects of will are expressed in these two sentences. In the first, will suggests intent and action, energy generated in the biological organism. In the second, it implies mental activity, the focus of desire. All of this is tempered with love. That is, the effect operates via the knots of love by which, according to Bruno, the magician is connected to other creatures and to the energy bonds (sympathies) that hold all things together. It also implies that magic should be used for beneficial ends; it should not break the bonds of love as, in Bruno's opinion, the Christian laws did.

Crowley made it plain that the most important part of magic is the careful refinement of one's wishes and desires, which must flow from truth as the magician defines it. Bruno called this the preparation of the personality of the magician. This "spiritual" dimension of the magic was abandoned as dangerous occultism—a result of the witch persecutions.

Crowley's philosophy is well suited for the development of individuation and relativity that is so much a part of postmodern thinking. It is existential—each act of the magician must flow from the truth she or he perceives in accordance with her or his true nature at each moment. It is relativistic; each person's truth, position in time and space, and set of impulses deriving from their past constitute different criteria for authentic action (Melton 1982).

In the minds of many Neopagans, the idea of will is often endorsed by references to popular science. I found four articles in Neopagan newsletters explaining magic in terms of quantum mechanics. "The basic reality of quantum universe is that it is only doing what the observer wills it do to," wrote Larry Cornett (1987, 3) in "Magick Is: Will Applied in a Quantum Universe" in a Canadian newsletter. Another Neopagan, Eran, wrote:

> Listen closely [to a quantum physicist] and you begin to hear things a High Priestess may have told you, things about the effect of will upon reality, about interconnectedness and relationships, correspondences lasting for all eternity between things that were once in contact. What you begin to hear is an explanation of the physics of Magic. (1986, 1:3)

Imagination

The creation of a clear and vivid image of the magician's desired outcome is a crucial first step in magic. Often imagination drives creative acts of manifesting an image in material form, such as in pictures or poppets (dolls) representing the persons on whom the magic is to work. Procedures such as those described as pneumatic and sympathetic in the Hermetic texts also operate through the imagination.

Some magicians believe the creation of the image of the desired outcome in the mind of the magician is sufficient in itself to set a magical transformation into action. Because the universe is, to them, entirely "mental" or sensate and intimately interwoven, Neopagans see no impediment to the transmission of an image from the mind of an adept magician through the system. When the magician reveals materialization of his or her mental image, such as a poppet or crafted talisman, for example, there is the added possibility of influencing the viewer by direct communication. Such an object would help the subject of the magic to imagine the outcome. In either case, imagination is the source of the image and the faculty through which its possible effects may be received. It is not surprising, then, that a great deal of magical training is devoted to developing the imagination.

Creativity

The craft of witchcraft is creativity, the fashioning of a physical thing or event. We have already seen that the Wiccan ritual is a template for the creative act. The boline is used for this practical work. Often the products of creativity are material art works which impress the minds of others, such as the larger-than-life props that are created for group rituals at gatherings, as we shall see in other chapters.

In spell-working, the magician may attempt to "draw down" the energy, powers, or associations of a deity by carving or drawing an image, making music, enacting a drama, or reading a poem. Spells may involve sewing of poppets to represent a person, carving messages or symbols on candles, or tying knots on a cord to "fix" one's mental image.

Creativity implies cunning also. I was told that effective magicians are those who are able to adjust their vibratory rate to accommodate to any circumstances in which they find themselves.[10] There are spells for invisibility, and there are ways of behaving that make one inconspicuous. There are complicated manipulations and mixtures of herbs, gems, and colors to attract a lover, and there are also ways of behaving that involve great sensitivity to circumstances that would attract erotic interest. All of these constitute creativity in the craft of witchcraft.

Psychic Skills

Only 5 percent of the respondents to my questionnaire mentioned psychic skills in their definition of magic. This is not to say that prophecy, divination, or other skills regarded as unusual are not valued by Neopagans. Magical training is intended to strengthen these faculties along with others such as astral travel. Many Neopagans say they have experienced premonitions or déjà vu or out-of-body states.

Because the credibility of these experiences is generally denied in the mainstream, those who believe they have had these experiences tend to repress their memories and feelings about them. The feeling of "coming home" that Neopagans often describe following their discovery of the Neopagan movement is, I believe, relief at finding others who also experience these unspeakable, yet—to them—real experiences. In the movement, they find others who either have similar "psychic" experiences or believe they are possible and good.

Most people are not boastful about the psychic skills they possess, and Neopagans tend to believe everyone has inherent psychic skills and the potential to develop them. If a person lacks psychic talent or aptitude, there are still other ways of working magic, such as cunning mentioned above, that do not require psychic ability. Psychic talents are, however, expected to develop and improve with magical work.

Many psychic skills regarded as extraordinary by others are not particularly unusual to the Neopagans who believe they are accessible to almost everyone. For instance, on the questionnaire I asked about the ability to see or manipulate auras. Most (89 percent) believed it is possible to see auras.[11] But when I asked respondents to define magic, only 5 percent thought to volunteer psychic skills—of any kind—as part of their definitions.

How Magic Works

In the free-form definitions, magic was defined by 30 percent of those surveyed as influence on physical reality or environment, by 10 percent as control or manipulation of natural forces, by 3 percent as influencing the thoughts of others, and by 2 percent as involving supernatural beings. Change of consciousness, mentioned by 19 percent, fits equally well among these effects of magic, although it can also be considered a way of describing the human faculties through which magic operates.

The magical procedures mentioned were: attunement with natural forces, 16 percent; healing, 7 percent; the use of rituals, 5 percent; spell working, 2 percent; prophecy, use of tarot cards, the use of crystals, and manipulation of auras, 2 percent each. Thirteen percent found it necessary to specify that their magic is used for positive purposes.

Direct and Indirect Manipulation of Energy

For Neopagans the energy manipulation aspect of magic operates in two fundamental ways: directly and indirectly. It is possible to (a) transfer energy from one's own body or (b) channel energy from an external source to another by physical contact, by being in proximity, or by projecting energy with the will over distances both long and short. The energy source may be (a) the individual's own body, (b) the Earth, (c) trees, plants, or other organic creatures, or (d) the sun, stars, or other celestial sources of light and energy. When the energy is derived from outside the body, the magician is the conduit rather than the source of the energy. All of these processes rely on the interconnectedness of the world.

Many ceremonies in Americanized Wicca involve drawing energy up from the Earth, generally by imagining fire from the core of the planet rising up into their bodies. (Theoretically energy follows thought.) In British covens energy is raised from the witches' bodies to fill the "container" of the circle, and be sent forth from it in the form of a "cone of power." Selena Fox believes that when attempting to give energy to another for healing it is important the healer serve as a conduit, not the source of the energy. Otherwise, the healer's own reserve of vital energy would be depleted.

It is possible, the Neopagans believe, to replenish one's energy by taking some from trees and nature—after asking permission, of course.[12] Energy must be kept moving. Illness and other problems are often attributed to blockages, repression, or stagnation of energy. Not only illness and unhappiness in personal and community life, but historical and social circumstances such as rigid social structures that contain and restrain energy by resisting change are examples of the adverse effects of hindering the flow of energy. Gardner's myth of the goddess' descent and the *Pimander* tale in the Hermetic literature tell that there must be death (of form) so that there can be rebirth, the forging of new bonds of love to create new forms.

Manipulation of indirect energy involves language, ritual, and other modes of symbolic communication, such as pictures or music, to generate vital energy in those who receive the magic. In such a case, energy is not transferred as much as it is ignited in the recipient by the process of symbolic communication. Referring to Azande magic, Evans-Pritchard wrote, "Witchcraft is like fire; it lights a light" (1937, 112). The evil eye and voodoo death are examples of indirect manipulation of energy, although we cannot rule out the possibility that practitioners of these magics also intended to project energy from their bodies (direct energy manipulation) at the same time. Surely the piercing glance, a stare, words, and gestures of the malevolent individual activate fear and perhaps other potentially harmful emotions and/or psychological responses.

Some spells, such as the creation and use of talismans, combine direct and indirect energy manipulation. When I required surgery, for example, a Gardnerian witch named Michael (of the lemon cake metaphor) created a healing talisman for me. By its geometric shape and color, the packet was intended to communicate (by indirect energy activation) a mental association with a specific body system. It was stuffed with herbs and gem stones that were expected to transmit their energy directly.

As Selena explained, a great deal of the healing powers of plants and minerals is attributable to the specific type of energy vibration they produce. According to the Neopagans, sympathetic magic operates on the theory that the vibratory rate of certain herbs and minerals are beneficial to specific organ systems with which their vibratory rates are in harmony, or sympathy, in humans and animals. In this therapeutic process the plants and minerals are believed to transmit their vibratory energy directly, independently of the magician or any symbolic communication with the subject of the spell.

In my case, the talisman was to be worn around the waist, next to the body, and it was intended to filter pathologic energy. A hematite stone on the side meant to be worn next to the body, I was told, draws to itself "negative" energy (I believe by this Michael meant toxic or disordered vibrations resulting from a pathological state). The pyramid shape of the stone theoretically directed the negative energy into the stuffing of the talisman where the herbs and gem stones would "filter" and purify the energy flowing through it. On the side worn away from the body Michael sewed a tourmaline stone that I was told would further purify the negative energy. In addition, the talisman was "charged" by Michael with energy which he told me he directed into the talisman with his will. No doubt he focused his will through the blade of his athame or a wand into the talisman, as I have seen witches charge or consecrate objects for magical purposes. He may even have chanted or recited a rhymed spell to further charge it with harmonious vibration.

The creation and use of the talisman entailed more than symbolic communication or even contagious magic, as Frazer describes it. I was not told much about the talisman until after I had recovered from the surgery. After I emptied the contents into a lake as Michael had instructed me to do, I asked about the herbs and gemstones that I found inside. Michael simply responded that they were the most useful ones for my needs.

Very complicated manipulations of energy flow were considered to be mobilized in the creation, consecration, and use of the little pouch. The herbs and minerals, although they were assembled and charged by the magician with his will, were believed to operate not symbolically but by virtue of their inherent energy vibrations. The intended beneficial interaction of the ingredients was the result of skillful orchestration or activation of bonds of love or attraction that might also be described as harmonizing their inherent vibratory rates. The deliberate manipulation of energy fields of living things (the herbs and minerals) transcended symbolic communication.

If the manipulation of energy or life force is significant in the magic of the Neopagans, I suspect that it is a significant and generally overlooked aspect of the magical intent of other practitioners that has been described only in the terms of symbolic communication, sympathetic, or contagious magic. One exception is Marett's discussions of mana as something resembling life force in humans (1909).

In this and the preceding chapter we have seen that witchcraft and Neopaganism together with other popular occultisms constitute a revival of a rich and ancient tradition that supports individual initiative in acts of magic in relation to a religious perspective that embodies a divine living and responsive universe. We turn now to a closer look at the Americanization of the Western spiritual tradition.

Chapter Eight

The Transforming Influence of American Gatherings

By devising large outdoor gatherings American witches created a loosely knit national community with a shared set of beliefs and both oral and written traditions. Largely as a result of the ritual dramas that evolved at these gatherings, Americans converted Gardner's more rigid ceremonies into inventive rituals, so that the religion of witchcraft broadens into a more general Neopaganism that serves strikingly different purposes. Rather than performing established religious ceremonies, American witches employ techniques that liberate the imagination and spur improvisation and invention.[1]

In the 1970s, meetings that resembled seminars or conventions were organized in hotels for individuals who were interested in various aspects of the occult. By the mid-1970s these events had evolved into the outdoor camping festivals that I attended. The first flurry of this kind of gathering was in California in the mid-1970s. By 1985, Adler wrote, there were at least fifty annual regional or national gatherings with a pagan or Wiccan focus (1986).

The impetus for one gathering in the midwest was the tensions that were building between local groups in the Chicago area. Most of the groups were of the English-based Wiccan tradition. However, friction developed between conservative Gardnerian groups and those that had begun to modify his version of the Wiccan tradition. Eventually the Gardnerians and the innovators made their peace, and now witches of both persuasions enjoy gatherings together. They make good-hearted fun of one another's style, but I have seen no evidence of conflict.

In fact, a great deal of cross-fertilization has been the result. The stronger influence today is in the direction of softening the rigid structure of English Wicca with the spontaneity, inventiveness, playfulness, and greater political focus that distinguish the American Neopagan festival style of religious celebration. There now exists a national Neopagan community with a shared body of chants, dances, and ritual techniques (Adler 1986). Formal hierarchical English Wicca persists but, largely as a result of the gatherings, a more pervasive, distinctly American Neopaganism has emerged.

While covens consist ideally of a fairly stable membership of no more than thirteen members, the gatherings—which are more like religious retreats or conventions than intimate meetings—are attended by hundreds of individuals. Over the years Spiral Gathering in the state of Georgia once accommodated 120 guests; presently about 75 people attend. The largest gatherings—Pagan Spirit Gathering and Rites of Spring drew from 300 to 500 participants. In the last few years 600 to 700 individuals have attended Rites of Spring. Although the faces change at gatherings, there is a core group that constitutes about half of the attendees at most gatherings.

Because the gatherings occur only once a year, and there is as much socializing as worship or magic, they resemble family reunions. Bonds are established among individuals living long distances from one another, and these are sustained through computer networks and by correspondences of several years' duration—letters and greeting cards on the sabbaths, and occasional telephone calls. I first met the Neopagans, with whom I maintain contact in these ways, at Pagan Spirit Gathering in 1983.

Pagan Spirit Gathering, 1983

My first experience at Pagan Spirit Gathering (PSG) was one of immersion in a new and strange experience. I didn't study it; instead I allowed myself to respond to the drama and playfulness of it. The following description is impressionistic. Although most of my comments have been formulated in retrospect, it nonetheless serves my purpose of illustrating the dramatic effects of American culture on British witchcraft.

PSG, which takes place in Wisconsin on the summer solstice in June, is organized by Selena Fox of Circle Farm in Wisconsin. For several years it had been the largest of the American gatherings, attracting 400 to 500 Neopagans from all over the country, Canada, and Europe. While other gatherings have surpassed it in size, PSG remains the most eclectic and its popularity continues to grow.[2] PSG is presently organized and run by Selena, her husband, Dennis, and a handful of volunteers, some of whom live and work at Circle.

The 1983 PSG took place in a newly mown field of straw situated on a lake near Madison, Wisconsin. The land was made available by its owner, an anonymous Neopagan. I enjoyed the comforts of my friend Deborah's recreational vehicle, while most of the attendees, over 400 of them, sheltered in tents.

Open House at Circle Farm

More than 100 of us arrived the day before the official start of the gathering to attend an open house at Circle Farm. The field surrounding the old farmhouse was dotted with tents and 20 to 30 guests who looked like hippies ranging in ages from about 20 to 70 years old.

During the afternoon Selena led a tour of her herb garden. Jim Allen, who was then Selena's partner, made Kirlian[3] photographs of our hands. We met 30 or 40 Neopagans from all over the United States, including Crystal, a flashy ceremonial magician who drew me aside to demonstrate his magical prowess.

He showed me how to dowse energy fields with bent coat hangers. Dowsing is a technique that had been used to find underground water or minerals with the use of a divining rod. Holding an L-shaped wire in each hand, Crystal approached trees, plants, Selena's dog, and people to show me how the wires would swing away as he approached the vicinity of their energy fields. It worked for me, too (perhaps by hypnotic suggestion).

Crystal pulled scarves out of nowhere and coins from behind my ears, and displayed the artifacts of his more serious magic: his ritual tools and ceremonial robe, all of which his magical order required that he create. I was also treated to a reading from his secret Book of Shadows.

That afternoon's events served as an introduction to the Neopagan concepts of immanence of divinity and energy. When Selena "introduced" her herbs to us on the tour of her garden, it was clear that in her estimation each possessed an inherent divine life force and specific affinities (sympathies) with other parts of the natural world including planets, seasons, and human organ systems.

The herb garden completely surrounded the old farm house, "protecting it with the serene and powerful energies of the plants," Selena said. "A plant should never be harvested without first gaining its permission," Selena explained, as she gently broke off a few leaves for us to taste, smell, and feel. (She had prepared the garden for the tour before we arrived.) Several of us wondered how a plant might indicate its permission to be harvested. "Oh, you can feel it," she replied. "It will either feel right or wrong to do it." Offerings of tobacco are generally appreciated by the plant spirits, she continued, and, of course, plants respond to human love and attention, as do all living things, by flourishing.

I learned that day that Neopagans include minerals and gems among the living, after watching stones and talismans reveal blue-white halos in the Kirlian photographs made of them with primitive equipment in the barn. Within a few hours of my arrival at Circle Farm, belief in Starhawk's poetic words about the consciousness of immanence had been vividly demonstrated for me: "the world and everything in it as alive, dynamic, interdependent, interacting, and infused with moving energies; a living being, a weaving dance" (Starhawk 1979).

By the time we organized a potluck supper, some "Big Name Pagans" (BNPs) arrived. Although Neopagans despise the very idea of leaders and followers, they do recognize celebrities. BNP is a tongue-in-cheek term which refers to individuals who are recognized for their talents or services to the community. As a result of the festivals, many local musicians and organizers of large group rituals and gatherings have acquired a national reputation as BNPs. Starhawk and Margot Adler are recognized for their authorship of widely read books. Adler reported that by the end of 1985, Starhawk's first two books had sold a combined total of about eighty-thousand copies;[4] the first edition of Adler's *Drawing Down the Moon* sold thirty thousand copies.

Selena Fox is on a par with these authors because of her Circle networking service, the PSG gathering, her skills as a healer, and her talent as a performer of Neopagan music. For several years, since public interest began to gather around the emerging cult of witchcraft, Selena has been visible in the media. More recently, she has appeared on television talk shows and in courts of law as a spokesperson for the movement and protector of the religious freedoms of Neopagans, including her own right to operate a Neopagan church on Circle Farm.

The category of BNP merges into one that the Neopagans have not yet named, but I think it would be the present-day equivalent of "tribal elder." Surprisingly few of these are high priestesses or priests of the English traditional covens. An exception is Haragano, of Seattle, Washington, a wise, competent, and humorous "matriarch," whose famous psychic skills will be mentioned later. Haragano's husband, Tiller, who is a charming musician, comedian, organizer, and community peacemaker, is another example. Oz of Albuquerque is honored as an expert dancer and authoritative priestess. She creates elaborate rituals from inspirations received in trance states from the deities she serves. Amber K, a healer and organizer of the first Wiccan seminary, is another example of the Neopagan equivalent of tribal elder.

After the evening's potluck supper, more than a hundred of us gathered in the meadow where Selena led a simple but very impressive ritual. As we turned to face each direction, she invited everyone to salute the guardians of the watchtowers of the cardinal directions by singing three times, "Spirits of the north [or east, south, or west], come." When, by this simple collaboration, the circle between the worlds was established, the group sang a chant to raise energy to fill the circle. Selena invited everyone to invoke (or draw down) whatever deities were important to them by calling out their names.

When silence gradually returned, twenty or more deities had been invoked—deities of Greco-Roman, Norse, Celtic and African derivation, as well as others I did not recognize. Selena asked the multitudes of deities to bless the gathering and those who were journeying to it.

Then Selena asked for the names of people or places the participants wished to empower with the raising of a cone of power that she was preparing to orchestrate. Theoretically, some of the energy would be directed to the desired destination by individual thoughts at the moment of their release.

Several people mentioned a baby whose kidnapping was then in the news. Another person mentioned a mock witchburning that a fundamentalist Christian group was planning to perform that weekend. Groans and sighs signaled that the group's energy (and emotional excitement) was already beginning to rise.

Selena reminded the group that while the gathering was in progress Starhawk was leading a demonstration to stop the opening of the aforementioned Livermoor nuclear power plant near the San Diablo fault line in California. I discovered later that Starhawk conducted witchcraft rituals as part of her political demonstrations and that when she and other demonstrating witches got arrested, they taught the prison inmates how to conduct rituals to raise and release energy. Blessings and protection were to be sent to the demonstrators that evening and at all the rituals throughout the gathering.

Selena then started a chant naming several goddesses: "Isis, Astarte, Diana, Hecate, Demeter, Kali, Inanna." The group moved faster and faster in a clockwise direction, or deosil (meaning following the natural rotation of the earth), while drums, tambourines, and various other percussion and wind instruments set the gradually quickening pace of singing and dancing around the circle.

At the moment when the group's energy was elevated to its peak, the chanting erupted into cheers, howls, screams, and animal calls, followed by ripples of contented laughter and sighs of exhaustion. The celebrants were content that a powerful cone of power had been created and released.

That evening was the first time I had experienced the raising and releasing of the cone of power. The orchestration of the rise to crescendo and the release of the energies of over a hundred people are impressive. Later, a high priestess described it this way: "A high priestess is a psychic cheerleader; she guides and paces the rising of the group's energy, and she must be able to feel the moment when the peak of excitement is reached and signal its release. A second in either direction can spoil the cone of power."[5]

Drummers orchestrate the rise and release of the energy for large rituals; occasionally the presiding priestess or priest leads the drumming. At some rituals I have witnessed the virtuosity of well-rehearsed groups of twenty to thirty drummers playing together. The prominence of percussion in orchestrating group energy in Wiccan rituals is uniquely American and, I would surmise, a result of the large gatherings that have developed here.

After the release of the cone of power, the group settled into silence for a few minutes before Selena asked if anyone wished to tell about any visions they had experienced during the raising and releasing of the cone of power.

I was most impressed by what Haragano reported. She "saw" three women traveling to the gathering in a red Ford Falcon. She felt that they were having problems and saw them drinking coffee in a diner while puzzling over whatever was holding them up. She said she thought she knew their names. Selena led the group in chanting the three names that Haragano provided and suggested that everyone visualize protective white light around the three women.

Two days later three women arrived at the gathering in a car they rented after leaving a red Falcon to be repaired. The names of two of the women were those that Haragano mentioned. I have been impressed several times since by Haragano's predictions and insights. "Been doing it all my life," she says; her point of view is that anyone can develop the skill. If people trust their intuition and use it a lot, it improves, as any human faculty would. Nonetheless, I found her own skill to be extraordinary.

At the gatherings I have most often seen divinatory talent put to use in Tarot readings or palm readings, but a few individuals have told me that they have been consulted to locate lost people and things by members of their local communities, generally by police departments.

When Selena directed the group to face each of the cardinal directions and bid the spirits of each direction farewell, the ritual was concluded. We dispersed into tents and campers, and the next day we packed up and moved to the festival site.

The Gathering

At the head of a tiny path, inconspicuously marked by a cloth with a barely perceptible star painted on it, a small group with a walkie-talkie greeted us. They inspected our admission pass before they directed us down the path into the site.

Gatherings are generally publicized only in Neopagan newsletters. My friend Deborah learned about PSG by reading the announcement in *Circle Network News*, published by Selena at Circle Farm. Each participant must sign a waiver in which he or she agrees not to inform the media about the event. Secrecy and security are maintained to protect participants from the intrusion of the uninitiated and unsympathetic.

We found the site and checked in, much as one would at any retreat, and then explored the grounds. It was somewhat disconcerting to see so many naked people. Fieldwork is a double-edged process, particularly when examining one's own culture. The familiar goes unnoticed, requiring no exploration or explanation. When the unfamiliar inspires the researcher to undertake a clarification, one of the first steps is to explore one's own sense of the familiar and the exotic. "Why does it seem strange?" is the flip side of "Why do they do this?" or "What does it mean?"

Being uninitiated, though sympathetic, I found myself experiencing shock on many occasions. The sight of people in varying degrees of nudity dancing around a bonfire in the black of night in a remote field can activate fear responses in the Western mind influenced by a culture that for several hundred years has surrounded such images with the most sinister of associations. The exuberance and playfulness of the actual event contrasted so completely with these automatic responses that I experienced cognitive disorientation. Had I succumbed to depravities or was the leaping over fires and the rise and fall of ecstatic dancing and chanting as harmlessly invigorating as it seemed?

Nudity, among other things, represents freedom from cultural conventions. Neopagan gatherings, like other pilgrimages, are retreats from the constraints of quotidian existence. In sacred space (removed from the constraints of mundane existence) it is safe to shed clothing and other conventions linked with the secular world, as it is safe and efficacious to assume a different appearance by wearing masks or costumes.[6] It was not long before the costumes—ritual jewelry, robes, horned furry headdresses (to emulate the horned god), and masks—demanded more of my attention and wonder than the nudity.

In sacred space, where adornment is potent with significance, the costumes spoke clearly. Many Neopagans reveal a nostalgia for feudal grandeur in their laced bodices and flowing skirts, shirts with full sleeves, and tunics over tights. Others dress like gypsies or Native Americans. The majority, however, cannot be classified. Many people wear only an athame in a belt and sheath, a scarf, or jewelry. Those who wear shorts and tee-shirts (somewhat less than half the group) begin to look out of place, reminders of the world left behind.

Nudity at gatherings is fundamentally a symbolic statement of forsaking ordinary culture for an immersion in nature, much as it would be at a nudist beach. Although many Neopagans welcome sexual liaisons at gatherings—generally considered a deeply significant religious sacrament—nudity is not necessarily an invitation to have sex.

Because of the large number of newcomers who might not understand the sexual mores, and to protect participants from the spread of AIDS, the EarthSpirit Community was moved to issue a guide to appropriate behavior for pagan gatherings at the 1988 Rites of Spring.[7]

In the last two years, concern about AIDS has caused conflict regarding the concept of sex as sacrament. In many cases even the practice of sharing wine from a common chalice has been abandoned in favor of the use of paper cups or dispensed with entirely as too dangerous a ritual practice in large groups.

From this digression into the subject of nudity and sex, let us return now to the layout of the gathering. Covens or groups that journeyed there together set up camps around a common fire pit. Many displayed banners with the name and symbols of their group: Athanor of Boston, Silver Web of Maryland, Tribe of the Phoenix of Georgia, Circle Jerk Camp, for example. The banner belonging to the gay men's camp featured Bugs Bunny.

There were two magnificent teepees, each about twenty feet high. One had a ring of rainbows painted around the outside. We were invited to see that the inside was lined with images of various goddesses, expertly crafted in soft fabric sculpture.

A strong sense of playfulness mixed with competent creativity was becoming apparent as Deborah and I toured the camp and saw the altars people had created at their campsites, the clothing and jewelry with which they adorned themselves, and the beautiful handcrafted wares that were displayed for sale under a huge army tent labeled "Tenthenge." Overall, the camp had the appearance of a gathering of tribes of gypsies.

On the first evening of the official festival, or gathering, the fire that was to serve as the symbolic center of the ritual circle (within the larger sacred space of the entire campsite) was lit in a ceremony in which Randy, the "Fireman," was the main actor. The fire was kept burning until Randy extinguished it at the concluding ceremony on the last day of the festival.

Many people stayed to talk, drum, sing, and dance around the fire each evening. The fire served as a symbol of the group's collective spirit. The ritual circle was the focal point of the campground; the fire represented its core. Each evening another spectacular ritual drama was presented there, and all day long people brought wood to the fire.

On another evening, the EarthSpirit Community staged a purification

Pagan Spirit Gathering encampment.

ritual in which a larger than life "Wicker Man," an effigy of straw, was set ablaze. Participants had been invited to bring debris from their homes as a symbol of what they wished to destroy or relinquish. The trash was woven into the effigy and burned with the usual ecstatic singing and dancing.

One evening the men and women celebrated separate rituals: men's and women's mysteries. While the women splashed and sang their way through their mysteries (performed in the lake), they laughed at the sounds of the shouting, stomping men "relieving their endless aggressions."

Although all rituals are intended to effect some "healing," by which the Neopagans mean any beneficial magic, two rituals were specifically referred to in that way: the web-building ritual, described earlier, for healing the earth and a more overtly healing ritual—in terms of transforming pathological physical states—which was facilitated by Selena one evening.

To heal the physical ailments of individuals who were present, Selena instructed the group in a technique resembling therapeutic touch. Every person present was considered capable of drawing energy up from the earth down from the stars, and through their bodies to effect a healing in others present.

To heal those not present, energy was sent by releasing a cone of power, and it was conveyed by contagious magic through photographs or small belongings or symbols of the person that were brought to the ritual.

Finally, energy was released into the Earth when everyone lay down on the ground and visualized the residual energy draining out of their bodies into the "body" of the Earth. The energy source for this ritual was external to the participants; energy from the Earth or sky was "tapped," so that the participants would not be personally depleted.

One evening a talent show was staged. There are many competent musicians, bards, poets, and comedians in the Neopagan movement, and there is also a distinct style of Neopagan music—a cross between Celtic bardic songs and the folk music that was popular in the 1960s. Neopagans have a charming sense of humor about their beliefs and practices that enlivens their performances. Numerous other rituals, including two "handfasting" (marriage) ceremonies took place. On the morning of the solstice a tiny band of early risers chanted and danced while the sun rose.

Peter the Big Blue Fairy's Full Moon Ritual[8]

The most elaborate was the full moon ritual. It involved about twenty dancers, as many musicians and singers, and elaborate props. Everyone sang original chants that the entire group had learned and rehearsed each morning at the "village meeting." The ritual was designed by Peter Sonderberg who calls himself "Peter the Big Blue Fairy." Peter, who thinks of ritual as a form of theater, brought his considerable dramatic gifts and experience into the creation of this culminating ritual drama.

This ritual event is an example of the transforming influence of American culture on British Wicca. Gardner's rituals are formulae that must be performed in rigorous accord with the "ancient" traditions; otherwise, the theory goes, the gods will not be pleased or they will not come and/or the magic will not work. On the other hand, the more innovative rituals generally presented at gatherings are devised to evoke powerful responses in the participants, in whom divinity is assumed to be immanent.

The episodes of Gardner's basic ritual provided the structure for this very different one. The circle between the worlds was marked, not by one candle at each cardinal direction, but with a ring of flaming candles that the hundreds of participants were instructed to carry as they took their places in an enormous ring.

Celebrants entered through a human gate: a pregnant woman suspended on a litter between one black man and one white man, who served as the two supports of the lintel. The celebrants entered through the elegantly portrayed opposites that are recognized in Wiccan rituals and ultimately united in the great rite or ceremony of cakes and wine: black and white; woman and man; moon and sun; the pregnant fecundity of the woman and the virility of the men.

The black and white pillars have deep roots in the Western spiritual tradition. They derive ultimately from the twin pillars constructed in the temple of Solomon. The black and white pillars can be seen in the temples of the Masonic order and other secret societies. In the Hebrew Cabala, with which many Neopagans are acquainted firsthand, and even more through its incorporation into Gardner's Wicca, the black pillar represents severity, the white, mercy; and the "Middle Pillar of Mildness," or "Middle Way," is the spiritual path between the two extremes that represent other countless complementary oppositions (Gray 1984).

When everyone had entered the circle by passing through the "doorway" framed by the black and white human pillars, the pregnant woman was lowered into a chair beside the fire. The red spirals painted on her naked breasts and pregnant belly gave her the appearance of a life-sized fertility fetish. She represented the great mother goddess.

The guardians of the watchtowers were wordlessly invoked by four dancers wearing costumes of colors evocative of the elements: air, fire, water, and earth. Each danced to the accompaniment of a small orchestra of percussion and wind instruments.

The celebrants raised energy to fill the circle by singing Peter's original chant.

> And the full moon
> Is her vagina spread wide.
> And the full moon
> Is her vagina spread wide.
> And the wild realm of all possibilities,
> every possibility,
> Is pouring out.

The goddess was drawn down (invoked or evoked from within) by a parade of twelve women; each one embodied one aspect of the triple goddess who represents the three phases of the moon. As each one entered, she bowed before the enthroned pregnant high priestess, revealing with her dance, costume, gestures, or a short expression (such as "I am the giver of milk, she who comforts children in the dark of the night") that she represented either the new moon (maiden goddess), the full moon (matron), or the waning moon (crone). The "goddesses" then danced together: among them were "Hecate" in black-hooded cape; "Kali" with a gleaming scimitar balanced on her head; one portrayed the "Amazon" in leopard skin loin cloth, another, a businesswoman in a suit; another had flowers painted on her body; Haragano's skin was stained to look like the Venus of Willendorf. The "goddess" who entered last, a young homosexual man wearing rabbit ears and pink harem pants, represented Discordia, the goddess of chaos.

When this homage to the great mother goddess was finished, the queen of witches and goddess of the moon made her appearance. Wearing the traditional silver crown of a high priestess (with upturned crescent moon), "Diana" entered through the gate of oak branches where the human portal had been, accompanied by two men in long robes and a chorus of twelve others, all singing a song made popular by another Diana. Through the "ooo-ooo-ooo-ooo, aah-aah-aah-aah" that introduced the song, the crowd laughed softly at the spectacle of this emulation of Diana Ross and the Supremes. Because Peter the Big Blue Fairy (now one of the three Supremes singing beside Diana) was a notorious practitioner of an innovative Wiccan tradition devoted to Discordia, he was expected to be unconventional, bordering on sacrilegious.

When the priestess sang the lyrics of the love song promising that no wind or rain or any other thing could prevent her from coming to the beloved whenever she was needed, the laughter stopped. With the lyrics of the song "Ain't No Mountain High Enough," the priestess was delivering the charge of the goddess.

> If you need me; call me.
> No matter where you are,
> No matter how far,
> Just call my name.
> I'll be there in a hurry.
> On that you can depend and never worry. [9]

The full moon goddess was drawn down to speak with the lips of the singing priestess her covenant with the witches.[10] In the traditional charge, Aradia, avatar of the goddess, reminds the witches:

> Whenever ye have need of anything,
> Once in the month, and when the moon is full,
> Ye shall assemble in some desert[ed] place,
> Or in a forest all together join
> To adore the potent spirit of your queen,
> My mother, great Diana. (Leland 1899, 7)

Of course no mountain could be high enough to keep her away; the goddess is the mountains, the wind, rain and all things in the universe. The invocation to draw her down reads:

> Hear ye the words of the star goddess,
> The dust of whose feet are the hosts of heaven
> Whose body encircles the universe:

Once drawn down, Diana speaks through the lips of the priestess:

> I am the beauty of the green earth,
> And the white moon among the stars,
> The mystery of the waters,
> And the passion of human hearts.
> Call unto your soul,
> Arise and come unto me
> For I am the soul of nature.
> From me all things proceed
> And unto me all things must return.

Diana sang that she realized that the beloved must follow the sun, wherever it leads. However, if one should fall short, life holds one guarantee: she will always be there.

> I know you must follow the sun,
> wherever it leads.
> But remember,
> If you should fall short of your desires,
> . . . life holds for you one guarantee;
> You'll always have me . . .[11]

In a similar fashion the familiar charge advises: "Keep pure your highest ideals; strive ever toward it, let naught stop you or turn you aside . . . For mine is the secret door . . . the cup of wine of life . . . which is the Holy Grail of Immortality" (Farrar 1983, 172).

"Diana and the Supremes" sang the assurance that her love is constant.

> You see my love is alive,
> It's like a seed that only needs the
> thought of you to grow.[12]

In the traditional ceremony the priest draws down the moon with similar references to plants:

> I invoke Thee and call upon Thee
> O Mighty Mother of us all,
> Bringer of all Fruitfulness, by seed
> and by root.
> I invoke thee, by stem and by bud.
> I invoke Thee by life and by love
> and call upon Thee to descend into this,
> Thy Priestess and Servant.
> Hear with her ears, speak with her
> tongue . . ." (Bell 1974, 157)

The idea that humans are linked to the divine universe through the mind is recognizable in these lyrics as well. When the moon is drawn down, human and divine are made one.

At the completion of the song/charge of the goddess, Diana took her place at the opposite side of the fire from the pregnant priestess, and the goddess was considered amply drawn down in all her aspects.

The god or sun was then drawn down as several young men danced through the gate and around the circle, wearing horned headdresses to emulate the horned god as animal, Cernunos, Dionysus, and other of his forms.[13] They cavorted like a herd of frisky ungulates. Finally they collapsed in exhaustion at the feet of the many representatives of the goddesses who were assembled in a ring around the central fire.

Then the great rite was performed. The "blessedness" that results from the conjoining of opposites was, in this case, the planting of seeds in the Earth. The goddess' representatives—except for the pregnant moon goddess and Diana, who both remained enthroned at opposite sides of the fire—gathered into large bowls the seeds that each person had been given as he or she entered the gate. Each dropped their seeds into the bowls, serving as a cauldron or chalice, and said what they wished to "plant" for the future (peace, companionship, and other boons). The many goddesses emptied the contents of the bowls as a libation onto the Earth in front of the pregnant full moon goddess around whom the "gods" crouched on the ground. The god figures quickly descended upon the seeds, planting them into the soil with a swimming, squirming, spermlike dance. The opposites were blended: the male (seeds) penetrated the female (Earth) to initiate a transformation (new crop).

The ritual ended with the raising and releasing of a cone of power in a spiral dance. The circle of participants were led into the center to dance around the fire and spiralled back out again while singing to the beat of the drummers. With howls and cries the cone of power was released, representing, not only the energy raising of this ritual, but the culmination of the five-day-long gathering. Excess energy was grounded—allowed to flow from the energized and exhausted bodies into the Earth—as the celebrants lay panting on the ground. Gradually drumming and chanting started up around the fire and most of the celebrants returned to their camps to feast.

On the following day Randy, the Fireman, extinguished the ritual fire as ceremoniously as he had lit it. The pagans broke down the camp and said their emotional farewells. Then these pilgrims returned home from a pilgrimage site that existed only in their memories, leaving their seeds to sprout in the deserted straw field.

Chapter Nine

Growth of American Neopaganism from the Roots of British Wicca

Hundreds of years before Gardner's witchcraft was imported from Britain, the colonialists brought with them the fear of witches, as well as a few witchcraft covens, and some groups that took inspiration from paganism as an alternative to Christianity. They imported occult traditions, including Renaissance esotericism and practices such as astrology, palm reading, and magical healing (Butler 1979; Demos 1982; Godbeer 1992). Following the first world war a number of occult movements developed much as they did in Europe.

British Wicca fanned the embers of diverse peripheral occult traditions and provided a structure for unifying them. Many individuals who possessed, or wanted to possess, psychic skills and those, like Lady Cybele the weather-worker, who already practiced folk magic found in British Wicca a name for their beliefs and practices, along with myths and rituals that vindicated their unique perspectives and a language of symbols through which they might express themselves.

At the same time, news of British Wicca inspired others who had no prior interest in either magic or the occult to seek membership in covens and to think of themselves as witches. Coven membership provided identity and intimate relationships with small local groups that could easily serve as a substitute for the family, which had become increasingly atomized. It offered a novel way of developing personal power and status and fostered experimentation with new forms of authority and cooperation.

British Wicca was readily, though not uncritically, adopted by many Americans. As we have seen, Americans eagerly refashioned it to

141

accommodate their own culture. Cult practices became less formal, more inventive, democratized (in many covens the members take turns acting as the high priestess or priest), and less hierarchical (levels of initiation were abandoned in many cases). Other pantheons, such as Norse, Welsh, and Minoan, were superimposed on the fundamental structure of Gardner's Wicca.

British Wicca was transformed into a very different kind of religion in America, largely as a result of four factors: (1) the ritual style that developed at large gatherings, (2) the incorporation of revived shamanism as a counterpart to the kind of work and worship associated with the culture heroine, the witch, (3) a different conception of the Earth as a living, conscious divine being, and (4) the superimposition of the psychotherapy model onto Gardner's Wicca and its application to political activism initiated by the very influential witch, therapist, and political activist, Starhawk. These modifications do not change the witches' position of conceptual opposite of "right society." The Neopagan, "shamanic witches'" Earth religion is transcendent Christianity turned inside out.

Both British and American Wicca take as their more authentic cosmology the Old Religion. The mythic themes of agriculture—cycles of birth, death, and resurrection—and those of the celestially inspired city-states remained significant, but the lore and techniques of shamanism became much more important in America than they had in England.

In Europe, Hermeticists and alchemists, who pursued the quest for personal visions and empowerment by resort to the intellectual magic of the Western spiritual tradition, considered themselves ceremonial magicians, rather than witches (practitioners of the more folk-communal witchcraft religion). In the United States, elements of ceremonial magic were absorbed into Wicca so that the communal rites came to stress "enlightenment" via the achievement of altered states of consciousness, self-perfection, and the empowerment of individuals.

While ceremonial magic underwrites the transformative powers available to individual adepts (shamams), the agricultural lore endorses the potential for groups of individuals to work magic—"raise and move energy"—collaboratively, under the guidance of initiated priestesses and priests. The inclusion of shamanism characteristic of the religion of small hunting and gathering societies into American "shamanic Wicca" affords the opportunity—or the as yet unmet challenge—for individual adepts to collaborate in their magic as equals without benefit of ordained leadership.

The marriage of these two approaches to magical work—the communal energy-generating characteristic of agricultural rites and the individual pursuit of power and visions associated with shamanism and ceremonial magic—has not been an easy one. Learning to collaborate effectively as a group without sacrificing identity, autonomy, and individuality is an ambitious goal. At this point, the efforts are more impressive than the achievements in the sphere of social organization. We will have the opportunity to explore one example of success in chapter eleven.

The cohesive forces operative in these social groups are of a wholly other order than those of communities that require the subordination of the creativity of the many to the guidance of the few, such as is the case in Gardnerian covens. Here the high priestess is clearly the authority. Social relations on the level of the small local community or coven are, in general, less successful than the more distant and intermittent relations among witches on a regional and national level.

A social movement under construction, American witchcraft is somewhat unstable. This very instability is the source of its greatest virtue—flexibility—as well as its most debilitating flaw—disorganization.

The prevalent worldview, which witches regard as inauthentic as well as pathological, derives from patriarchal Christian society. It is faulted for being monotheistic, male-dominated, and uncritically oriented to positivist science and production. A particularly pernicious element of that "pathology," in the estimations of American witches, is the abandonment of individual initiative in favor of reliance on state authorized professionals.

In the late 1970s when professional medicine suffered a loss of confidence, personal healing of a medical and psychological nature became a significant issue and focus of magical work. On the social level, healing became a blend of magical techniques, along with political protest and legal measures, to defend and protect the environment and to accommodate religious freedoms.

Witchcraft also served as a vehicle for expressing the social protests and cultural transformations of the 1960s: civil liberties, feminism, ecology, and peace. In the 1970s gay and lesbian rights became important in the Wiccan movement along with a concern with healing. Rituals were modified to express these themes, and American witches adapted the techniques of raising energy, spell working, and trance work to the goal of "healing society."

Although the British witches enliven the intellectual magical tradition with folk dances and games, their central purpose is communion with the gods and achievement of an apotheosis (deification) through a mythic palingenesis, that is, a journey of the soul. Healing spells are included in the British Wiccan repertoire, but to a lesser extent than in the American rituals, all of which are described as effecting a "healing" in the broad sense of restoring harmony within individuals and groups and ultimately the world.

Thus, in the United States, Wicca has turned toward expanding the witch as culture heroine into her predecessor, the shaman, whose emblematic ceremony is the curing rite (Lessa & Vogt 1979). As is characteristic of the religions of agricultural societies, Wiccan priestesses and priests perform codified and standardized rituals at the proper time within the annual ceremonial calendar. Shamans, magico-religious specialists of the less formal hunting and food gathering societies, conduct ceremonies on a non-calendrical basis whenever healing— broadly defined as the Neopagans do as restoring balance—is required for individuals or the whole of a small society.

Shamanic Witches

Many Neopagans think of themselves as shamans or "shamanic witches." Workshops on shamanism are offered at nearly every gathering, and Neopagan periodicals are replete with articles on the subject. A special section devoted to shamanism in *Circle Network News* (Winter 1984) included the interpretations of six authors. Noel Anne Brennan, who has a master's degree in anthropology, pointed out the important distinction between the individualistic religious expertise of shamans and the socially authorized tasks of initiates of priesthoods. The importance attributed to individual visionary experiences in most branches of Neopaganism, along with the relative disregard for social rank, have paved the way for the *entrée* of shamanism, Brennan pointed out (1984).

While shamans of traditional societies gain their powers by surviving terrible physical and mental ordeals, present-day shamans, Brennan remarked, prefer vision quests with maybe a little fasting, or—I have learned—participation in workshops such as those given by anthropologist Michael Harner,[1] or the use of visionary drugs.

The Neopagans often interpret spontaneous crises of mental or physical health or other misfortunes as the shaman's crisis of vocation, which the shamans describe as being broken apart. Selena Fox reported:

> I journeyed alone into the Pit of my shadow self and came face to face with my problems and hang-ups; with my doubts, fears . . . words cannot express the misery, the utter despair I felt during this time. Yet coming apart was essential; it enabled me to break through the barriers . . . (1984, 15)

Contributors to the special section on shamanism in *Circle Network News* all point out that the potential to experience the shaman's ecstasy is a basic attribute of human nature. There is a need to develop that potential now because the planet requires it, the authors agree.

Here we encounter a novel animism that has no precedent in

shamanism or any other religious worldview. The idea that the planet is conscious, alive, and capable of motivating humans to acquire the powers of shamans or to modify their behavior in other ways has evolved recently in the thoughts of individuals presently facing, as Judith Anodea put it, "the threat of extinction and/or promise of apocalypse" (1984, 8). The incorporation of shamanistic techniques into the Neopagans' magical repertoire is, in the estimation of another author, a necessary response to "a need sent by the Bio-sphere of Earth to those attuned to its need" (An Doile 1984, 12). The technique that Neopagans associate with shamanism is drumming to induce visionary journeys (trances) in which they seek commerce with spirits, mostly animal spirits.

The Old Religion envisions a divine moving universe, but the idea of an ailing personified planet that communicates with and acts directly upon humans on its own behalf is new. This expanded animism is at the opposite pole from the notion of a transcendent Christian divinity. Inspirations arise from the seductive material Earth, the domain of the Christian Satan.

Neopagans must learn to journey, as the shamans had, beyond "the limitation and security of our present world, to enter another world, about which we know nothing" (Anodea 1984, 8). This is not the known world of the gods, mighty ones, and the spirits of British Wicca. The goal is to "upstage the conscious mind that holds our world in limitation, and regroup on a new plane, more suited to our purposes" (Anodea 1984, 8).

The Neopagan shamanic witches foresee a collaboration of shamans, something that would have been impossible for the fiercely individualistic shamans who were one anothers' deadly rivals. Together they will transform the world by sharing and acting upon their visions. "The worlds that lack support will eventually diminish, and our creation of another plane is the new cycle growing in the shade of the old" (Anodea 1984, 8). British Wiccans would use their worship and magic to enlist the aid of their gods to protect and restore the world; Neopagans would use theirs to invent a new one from the ground up, in response to the expressed desire (in their estimations) of their goddess, the Earth itself.

The capacity to experience the shaman's ecstasy may remain within the repertoire of human experience; after all, Eliade contends, the human nervous system has not changed (1964). However, today's society lacks the beliefs and practices that foster development of and sensitivity to these human powers, and it denies them respect and confidence. Neopagans are reinventing these elements of culture in their experiments with mind-expanding techniques in local covens and at their large outdoor gatherings.

It is ironic, this revival of the world's oldest religion, shamanism, by members of the world's most advanced society. The shamans' unique claim to power and knowledge resonates with the postmodern confidence in subjectivity, relativity and individualism. The shaman's ecstacy has come full circle.

The Transforming Effect of Gatherings

Gatherings, like PSG, are uniquely American. Gardner reported that the British witches used to gather several related covens to celebrate together on occasion, but these covens differed from American gatherings in that they were smaller groups and they had a more hierarchical structure. Either the witch queen and king (ultimate founders of the collection of assembled covens) would perform the ritual along with eleven other witches for others to watch, or several circles of thirteen persons would perform rituals simultaneously with the witch king "keeping the rhythm" (Gardner 1954). As we saw in chapter one, a collaboration of another sort was described by Lady Boadecia; several covens performed rituals in concert, though in separate locations, to halt Hitler's advance into England.

Each year the American Gardnerian witches conduct a "family gathering." It is small, and the ceremonies are formal orthodox Gardnerian rituals open only to those who can provide credentials of initiation into a bona fide Gardnerian coven. The Neopagan gatherings— pilgrimages to nature—that are the setting for networking and theatrical rituals are uniquely American.

The term *Festival Movement* was the topic of a panel discussion at an annual Neopagan gathering in Ohio called "Winter Star." One speaker, Jeff Rosenbaum, described the function of the gatherings as responding to the need

> . . . for people to have sort of "space-stations" or safe places where they can go to learn and to become illuminated, to recapture that sense of being in reality rather than being asleep and dreaming in this world of illusion that we get fed by various people that are giving us the information that we base our reality-view on.[2]

Using Gardner's rituals as a foundation, American witches create "safe spaces" within which they awaken their imaginations to create a more authentic reality. To this purpose the full transformative potential of ritual is turned loose in the theatrical rituals performed at gatherings.

The Transformative Potential of Rituals

The British and American witches present their alternative cosmology through the potent social process of ritual.

Anthropologist Victor Turner located the transformative power of rituals in the condition of liminality and characterized this potent phase of experience as "an interval, however brief, of *margin* or *limen*, when the past is momentarily negated, suspended, or abrogated, and the future has not yet begun, an instant of pure potentiality when everything, as it were, trembles in the balance" (1982, 44).

This potent marginal condition exists in all kinds of societies as the Achilles heel in the structuring process, which Turner described as the process of containing new growth in orderly patterns or schemata of social structure. In the "antistructural" moments of liminality, there is a "liberation of human capacities of cognition, affect, volition, creativity, from . . . normative constraints" (1982, 44).

Rather than periodic refreshments between phases of social structure that processual rituals generally provide, liminality at gatherings is intended to facilitate the discovery of a radically different point of view that might point the way to a revision of self and society.

Both English and American rituals make use of the same threshold—the consecrated circle—that celebrants cross to enter the betwixt-and-between ritual space, or condition, and to shake loose the constricting paradigms of Western culture, especially those arising from Christian patriarchal culture. These would be the preeminence of the profit motive, the concept of manifest destiny, and the supremacy of science, technology and professionalism, to name a few. In ritual space, where cause and effect are thought to operate on radically different principles, anything seems possible. Visions of alternatives to the status quo seem attainable and feasible; individuals feel empowered "in the company of the gods" to imagine alternatives, to believe in their visions, and to establish a resolve to reenter the social structure changed and strengthened by the illuminations received in the ritual space.

American witches liberate the innovative and evolutionary potential of processual rituals which Turner compared to that of evolving biological forms. "The besetting quality of human society," Turner wrote, "seen processually, is the capacity of individuals to stand at times aside from the models, patterns, and paradigms for behavior and thinking, which as children they are conditioned into accepting, and in rare cases, to innovate new patterns themselves or to assent to innovation" (1974, 14–15).

The present resort to living rituals and performed religion resonates with other historical periods of ideological shifts when the Western spiritual tradition enjoyed resurrections into visibility. The Western spiritual tradition has for a long time provided an alternative cosmology to that of the Christian state in Western society. The Christian view is of a static world that is susceptible to change only at the hands of the Christian God. Attempts by humans to participate in changing the world, according to the latter view, constitutes heresy, or in the sixteenth and seventeenth centuries, the crime of witchcraft.

All cultural innovations evolve in the imaginations of individuals. The Wiccan religion inherited from the older Western spiritual tradition techniques for developing the capacities of creativity (the craft), imagination, and will that are needed for such a *poesis*. Neopagans introduce the post-industrial progeny of the liminal, the liminoid,[3] genres: song, poetry, dance, and drama, to serve as springboards to hurl the celebrants into the open-ended experience of the shaman's ecstasy. Vivid dramas present novel themes and new perspectives, and the celebrants are released into silence to see their personal vision at a crucial point in nearly every ritual I experienced at gatherings.

Many of the same techniques for creating open-ended mental flexibility and an activation of creativity are used in other religious and thought movements to break through established thought patterns. In most of these movements the leader, teacher, or guru (in Gardner's Wicca, a high priestess or high priest) provides an unambiguous new pattern for the transformation, just as tribal leaders provided the clearly defined new role for those undergoing initiation in early horticultural and agricultural societies.

The rituals of present-day witches, though, provide few cues. There are only two laws that are uniformly recognized: the threefold law that one's effect on the world returns threefold in kind, and the Wiccan Rede: that ye harm none, do what thou wilt; love is the law. Interpreting these laws comprises a great deal of the responsibility of the high priestess in traditional Gardnerian covens; Americanized witches, on the other hand, prefer to rely on their own judgement.

For Neopagans the goal is beyond and through liminality into ecstasy. These excursions into liminality are more hazardous because of the lack of uniform acceptance of any formula for the desired, more authentic cosmos. The greater danger in American-style Wicca is matched with a greater potential for change than the English version. As Starhawk puts it, "Where there's fear, there's power!" (1982, 47).

Planet as Divinity

In the Old Religion, the gods are accessible to the magician. They may be distant from humans—the Egyptian decans were representatives of the astrological sectors of time and space, and the Sumerian gods were the great planets moving among the lesser gods of the fixed stars—but because the human soul partakes of divinity, it is, theoretically, possible for the initiated to make contact with them. The agricultural rites

Ken Deigh invokes Pan at Spiral Gathering, 1990. Photograph included with the permission of Ken Deigh.

characteristic of Gardner's Wicca are more "down to Earth." Although celestial deities are honored, rites are addressed to those supernatural forces immanent in the Earth and its creatures: elementals, fairies, and spirits of trees and animals. The rocks and trees that early Wiccans were criticized for worshipping in the ninth and tenth century canons were embodiments of divine forces that might help witches to achieve practical boons for human life on Earth.

The planet is the ultimate deity of American Neopaganism. The great mother goddess of the early planters and hunters—the source of animals, plants, and indeed all of life—is for them the blue and white planet photographed from space, the ground on which they dance in their rituals. For Neopagans, the seas and rivers are literally the living circulation of an organic entity, the suffering and dying Earth. The danger of pollution and nuclear hazards are often spoken of in terms of the deficiencies of the Earth's immune system.

The ecological core of Neopaganism was formulated, if not devised, by Tim (Otter) Zell, who established the Church of All Worlds in the early 1970s. *The Green Egg*, the periodical generated by this group, was the first and most influential, nationally circulated Neopagan publication. This magazine published the dialogue between Zell and George Lovelock, originator of the Gaia hypothesis (that the planet is a living organism). The Omega principle—that the Earth is a conscious being—of Teilhard de Chardin is nearly as significant an element in the ecological lore of Neopaganism as the Gaia hypothesis. The Neopagans have created a body of lore and a tradition of worship and magic based on these philosophic ideas.

The relationship between the Earth and the Neopagan is reciprocal as is the relationship between Gardner's witches and the mighty ones. The recent "pathology" of the Earth has resulted in the newer idea that the Earth is in urgent need of healing.

In most religions, worshippers ask for healing and blessing from gods. In American Wicca, by contrast, the great mother goddess requires healing and blessing from her worshippers. Like the wounded king of the grail legends, she requires the success of the hero's quest to be healed, and, like him, the goddess receives succor from her worshippers. This is quite opposite to the redeeming sacrifice of Christ for his people.

The great goddess of the Neopagans is victimized—by the patriarchy—and must be redeemed by her "children," who are the extensions of her physical substance. Regardless of their superficial themes, all the rituals enacted at the gatherings have as their fundamental purpose the healing of the Earth.

This is not to imply that the Earth goddess is powerless. Boons and blessings are asked of the Earth and her powers are venerated and feared. Volcanic eruptions and earthquakes are seen as expressions of the Earth goddess' awesome power. Beyond the solar system, the universe is regarded as accessible, populated with "neighbors" one might call on for help. Photographs from space missions as well as the Neopagans' fondness for science fiction provide inspiration for this idea. I experienced a ritual in which about a hundred people called out to the Andromeda galaxy, "Help!"[4]

Neopagans believe they may collaborate with sacred universal forces, and they feel that, like the bold shamans and enterprising witches, they can, and should, use their "healing" powers to heal their creator, the planet.

Reinventing Morality

The sociologist Robert Bellah reported that there is a pervasive trend in America toward a greater individualism, especially in interpreting religious beliefs and in defining moral issues (1985). The knowledge that humans have the power to change their world increases their responsibility, Bellah claimed. At the heart of the quest for salvation is a concern for adequate standards of action and a search for personal maturity and social relevance, rather than the older doctrinal orthodoxy and insistence on moral purity. Although the situation is often characterized as a collapse of meaning and a failure of moral standards, Bellah is encouraged that the predicament offers unprecedented opportunities for creative innovation in every sphere of human action (1985).

While Bellah wrote optimistically of opportunities for creative innovation, he takes the conservative position that a resort to the "biblical" and "republican"⁵ strands of American culture must be the starting point. Neopagans, on the other hand, are counting on novel answers that come in the visionary shamans' journeys and experiences of gnosis or ecstasy.

In British covens, the high priestess and high priest provided the valuable services of assisting coven members in interpreting visionary experiences and aiding them in finding a safe and an ethically sound approach to acting upon them. They teach coven members what constitutes magic that will truly harm none and help them envision the threefold repercussions of any magical or mundane action. Having dispensed with hierarchy, the American witches have cut themselves adrift with few sources of support and guidance in their personal quests for the ethical and fortunate life. Here is where strong community could substitute for leadership.

Neopagans seek inspiration in pagan or "primitive" religion. All the perspectives that find expression in the religions of the earliest societies are found in Neopaganism, including naturalism, animism, spiritualism, and totemism. These flow from a fundamental idea that the world is alive, interconnected, and responsive.

In primitive societies, religion encompasses philosophy, theater, science, ethics, diversions, and other behavioral spheres that recent Western civilization has segregated. By reunifying the many facets of religion Neopagans hope to create an institution of culture that will provide the knowledge, inspiration, and joyous experiences that inform a new definition of the moral life, one that assumes the vitality and sacredness of the Earth.

Leadership

In American Neopaganism the authority of the priesthood is displaced by expertise in group dynamics. In coven meetings as well as at gatherings the effectiveness of rituals is contingent on the orchestration of group energies more than the rigid observance of arcane formulae.

Because the British acknowledge their social stratification and monarchy and honor tradition generally, subordination to the leadership of a coven's high priest and high priestess or to the "witch king" or "queen" of clusters of covens was an acceptable process for achieving group cohesion. The British are also better prepared by long tradition to function within levels of initiation than the more mutinous and individualistic Americans.

In the communal rites of British Wiccan rituals, each person—not only the presiding hierophants—contributes his or her energy, dances, sings, leaps over the flaming cauldron, spins the Yule wheels, and participates in other ritual acts. Every covener may experience the presence of the elemental spirits, the mighty ones, and the goddess and god.

Still, the high priestess and high priest serve the covens in the capacity of an accredited priesthood. The gods communicate only indirectly with the coveners through the high priestess or priest when the moon or sun (goddess or god) is drawn down. Although each witch is deemed a priest or priestess after achieving initiation into the first degree, only those who pass through all levels to achieve the full apotheosis of becoming high priestess or priest are deemed worthy to serve as the vessel in the ceremony of drawing down. Gardner's Wicca is an intermediate approach to divinity between exclusive priestcraft and the "democratic shamanism" of the American witches.

Unlike the Minoan Sisterhood and other formal Wiccan traditions, initiation is not necessary in the Americanized covens; all are equal, and every new person present is deemed worthy to invoke the gods—or to evoke them from within themselves—and experience divine inspiration.

At the gatherings the priesthood is displaced by "stars" (BNPs), who enable others to have the religious experience—rather than experiencing it themselves for the benefit of others. The entire group collaborates in establishing the sacred circle. We saw how each person was invited to invoke the divinities of their choice in the ritual at the open house at Circle Farm.

In American Wicca each person, like the shaman, is deemed worthy of having personal commerce with the supernatural realm and to gain from their personal resources the vision of a world more authentic than the one they live in day by day. Worship often entails listening to the self (dreams or intuitions) or evoking archetypes or divine potential from within the self.

Celebrants are simultaneously audience and performers. Rituals at gatherings rely for their effectiveness on the collaboration of talented individuals as equals, under the effective but subtle leadership of an imaginative director. The flawless performance of established rituals, on the other hand, is the domain of the priesthood.

The Place Where Art and Worship Meet

Ritual theater is useful for addressing all levels and facets of the eclectic membership of the national community that attend gatherings, wrote Andras Corban Arthen, founder of the Massachusetts-based EarthSpirit Community.[6] It also provides an effective focus for a larger crowd. Theatrical expertise is required to accommodate several hundred people in large open space, he adds. In the rituals that take place at gatherings, larger-than-life props provide a strong visual focus on which participants can concentrate and with which they can identify from their various levels of involvement in "the mysteries."

An example of this is my own response to the rituals in which I participated at my first gathering. I realized retrospectively after my initiation into the Minoan Sisterhood, that Gardner's rituals—drawing down the moon, the great rite, and the raising of the cone of power— were being enacted in Peter's spectacular ritual. I was moved and impressed by the symbols and theatrical techniques at PSG, but I understood their significance on a more shallow *intellectual* level than others who at that time possessed a more thorough acquaintance with the religion than did I. On an *emotional* level the theatrical techniques are profoundly moving to individuals at all stages of acquaintance with the mysteries.

Festival organizers supplement their ritual dramas with skillful drumming, chanting, dancing, and other techniques for harmonizing group energies (heart, respiratory, and brain rhythms). These involve everyone in the action and are intended to heighten mental receptivity by effecting a shift to right-brain hemispheric dominance and autonomic nervous system "tuning" as described by physiologist Barbara Lex (1979).

"The Goddess hates to be bored," wrote Z. Budapest, a prominent California witch and organizer of large public rituals. The greater concern to provide a moving experience for the audience reveals the belief that the gods are integral to, rather than external to, the participants.

"Ritual is about energy and it pretty much doesn't matter what kind of energy, as long as it is alive . . . [it] is especially about the collective energy of its participants," Peter (the Big Blue Fairy) Sonderberg writes in his article about ritual as theater. He speaks of the importance of the energy exchange between performers and audience: "A show sends out its own energy, but its effectiveness is totally dependent on creating a rapport, an energy exchange, with the audience. These energy connections become even more important in the context of ritual where the participants are simultaneously actors and audience" (1985, 14).

In the rituals presented at gatherings there is a blending of secular and sacred symbols. In Peter's ritual, for instance, the goddess and god were represented in multiple facets, many of which related to the contemporary world. One of the Amazon goddesses wore horn-rimmed glasses and a business suit. For American witches, a godlike personality in the world must be achieved within the parameters of that world, not the idealized world of the mythic past. The charge of the new moon goddess ("Ain't No Mountain High Enough") gained considerable power because it was strikingly contemporary and secular.

American gatherings are pilgrimages to nature, to Earth—the goddess who is everywhere, everything. In primitive campgrounds it/she can be experienced directly. The journey there is often a long trip, but the pilgrimage is more accurately a separation from all that obscures nature. Nature is not the setting for the pilgrimage but the destination and object of the pilgrims' quest.

Generally speaking, all pilgrimages are healing events in that they reunite the alienated pilgrim with the cosmos. Beyond the relinking of humans with their source, overt efforts to heal perceived pathologies of both the individual and the planet are engaged in at Neopagan gatherings. The ritual dramas are often treatments of a kind.

Even when rituals communicate through the use of metaphor and analogy, the effect is intended to be actual and direct. Burning the wicker effigy (which was interlaced with garbage that had been transported to the gathering as specimens of the disease of the planet) was intended to effect an actual purging of the Earth's diseased tissue. Planting seeds that were charged with the celebrants' energy and their wishes for a healed Earth were more than efforts at sympathetic or contagious magic; the Neopagans were "operating" on the Earth's body, not merely symbolizing the action.

The greater concern for secrecy and the necessity for study and initiatory levels in the British witchcraft tradition are part of the idea that the Western spiritual tradition is a fragile, endangered reserve of potentially powerful information—a science, of sorts—whose efficacy is independent of the practitioner. Peter, the creator of the Saturday night full moon ritual, criticized this conservative approach by calling it "The "dinosaur syndrome." Those who would shudder at the inventiveness of his Saturday night ritual take the position that "our rituals have been handed down from time immemorial; we couldn't possibly change them" (1985). Most people who express this conservatism admit that the antiquity of contemporary Wicca is a myth. The Western spiritual tradition is the real treasure they wish to keep inviolate. Peter and other devotees of the newer, more inventive versions of the craft have their own myth: "We practice our craft as our ancient ancestors did—we make it up as we go along" (1985, 14).

The experimental nature of American witchcraft reveals the greater confidence of the Americans in the possibility of creating a *better* paganism than the ancient one inherited in the Western spiritual tradition, a Neopaganism which offers not only an alternative to Christian culture but serves contemporary needs more effectively. American witches have a greater tendency to believe that what is potent in the Western spiritual tradition is accessible to the refined faculties of intuition and imagination. By healing—restoring balance and well-being where patriarchal culture has created pathology—one is best prepared to receive needed insights and inspiration. With arduous study and spiritual discipline, one may gain the refinements of the imagination, will, and craft that are needed to bring those insights into manifestation. British witchcraft is a revival; American witchcraft is an attempt to create a new religion.

Chapter Ten

The Witch Is the Opposite of the Physician

As unauthorized healer, the witch character finds its clearest expression as the opposite of right society in the West. We have seen that the universal associations with the primordial character of the witch—darkness, animal familiars, emission of light, and malevolent intent—are enhanced in each place where the witch is believed in, by the local details of that society's notion of perversity and evil.

Witchcraft and other Neopaganisms are, in terms of Western notions, heretical—that is, the opposite of Christianity. In this chapter we will see that they are also the opposite of professional medicine. Neopagans have resurrected the legendary witch healer, victim of the European witch hunts, as their heroine along with her herbal pharmacopoeia and techniques of sorcery and midwifery.

As healers, Neopagans identify with the legendary witch, while the patient, who assumes the starring role in the therapeutic process, is identified with the character of the shaman, who gains power and knowledge from a heroic victory over suffering.

Symbol of Witch as Healer

The Neopagan—taking the legendary witch as a model—is the professional male medical establishment turned inside out. As a symbol, the witch is female and dressed in black; she operates with chthonic powers of the psyche in contrast to the physician's clear and rational domain of the scrubbed and well-lit examining room, hospital, and laboratory. The witch concocts remedies consisting of herbs plucked from the soil and minerals derived from the ground, while physicians operate in sterile environments with a purified pharmacopeia.

The contrasts are striking. The witch is a solitary, hermitlike character effecting sorcery in isolation, while physicians gain their prestige by association with lofty professional groups. The witch is self-sufficient; the physician, by contrast, is dependent on elaborate research institutions, hospitals, teams of subordinate professional and nonprofessional practitioners, and peripheral industries.

The witch possesses no authority, only skill; she enjoys no privileged social status; she performs with materials and tools that are available to anyone.

Physicians "conquer" disease; witches operate as midwives. They stand by, support, and empower the patient to heal her- or himself. While wealth is a symbol of the physician's success and effectiveness, lack of wealth is a symbol of the witch's honorable intent; she heals out of love and compassion, without thought of material enrichment.[1]

The witch is consistently associated with the color black and darkness (Needham 1978). The underworld is dark. It was once associated with the temporal past and the domain of the eclipsed rulers of the Golden Age (in Sumerian mythology especially) and the fertile darkness to which agricultural goddesses, like Persephone, and Gardner's goddess descended to learn the mysteries of death. The Christians discredited the underworld as the domain of evil. In a society that sees time as linear and progressive, there is little value in resorting to the past. Former gods become demons, and superseded belief systems are discredited as inferior, erroneous, or evil. As the opposite of right society, the witch symbolizes associations with this shady realm.

From their own perspective, witches represent nature as the Earth (dirt from the vantage point of their critics), while physicians represent culture and the benefits of purity and technology.

In the estimation of the witches, the opposition is potentially complementary. Enhanced by magical healing, the Neopagans feel, allopathic[2] medicine can be more effective and less iatrogenic.[3] In few circumstances do professionals share that view.

We have seen in chapter four that in the witch hunts in Europe, the witches came to be associated with quackery through the efforts of the emerging medical profession to discredit them. As early as 1441 the accusation of witchcraft against the duchess of Gloucester was in part "owing to her 'uncanny' knowledge of medicine and astrology" (Lea, as cited in Fox 1968, 86 n. 32). In the American colonies, the healer Margaret Jones was hanged in 1648 for witchcraft. Fiske describes her as having "had some sensible ideas about medicine. She disapproved of wholesale bleeding and violent emetics [the therapies practiced by the professional doctors], and used to work cures by means of herb tonics and other simple prescriptions." However, the sufferings of some of those she treated seemed to have continued, and their complaints might have ripened into accusations of witchcraft (Fiske, 1902 as cited in Fox 1968, 84–85).

Male healers were not exempt from persecution, it must be remembered, but physicians (all of whom were male) enjoyed extraordinary immunity. Historian Leland Estes remarks that he is unaware of any single university trained medical man being executed as a witch (1983 n. 52). Although Larner discovered victims of the craze in almost every other occupational and social category (including sixteen from the nobility), she too was unable to find evidence that a single physician, surgeon, or apothecary was executed as a witch in Scotland (1981, 89). Members of officially established medical groups in England were similarly invulnerable (Estes 1983, n. 52). This invulnerability was probably related to the physicians' self-confidence that was supported by ecclesiastical and civil authorities, and confirmed by scholars of demonology, all of whom believed that university trained physicians were best qualified to "diagnose" witchcraft. Thus, the professionals became associated with truth and competence, in contrast to witches and other folk healers who became associated with superstition and quackery.

Before the fifteenth century in many parts of the world, witchcraft had long represented the malevolent or black aspect of magic—the counterpart of divination and healing associated with white, or good, magic performed by socially approved shamans, medicine people, and other magical practitioners. In fact, the processes, and often the practitioners, were the same; the effect, however, was perceived as either witchcraft or healing, depending on one's position or condition relative to the magic performed.

As Durkheim wrote, magic derives from religion and uses the socially shared symbols in ways that are hostile to society (1915). From the perspective of society, then, magic is subversive. From the viewpoint of the individual practitioner or consumer of magic, it is a method of self-defense, although it may at times involve hostility to individuals and the larger society. As a resort to socially unauthorized technology and technicians, magic constitutes an act of defiance—if not one of overt hostility—to society.

The witch and the physician take opposite perspectives on health and illness. The physician specializes, that is, he narrows his focus to specific organ systems. The witch divines with Tarot cards or consults the astrological climate to broaden her perspective to include the social, spiritual, and natural conditions as far-reaching as the planetary forces in the solar system. She ponders the patient's past deeds (in this and former lives) as well as the effects of hopes and fears in regard to the future for the possible repercussions on the present state of health.

The Neopagans find the conventional definitions of health, illness, disease, and healing too limited, and the customary role of the physician (the very symbol of patriarchal oppression) is uniformly rejected as offensive and counterproductive. One Neopagan physician whom I was able to interview exhibited ambivalence and defensiveness in regard to the Neopagans' criticism of the authoritarian role of the physician, and of allopathic medicine in general. At "witch camp" in 1985 the physician, an allergy specialist, demonstrated some nontraditional diagnostic techniques that she had incorporated into her practice. She maintained, however, that it is dangerous to rely on any practitioner other than a professional medical practitioner for diagnosis and supervision of health care.

Attitudes of Americans toward Their Health Care System

While it does not occur to most Americans to consult a witch to help remedy their health problems, there is a pervasive dissatisfaction with the country's health care system. In the late 1980s adults in the United States, Canada, and Britain were given the opportunity to evaluate the performance and desirability of their own health care system and offer their perceptions of the other two systems. The study was underwritten by the *Health Management Quarterly* (*HMQ*) in conjunction with the Harvard School of Public Health.[4] Americans were found to be less satisfied than the British with their health care system and substantially more dissatisfied than the Canadians. Only 10 percent of Americans see their own health care system as working reasonably well; 89 percent see it as requiring fundamental change in its direction and structure. In contrast, only 42 percent of the Canadians, and 60 percent of the British expressed such criticism of their own country's system (Blendon 1989).

We have seen that, as a group, the Neopagans are exceptionally imaginative, and, as we would expect, they are quite willing and able to leap into the uncertainty of new options while the majority of Americans cling to the familiar. Increasing levels of frustration with the health care system in the United States is presently inducing desperate leaps of faith not only by the imaginative but by the conservative-minded as well.

The investigators in the *HMQ* survey were surprised to discover that the strong preference for change (as indicated by a receptivity to the idea of adopting the Canadian system) was shared by the mainstream of

American society, (the middle income population), as well as business and government executives (Blendon 1989).

Dr. Blendon commented that "Americans apparently are so frustrated and discouraged with their existing health care arrangements that 61 percent say they would favor a health care system resembling that now operative in Canada," where the government sets the fees charged by hospitals and doctors. In the 1960s when the Medicare and Medicaid programs were on the drawing board, such governmental intervention was broadly regarded as a violation of the free market economy.

Neopagans differ from members of the larger population in their opinions regarding what constitutes effective health care. Eighty percent of American respondents to the HMQ survey were satisfied with the kinds of health care services received by themselves and their families, suggesting that mainstream America's dissatisfaction lies with the cost of health care or the system of distribution, rather than the nature of the services rendered.

In 1994, President Clinton's administration planned to initiate reform in the health care system by focusing on the cost and availability of medical care. The favored approach would put physicians and insurers into competition with one another in the effort to provide the best and most affordable product to purchasing networks of consumers.

In his essay, "History and Health Policy," Daniel M. Fox wrote that two hypotheses are fundamental to the assumptions about modern medicine: the power and importance of biomedical sciences and the inexorable welfare state. Each assumes that progress in discovering and distributing biomedical knowledge will improve the human condition (1985). Clinton's "managed competition" is an effort to revive free-market forces rather than emphasize the government's role in regulating and delivering health care. However, responses to the HMQ survey reflected the kind of thinking Fox described. It may be because the questions were phrased in those terms. Sixty-one percent of the respondents said they would favor a system like that in place in Canada, described in the survey as "the government pays most of the cost of health care for everyone out of taxes, and the government sets all fees charged by hospitals and doctors" (Blendon 1989, 5).

The Neopagans expect more of health care than efficient and equitable distribution of physician-provided, technology-intensive medicine. Respondents to a more recent survey, the Time/CNN poll (1991),[5] criticized the health care system for endless waiting for care, being treated in an impersonal manner, and indiscriminate resort to "big gun medicine" (Horowitz & Lafferty 1991, 68). An article about the recent popularity of New Age medicine reported that dissatisfaction inspired 30 percent of those who were interviewed to resort to alternative therapies such as homeopathy, chiropractic, acupuncture and guided imagery (1991, 68).[6] As we shall see, the Neopagans resort to these alternatives and many others besides.

I asked respondents to my questionnaire to indicate which of three options was the most promising way to improve health care. Thirty-eight percent believed "better utilization and availability of non-medical therapies was needed"; the majority (52 percent) felt that "both medical and non-medical therapies are equally important." Only 9 percent selected socialized medicine.[7] Eighty-nine percent of the respondents to the *HMQ* survey expressed a preference for the socialistic systems of Canada (61 percent) and Great Britain (28 percent).

Neopagans as a group are dissatisfied with allopathic medicine. (Only two respondents believed professional medical care is more effective than nonmedical care.) The large majority of respondents (80 percent) felt that medical and nonmedical health care were both effective, each for different problems; 13 percent believed nonmedical health care was more effective than allopathic medicine; only 6 percent believed that both are equally effective in an unqualified way.[8] However, 93 percent visit a medical doctor or dentist from one to six times a year.[9]

The nonprofessional therapists consulted most frequently were: chiropractors, massage therapists, and spiritual healers. One respondent included resort to a prostitute as a therapeutic modality. (See table 7 for a breakdown of what percentage of the total Neopagan population surveyed resort to various nonprofessional therapies and the levels of satisfaction with the outcome.)

In addition to the therapies listed in table 7, the Neopagans include meditation, visualization, and hypnotic affirmations among their magical technologies. We will return shortly to the healing practices that the Neopagans perform for themselves and one another.

Assuming Responsibility for One's Own Health

Theoretically, at least, Neopagans are willing to assume responsibility for maintaining and restoring health for themselves and for each other, to the fullest possible extent. My field experience indicates that a desire for self-sufficiency is one of the greatest inducements to study magic.

As a measure of responsibility for personal health, I asked Neopagans about their level of physical activity and about their use of alcohol, tobacco, and other substances. I discovered that they did not differ significantly from their peers in this regard. Sixty-one percent indicated that they exercise regularly.[10]

Slightly more of the Neopagans consume alcohol and slightly fewer smoke tobacco than the larger population.[11] More Neopagans smoke

Table 7

Neopagans Resorting to Nonprofessional Healing Therapies

Type of Therapy	Percentage* of Neopagans Who Use It	Percentage* Satisfied with the Results of Treatment
Chiropractic	47	40
Massage Therapy	42	41
Spiritual Healing	23	21
Other**	18	18
Homeopathy	13	10
Acupuncture	13	10
Crystal Healing	12	10
Osteopathy***	5	4
Midwifery	4	4

*All percentages are of the total population surveyed.
**Included in this category are herbalism, therapeutic touch, rituals, patronage of prostitutes.
***Although osteopathy has been granted membership in the AMA, it is included artificially and for convenience among nonprofessional therapies.

marijuana and use visionary drugs than do members of the general population. While only 10 percent of Neopagans surveyed responded that they smoke marijuana often, 46 percent responded that they smoke it occasionally, and 44 percent indicated they refrain altogether.[12] Only 9 percent of the larger population indicated that they use marijuana.[13] It is significant to remember that my questionnaire was administered in a less judgmental context than that in which the national statistics were gathered. Sixty-six percent of the Neopagans refrain altogether from the use of mind-altering drugs. Slightly more use drugs for visionary purposes (46 percent) than for recreation (34 percent).

Neopagans tend to be hedonistic, as we have seen, but they also believe that the use of mind-altering substances of a visionary nature enhances spiritual growth. The "Eightfold Path to the [spiritual] Center" in Gardnerian and other British Wiccan traditions includes "The correct and controlled use of drugs (hemp [marijuana], mushrooms, ritual wines, whiskey [known as the 'elixir of life']), and incense." The Eightfold Path is essential in all the workings of the craft, Lady Sheba writes in her Book of Shadows. Other paths include intention and concentration of intent, mental imagery, and the projection of the astral body. The various paths can be combined or used separately in working magic (Bell 1974, 9).

The controlled and correct use of these substances is regarded as only moderately harmful to one's health, and only if one neglects dietary and other simple restorative measures, while the benefits (in regard to enlarging one's understanding and magical effectiveness) are considered well worth the risks. Such is not the case with more routinely prescribed mind-altering drugs such as valium, I am generally reminded in disussions regarding substance use.

Neopagans are conscientious about their diets. Forty-four percent refrain from eating red meat, and 22 percent eliminate poultry from their diets (10 did not respond). I am not able to ascertain, however, to what extent these dietary restrictions represent health consciousness as opposed to a humanitarian concern for animals. Twenty-one percent eliminate dairy products, which, I believe, we can assume represents an effort to improve health.

For many Neopagans self-sufficiency in matters of health maintenance does not consist in moderation. They maintain a high degree of confidence in the body's ability to restore itself after periodic indulgence in rich foods and the occasional use of drugs and alcohol. The harmful effects of stress and toxic effects of environmental pollution, along with any other factors over which they have no personal control, trouble them much more. Control is of the essence in matters of health as in all aspects of their lives.

Explaining Illness

Along with the physical experience of illness comes the need to understand *why* there is the suffering. Bio-medical explanations—that provide a mechanistic view of the human body as a physio-chemical system—are the most satisfying for most people in Western society. Within this framework, health is essentially freedom from disease, that is, the absence of derangement, malfunction, or disorder that might result from disturbance of homeostasis, hereditary error, or intrusion by foreign substances such as germs and chemicals. Such an explanation requires the expertise of scientists. However, the diagnoses that physicians and their scientific colleagues produce are more useful for orienting themselves, rather than the patient, toward a line of action.

For Neopagans, biomedical diagnosis describes the suffering—it doesn't explain it. Along with some guidance toward a remedy, they need to incorporate the suffering into a mythology that relates to his or her unique biography and answers such questions as "Why me?"; "Why now?"; and "Where is there in this challenge an opportunity to learn or grow?" Even if the cure includes mechanical and/or chemical repair that can best be accomplished by medical professionals, the larger issue of "what is to be learned and transcended" will involve the patient and a spiritual advisor in a more emotional and cognitive, and equally significant, element of the cure.

The Greek *paideia*, "the *art* of civilization," approaches the idea of health entertained by Neopagans. Medicine of the Hippocratic era was based on the idea that the physical nature of humans was inseparable from the nature of the environment. Health was a natural quality arising from a dynamic balance of humans and their environment. In highly complex societies, on the other hand, there arose the illusion—deriving largely from the Christian worldview—that human life was outside natural limitations. The object of the art of civilization is the development of the character and qualities of life in which people might realize their fullest potential within and in relation to the social and natural worlds. In the Renaissance, paideia became the spiritual path of the magus. Health, in these terms, is essentially self-realization and creativity; illness is anything that disrupts it.

If humans are seen as integral to the natural environment that is itself capable of adaptation and evolution, then, above all, maintaining health requires flexibility. According to this point of view, periods of ill health are not necessarily mistakes or failures; they may be natural stages in the ongoing interaction between the individual and the environment. Like the shaman mastering the crises of breaking apart or magicians perfecting themselves, the object is not merely survival or relief from suffering, but the acquisition of knowledge and power by transcending suffering.

The decision to consult one or another type of healer first is important, because it is in the initial consultation that the condition is explained or diagnosed. Consultation with a professional first may indicate receptivity to a biomedical diagnosis, although it would not necessarily be considered sufficient explanation. Consultation with a nonprofessional healer first may indicate the preference for a spiritual interpretation of the misfortune or the hope that this kind of treatment—which is generally less expensive, less invasive, more aesthetic, and more person-centered—will be sufficient.

In an effort to discover how the Neopagans combine their mixed approach to healing, I asked respondents to the questionnaire to tell me for which conditions they rely only on each other and nonprofessional healers and for which condition they resort to professional health care (see table 8). I asked them to review a list of conditions (see Appendix) and indicate what kind of healer they preferred for each. Then I asked respondents to indicate those conditions for which they would consult both types of medical practitioner, and which type they would consult first (see table 9).

Many of the conditions for which Neopagans prefer to consult

Table 8
Conditions for which Neopagans Consult Only
Nonprofessional or Only Professional Healers

Nonprofessional Consultations

Condition	Number of Responses
Anxiety attacks	95
Persistent bad luck	93
Severe depression	78
Mild depression	78
Paranoia	62
Headache	61
Schizophrenia	59
Mild burns	56
High blood pressure	49
Infertility	49
Pregnancy & childbirth	47
Diarrhea	41
Cold or flu	38
Nausea	34
Hemorrhoids	33

Professional Consultations

Condition	Number of Responses
Appendicitis	114
Fractured bones	109
Venereal disease	102
Hepatitis	97
Kidney disease	95
Toothache	94
Heart attack	90
Impaired vision	89
Pneumonia	87
Severe burns	83
Diabetes	81
Childhood diseases	73
Hernia	71
Bladder infection	69
Heart disease	69
AIDS	60
Athletic injury	61
Cancer	45
Sprains	39
Ulcers	36
Hemorrhoids	33

Table 9

Conditions for which Neopagans Consult Both Professional and Nonprofessional Health Care Practitioners

Selection of **Professional** for First Consultation

Condition	Number Who Would Consult a Professional First
Fractured bones	56
Heart attack	53
Appendicitis	52
Severe burns	52
Impaired vision	50
Venereal disease	48
Hepatitis	46
Diabetes	46
Heart disease	44
Kidney disease	43
AIDS	43
Hernia	41
Toothache	41
Cancer	38
Pneumonia	37
Childhood diseases	35
Athletic injury	34
Bladder infection	31
Abortion, unwanted pregnancy	30
Sprains	28

Selection of **Nonprofessional** for First Consultation

Condition	Number Who Would Consult a Nonprofessional First
Headache	45
Pregnancy & childbirth	43
High blood pressure	43
Infertility	38
Severe depression	37
Anxiety	36
Ulcer	35
Paranoia	34
Schizophrenia	32
Mild depression	32
Mild burns	29
Cold or flu	28
Persistent bad luck	27
Hemorrhage	20
Nausea	18
Diarrhea	18

nonprofessional healers are those that might respond to treatments with which they can bypass the gate-keeping function of professional physicians—that is, with medications and treatments such as massage or herbs or meditation, all of which are accessible without prescription. Other conditions might be considered emotional or psychological in nature. These conditions are particularly responsive to magic that involves movement of energy and change of consciousness. Such conditions as bad luck and infertility might be regarded as primarily spiritual rather than physical challenges. The conditions for which Neopagans would consult only professional medical practitioners are those for which access to prescription drugs and specialized treatments such as hemodialysis, surgery, or dental technology find no substitute in the repertoire of nonprofessional healers.

Because respondents said they would consult both types of healers for so many of the conditions, we may conclude that for the most part, nonprofessional techniques and those offered by mainstream medicine are regarded as supplements, rather than substitutes, for one another.

The self-reliance valued by the Neopagans cannot, then, be regarded as a sufficient substitute for a more equitable distribution of affordable professional medicine. We may say that Neopagans have an advantage over many others in American society who believe there is no substitute or supplement to allopathic medicine.

Supernatural Causes of Illness

The Neopagans share with a large majority of other pagans around the world belief in supernatural causation of illness. George Peter Murdock (1980), who discovered in his anthropological cross-cultural survey that supernatural causes far outweigh natural ones in significance, divided supernatural causes into three groups: mystical, animistic, and magical. Mystical causation included fate, ominous sensations, contagion, and mystical retribution. Neopagans take the position that fate is susceptible to human intervention. Although ominous sensations are generally interpreted as significant warnings of what may happen, it is not my impression that Neopagans regard them as the cause of any misfortune.

The concepts of contagion and mystical retribution, however, do have a place in the Neopagan idea of causation. Because the universe, according to the Neopagans, is interconnected, all magical workings are regarded as operating to some degree on the principle of contagion. An interesting example of this belief is a practice that was described to me as a method for containing a person's adverse magical influence by blocking contagion of it.

A person who drains the energy of others, leaving them feeling depleted or tense, is called a "psychic vampire." One coven performed a spell called "the bubbling" in which a "vampire" was collectively visualized by the members as contained inside a bell jar. In this way, I was told, the vampire's draining effect on others was obstructed. As a result, the vampire became uncomfortable, at which point the coven "removed the bell jar" and instructed the woman to try to change her behavior. She eventually did learn to control her draining effect on others.[14]

The threefold law is an example of mystical retribution. Because the cosmos, or, at least, the Earth, is constantly engaged in the dynamics of maintaining equilibrium, every act has repercussions. It would be unusual if there were to be a direct connection among those events and people. Often, Neopagans believe, retribution takes many lifetimes to come full circle, and it may involve groups rather than specific individuals.

For example if someone humiliated a friend, he or she might receive an even more extreme insult at the hands of another person he or she trusts, or perhaps three or more similar unkindnesses would come his or her way.[15] The threefold law operates according to the principle of cause and effect that was described in chapter seven. Every cause has its effect, which is not to say there is an equal and opposite reaction. The principle includes chance, the apparent face on the workings of mysterious but consistent universal laws that operate on many different planes of existence.

Animistic causation includes soul loss and spirit aggression. Soul loss is more often thought to be the result of human rather than supernatural causes, however. It was explained to me in this way by Earil, a shamanic witch: It is possible to kill or remove an essential part of our personality, or soul, if we believe it is the cause of suffering or punishment. I have also heard Neopagans name soul loss as the cause of AIDS. This theory posits that individuals who are despised for their sexual preference, or another essential part of the self, are robbed of their souls. This can depress the immune systems and render the person vulnerable not only to a virus but also to self-hate. This would be described as a combination of soul loss and spirit (of hate) aggression. A Neopagan psychiatric nurse told me he is approaching the treatment of adolescent patients by resort to the idea of soul retrieval.

Animistic causation includes spirit aggression. All manner of disembodied spirits are believed to exist in the supernatural realm, and most of them are attracted to the physicality that they lack. Procedures, such as the creation of a magic circle, or rituals to surround the body with a protective energy field are intended to safe-guard against aggression of the spirits when one crosses the threshold into sacred space.

A similar concept, "loss of one's center," does have considerable currency. Loss of one's center means that in the face of threats to one's physical, mental, psychological, or spiritual integrity, a person may become disconnected from the natural or social world and as a result, lose one's balance or equilibrium. In this condition of broken harmony with one's world, the natural circuits of energy (vital life force) within the individual and between her or him and the environment are considered to be disrupted, blocked, or imbalanced, all of which renders one susceptible to illness.

While I have had only one informant confess to deliberately performing harmful magic, fear of it is nonetheless pervasive. The young man in question claimed to have caused his college homecoming weekend to be rained out and to have caused a house to burn from a distance. When I experienced several months of unrelenting frustrations during my active membership in the Minoan Sisterhood coven—including a few car breakdowns when attempting to drive to meetings—the high priestess suggested in an oblique way that I may have been the victim of adverse effects of hostility, although we both doubt that anyone in the coven actually performed harmful spells.

Of course magical causation by sorcery and witchcraft are the normal daily fare of the Neopagans. In response to the question "Do you believe people can make others sick or injured with their will or thoughts?" Seventy-eight percent responded positively. Another 7 percent responded that the vulnerability of the object of the magic is a significant qualifier; 15 percent responded negatively.

In response to the question "Which is most determinative of your state of health?" 69 percent of the Neopagans responded that the condition of the body, mind, and spirit were equally determinative; 12 percent indicated that the condition of the spirit was most important; 8 percent indicated that the condition of the mind was the most significant; only 3 percent believed that the condition of the body was the most significant factor.[16]

Opposing Conceptions of Health, Illness, and Cure

As the conceptual opposite of the physician, the witch represents an alternative perspective on the nature of the therapeutic process. Historically, members of the emerging medical profession distinguished themselves from the folk healers—many of whom (as noted earlier) were persecuted as witches—by their more aggressive stance as conquerors of disease, "the enemy," while the folk healers persisted in midwifing their patients through the "natural process" of illness. The folk healers maintained a confidence in the body's inherent ability to heal itself and in remedies deriving from nature—herbs and minerals, for example. Physicians took the position that their "scientific" knowledge and technology were required to coerce the imperfect body into a cure and to improve on the filthy and superstitious remedies deriving from the Earth with their technology (most notably the lancet for bleeding and the forceps for birthing).

Opposing approaches to healing follow logically from these contrasting views, as we will see in the following chapter in which the witch's craft of healing will be explored in detail. Put quite simply, the healer is active but supportive; the most powerful determinative role is that of the patient. It is not surprising, therefore, that 84 percent of the questionnaire respondents indicated that the resistance of the individual is a more determinative factor in the severity of an illness episode than the severity of the invading organism or disease process. A sufferer, in this view, is a potential hero or heroine rather than a helpless victim who must be rescued by a professional.

The Role of the Healer

In the mid-1970s a physician, Eric Cassell, claimed that the most important tool for healing is the physician's symbolic role of omnipotence (1976). More recently, another physician, Melvin Konner, was moved to protest that doctors are not the enemy, "most are making low to reasonable incomes doing the hardest job in the world—and the one that requires the most training" (1991, 41). The statement summarizes the defensiveness that has recently displaced the omnipotence Americans granted their physicians so willingly.

"The patient is the arena over whose ground the doctor and his allies do battle with disease—the pot in which the surgeon plants his morning glory," Cassell wrote (1976, 203). He contrasted the physician's omnipotence to the patient's loss of control over his or her life. Cassell (1976) also contrasts the physician's realm of reason to that of the patient's loss of reason; the physician's firm connection to the world of health and high socioeconomic status to the patient's disconnection from the realm of the healthy; the physician's confidence to the patient's anxiety; and the physician's control to the patient's dependency.

In fact, Americans had to be taught to yield to such an unequal relationship. The rugged individualists of the American colonies did not submit gladly to the authority and privilege of physicians. In the Jacksonian era, Dr. Thanson, an "irregular" (not a university trained doctor) summed up the belief of most Americans in one of his home health care manuals when he wrote that the common person must "throw off the oppressive yoke of priests, lawyers, and physicians and assume his rightful place in a truly democratic society." As the educated elite, male physicians attempted to establish supremacy; women— housewives and practitioners of alternate therapies such as hydro- therapy—opposed them, literally with a missionary's zeal (Starr 1982).

The idea that science is a superior form of knowledge gave the "regular" physicians (those who were university trained) the edge. By the 1890s individuals were forced to defer to the expertise of the educated doctors because the science of medicine had become too complex for common people to comprehend (Starr 1982). The pharmacopeia and technology of modern medicine—like a shaman's tricks and paraphernalia—dazzled the American public.

This shift in popular opinion was largely attributable to the powerful monopoly achieved by the American Medical Association and the influence of the Laskar Lobby. With considerable wealth and expertise in advertising, this private lay lobby was able to establish medical research as a compelling social cause. In the late 1940s most Americans abandoned self-healing practices and belief in their efficacy, and placed their confidence instead in the unique status of physicians and scientific medicine (Starr 1982).

The extent and type of authority that American physicians have at- tained for themselves is unique.[17] American consumers were considered so unqualified to evaluate or, for that matter, even to comprehend the health sciences that their opinions were not sought until the late 1980s when researchers of the *HMQ* study asked lay persons to offer their opinions and when I surveyed those of Neopagans. Both of these studies, as well as other more recent ones, reveal that people feel qualified to identify failures in the health care system and to challenge both the methods and motives of physicians.

Passivity and unreasonableness are no longer automatically associated with the patient's role. Many patients and their lay and professional advocates are advancing the patients' right to collaborate in the design of their care. Some physicians are supportive of this trend also. Neopagans take an extreme position: the authority of the physician is counterproductive in a therapeutic relationship; it obstructs the healing process.

In the 1970s, when physicians' omnipotence was intact, Cassell likened their role to that of the shamans in non-Western societies in that both substitute themselves for the passive patient in combat with disease (1976). The person of the healer is itself a potent symbol, Lévi-Strauss demonstrated. Because of their marginality and other extraordinary attributes, healers are able to mediate between their patients' experiences and the cultural belief system. The great shaman, Quesalid, whose story

Lévi-Strauss (1963) told, shifted the community's confidence away from the other shamans through artifice, the "bloody down." Other shamans produced only a puddle of saliva as evidence that they had sucked out the patient's sickness. Quesalid bit his tongue to bloody a piece of down kept in his mouth in order to present more impressive evidence of his cure. By virtue of this "trick," he became a great shaman. His greatness was not attributable to his ability to heal his patients. Quesalid was able both to heal his patients and to become a great shaman because his dazzling artifice persuaded his community to believe in his greatness.

In fact, the object of shamans' performances is to overcome the patient's passivity, to mobilize his or her own aggressive response to the disease—although the responses are to a large extent unconscious processes. The shaman demonstrates that the battle is won so that the victory is activated in the patient's body.

The extent of the patient's passivity in Western medicine is unprecedented. It is more likely attributable to the patterns and ideals associated with the consumer economy than to the necessities of the therapeutic relationship. Where all products and services are commodities—including care of the sick—and ordinary citizens are considered infinitely malleable and susceptible to advertising and the advice of professionals, passivity is expected. The patient's only power is in selecting to whom and for how much he or she will yield control when he or she is sick.

Psychotherapist Jerome Frank (1974) also equates the role of the physician with that of the shaman. Hope is aroused by the healer's personal attributes, he writes, but even more so by his paraphernalia, which gains power from its culturally determined symbolic meaning. Although medical science and technology cannot be reduced to mere artifices, Frank rightly compares them, as cultural symbols, to the shaman's tools and tricks in regard to their power to impress the patient.

While Cassell and Frank were correct in observing the similarities of physicians to shamans on the basis of their "different" status and the glamour of their paraphernalia, they overlooked some important differences that, in the estimation of Neopagans, make physicians less effective. The shaman's suffering creates a bond of understanding and sympathy with the sick that comes from personal experience with the patient's state. Anthropologist Joan Halifax refers to shamans as "the wounded healers" (1979). Once they have survived and healed themselves, they may learn techniques from a senior shaman. However, first they must earn the right and the power to heal others by restoring order and health to their own lives.

In contrast, the difficult "breaking apart" or the "crisis" of contemporary medical education, separates physicians from their patients, who become adversaries in economic as well as social relationships. The training of physicians is so arduous (because as a professional group they support that style of education and they limit access to medical training) that it leaves most physicians with the feeling that their patients have a responsibility to reward them for their many years of difficult work and study. This is in utter contrast to the mystical love elaborated in the Western spiritual tradition.

The adversarial nature of the therapeutic relationship contributes to the high cost of medicine in the United States. Defensiveness on the parts of physicians and patients results in high insurance rates to protect patients from the prohibitive cost of care and to protect physicians against malpractice liability. Defensiveness on the part of physicians results in overuse of expensive diagnostic services. More trust and shared responsibility in the therapeutic relationship, such as that sought in alternative therapies, could hinder the growing cost of health care.

Physicians maintain a remoteness from the experiences of their patients. Subjective experience with suffering does not figure among their qualifications as it does for shamans. Physicians are expected to remain firmly connected to their consensus reality, science, which is not necessarily shared by the patient. Shamans gain familiarity with other realms of reality and with the patient's experience in altered states of consciousness. Physicians, on the other hand, gain mastery of an awe-inspiring body of theoretical knowledge and learn technical skills in order to gain the approval and permission of their peers—not the community of their potential patients.

Psychoanalysts resemble the shamans slightly more in that they must be psychoanalyzed themselves to earn the qualifications to analyze others. Physicians, on the other hand, maintain an unequivocal connection to the world of the healthy; they neither gain nor lose credibility or other "power" as a result of personal experience with suffering.

Shamans bridge disparate worlds. They represent at the same time the patient's subjective experience of illness and the world of health and consensus reality that the sick hope to reenter. Physicians are less able than shamans to integrate their patients' misfortunes into a shared belief system. The patient participates only to a limited degree in the privileged belief system of the professional. Shamanism is, for the most part, a religion of classless societies. In Western society medical education is most accessible to the privileged (in terms of wealth and other circumstances that favor academic achievement) and graduates of medical training are rewarded with power, prestige and, generally, exceptional wealth. They are, consequently, true peers only to others who enjoy high socioeconomic status. They represent the "real world" only to a very small number of their patients.

Cassell (1976) named another "useful" barrier that exists between physicians and their patients. The physician represents reason in contrast to the patient's unreasonableness. Reason flows from the discipline of science—a privileged sphere of knowledge—the pinnacle of which is medical science. Thus, the barrier is the scientific knowledge which creates a gap between the physician's and patient's frame of reference about the illness. Much of medical science is as foreign and arcane to laypersons as the shaman's spirit flights are to his people. In this sense there is some similarity between the shaman and the physician; the role of the healer implies access to privileged knowledge. For Neopagans, however, this barrier is an unfortunate impediment to the empathetic communication they see as vital to the therapeutic relationship.

In fact, shamans do not consider their patients to be unreasonable; reason and science have nothing to do with the healing process. The shaman's challenge, like that of the healing witch, is to participate in the patient's chaos of physical and mental derangements and to draw it into the realm of the comprehensible—to classify it and render it meaningful for the patient and the community. The community is assumed to be capable of understanding the shaman's diagnosis. This process of naming and classifying is intended to mobilize the self-healing mechanisms of the patient and the community. Not diminished or infantilized into a position of unreason, the patient (the momentary focus of a disharmony) is, rather, an object lesson for the entire community.

The authority of shamans and physicians differs on another issue. Shamans are continually justifying their position, which lasts only as long as their charisma and record of success. The authority of physicians, once established by membership in a professional association and licensure, persists whether or not they have charisma. As long as physicians are supported by their peers—for whatever reasons—their authority as healers remains intact. For example, lately Americans have become so frustrated by the expense of health care and the inefficiencies in the system of its delivery that they are quick to sue doctors for malpractice. Yet, as long as doctors are supported by expert witnesses (their peers) their authority remains constant.

The normal world that professionals represent is, in the estimation of Neopagans, a sick world. The physician's omnipotence and indiscriminate use of costly paraphernalia are the very embodiment of the patriarchal oppression that they see as the source of the sickness of modern society.

Disdain for the authoritarianism of professionals and a belief in the necessity for patients to assume responsibility and control over personal and social ills was illustrated in an Earth healing ritual I experienced at a pagan gathering in 1985. In this ritual the Earth was the patient.

Earth Healing Ritual

The ritual began with a lovely dirgelike chant led by Deirdre, high priestess of the EarthSpirit Community and wife of the aforementioned Andras. The few hundred celebrants were gathered in a circle in a field and responded to Deirdre's song as they had been instructed:

> Deirdre: The Earth is the healer.
>   All: I am the Earth.
> Deirdre: The Earth is our mother.
>   All: I am the Earth.
> Deirdre: The Earth is a fountain.
>   All: I am the Earth
> Deirdre: The Earth is a mountain.
>   All: I am the Earth.
> Deirdre: The Earth is in sorrow.
>   All: I am the Earth.
> Deirdre: The Earth is in joy.
>   All: I am the Earth.
> Deirdre: The Earth, She is crying.
>   All: I am the Earth.
> Deirdre: The Earth has a song to sing.
>   All: I am the Earth.
> Deirdre: I am a blackbird.
>   I am a river.
>   I am a healer.
>   I am a mother.
>   What is the Earth?
>   All: I am the Earth.
> Deirdre: Who is the Earth?
>   All: I am the Earth.
> Deirdre: We are the Earth.
>   All: I am the Earth.
>   I am the Earth.
>   I am the Earth.

Following that, the cardinal directions were addressed. Amber K faced the east and said:

> We invoke you from within and call you from without, and ask you to help us understand how we share in the creation of the poisoned air, psychic cesspool, and dangerous random thoughts that fly about in the air.

She concluded by asking the spirits of the east to help us to understand what we could do to remedy the environmental hazards to the air, the element associated with the east.

Addressed to the element Earth, the invocation in the north included this phrase:

> We ask that we each become aware of our personal role in the scarring
> of the Earth. . . . Let us recognize how our daily habits determine
> patterns of consumption that drive the machinery of pollution.

When each of the directions and their elements had been addressed, Amber K invoked the Earth by the name of the goddess, Gaia. Then she instructed the celebrants to shout out the descriptions of the destruction of the Earth that they had seen. "I have seen whole mountainsides stripped of every tree," someone cried out. "Rivers are clogged with poisons and dead marine life," shouted another, then "The air is thick with the filth emitted by greed." The celebrants began to moan and sway; energy was beginning to rise in response to the impassioned outcries coming simultaneously from all points in the circle. "Friends and friends and friends die of the Earth's cancer."

A woman came forth out of the circle splashing the blood-colored contents of an enormous stainless steel basin, on the ground and crying, "I have seen the blood of the Mother [goddess] spilled out upon the ground." Another person cried out, "Who will come to the aid of the Mother?" Loud responsive cries of "I will!" marked the peak of the release of energy, when a group broke into the circle shouting, "Make way!" An opening was made to admit the strange procession.

Five or so men all dressed in white lab coats and bedecked with stethoscopes, tourniquets, and other customary doctors' paraphernalia marched officiously to the center of the circle, ranting and squabbling among themselves. They were attended by a woman dressed in a nurse's cap and uniform, who fussed and fluttered around the "doctors," mopping their brows and making other gestures of servility. Following this group were two men dressed as orderlies and carrying an enormous band-aid the size of a small rug. The doctors argued vehemently over where the band-aid should be applied; the nurse hovered nervously while they snarled at her and debated peevishly among themselves.

At last an order was given by the "head doctor." While the band-aid was being applied according to the doctor's order, a "trickster" burst into the circle. His body was painted with grey and white stripes and he wore the horns of the Hopi Hano clown. The clown frightened and chased the medical team, who finally broke out of the circle and fled, still squabbling.

At that juncture, Amber K reappeared and restored the mood of solemnity saying, "It is easy to say the destruction of the Earth is caused by others. We need to take responsibility for our own part." She instructed the celebrants to decide what each would do to heal the Earth. Everyone was given a band-aid to place on one another's "third eye"[18] while recipients pronounced their intentions. Then, everyone either kneeled or lay down to communicate their intentions to the Earth. At this point, the Hano clown returned and cried out, "The body of the Earth is open; you can go and do this thing now."

Amber K asked the celebrants to rise, face outward, and close their eyes. She began to sing a lovely chant that resembled a lullaby; the celebrants joined in. "Open your eyes," she then said. "Go forth and do the thing you promised you would do to heal Her." In that way the circle dispersed without ever being ritually dissolved. The healing energy that the celebrants raised was to be carried into the larger world to empower the celebrants to keep their promises to work for the healing of the Earth.

In this ritual the physician's omnipotence was parodied, as was his medical technology, the pathetic band-aid, which, like the shaman's impressive paraphernalia, serves to establish his authority over the patient. The Hano clown indicated that professional physicians, like priests in solemn rituals, must not take themselves too seriously. In healing there is need of more humor, passion, sensuality, love, and art. The physician's omnipotence was derided as a thin veneer of pomposity obscuring actual confusion and incompetence. The doctor—symbol of the false bravado of science and technology in general—represented the professionals, legislators, and other experts on whom society depends to remedy environmental hazards as well as personal health needs— even to devise its version of "reality."

That a person's health can no longer be considered in isolation from the environment was also made plain. Most significant of all was the point that unqualified reliance on authorized persons must be forsaken in favor of the concerted action of "unauthorized" healers. Each person must do what she or he is able to do and must use whatever talents and powers he or she has. The role model for these healers is the legendary witch who had been persecuted for healing without a license.

We have seen that the witch healer is the conceptual opposite of the physician. Neopagans, who identify with the legendary witch, differ from physicians and most members of the larger society in their definitions of health and illness. They reject physicians' omnipotence and view most other features of the professionals' role as counterproductive. In their estimation, the heroes and heroines are the patients, and the true healers are those who approach their task more like the legendary witch.

Chapter Eleven

The Craft of Healing

W hen I injured my thumb at the Rites of Spring Gathering in 1985, I was relieved to learn that Lyra, a well-respected healer, was on duty in the "Healer's Hut." I had tripped while carrying firewood, and one of the heavy logs had landed on my thumb causing instant agony, in the throes of which one perceives bursts of light, spirals, and exclamation points as in the comic strips.

Lyra is a nurse supervisor in a nursing home and high priestess of a coven that specializes in the magical skills of healing. Like most Neopagans, she is not adverse to combining the best of allopathic medicine with techniques that are less well understood in terms of biomedical premises, and she gives more attention to the psychic and energy levels that tend to be neglected—even denied—in allopathic medicine.

I served as Lyra's assistant during some of my tours of duty in the health tent at the first gathering I attended. She was in a wheel chair that summer with her leg in a heavy cast, recovering from a fracture she sustained by falling at another gathering.

Because I had been a nurse, she assigned to me the straightforward tasks of changing wound dressings and applying calamine lotion. She taught me to use the juice of the yucca plant for sunburn and bites. I watched as she stirred up a foul-looking wad of herbs and honey to apply to a sore gum. The satisfied patient who was receiving a second dose reported that the application had been soothing and had reduced the swelling.

I watched her assign a "listener" to sit with people who were "fried" from too much energy shifting. She explained that gatherings are hard on the nervous system. Intense stimulation can fry the brain, she explained, especially if one is inexperienced with moving and balancing energy. She pointed at the tent where fried people were lying on mats

179

with listeners in attendance. Some were weeping, some released anxiety in high pitched chatter, others sipped a soothing herbal tea, or rested in dazed silence.

That day of the wounded thumb, I was Lyra's patient. She placed one of her forefingers at the tip of my throbbing thumb and the other at its base, closed her eyes in silent contemplation for a few seconds, then pronounced her diagnosis: "It's broken." How did she know? I wondered. "I passed some energy through it, from one of my fingers to the other and I felt the blockage," she explained. I was impressed. "You might want to get it x-rayed when you get home to be sure," she continued, "but I'm pretty sure . . . In any case," she went on, "the only thing to do now is dress the superficial wound, splint the thumb, and put ice on it." After she did all of those things, she directed me to a cot and told me to lie down and "let your energies settle." After all, according to the Neopagan disease model, it was not only my thumb that was injured, but my etheric body had been traumatized as well.

In fact, I was in a highly excited state that resembled anxiety except that it was mixed with euphoria. I was also worried about the preparations I needed to make for the performance piece I was due to present in an hour or so.

Lyra assigned a young woman to keep an eye on me. My gentle attendant made me comfortable on the cot. A young woman on a cot nearby who was sipping an herbal tea to quiet her menstrual cramps, started a conversation. I became so engaged in our chat that I forgot about time altogether. It gradually dawned on me as we spoke of other things, that, OK, it was only a finger, but my body was actually *broken*. The meaning of that was beginning to unfold with all the shocking implications—so seldom admitted into consciousness—that the human is so fragile a form in a world of hard stones and heavy logs.

I was beginning to resent the intrusion of the woman's conversation. There were things I would not be able to do, I was realizing. Who might I rely on to help me? What a miraculously efficient thing a human body is when it isn't broken; how powerful and adept fingers can be— particularly mine that had performed such delicate operations as a nurse or artist. How long was it going to hurt like this? Would this interfere with my artwork; would my hand ever be the same? My mind ruminated thus as I tried to appear attentive to the conversation.

Lyra returned to check on me. By then I had arrived at a more appropriate—rather solemn—acceptance that I was injured and would be experiencing considerable pain and inconvenience as a result. I had felt the "pangs of the scourge," not in punishment, rather as a part of the natural vicissitudes of life in a world composed of dense matter. Suffering yanks one into the present moment and into all moments; it is the opportunity to take an in-depth deep look at the condition of being human on planet Earth from the vantage point of heightened perceptions. Lyra considered the psychic impact of the damage to my hand a significant part of the problem—which is also opportunity—that she needed to address with her healing. Not until she ascertained (by the look of my aura, she said) that my energies had settled, did Lyra dismiss me.

I got to my presentation on time, and my performance anxiety provided a welcome distraction from the pain. The steady throbbing of my thumb was an ironic back-beat to the story I enacted. It was a true story of a Siberian shaman woman, who, like all shamans, acquired her power by surviving suffering. When the performance was finished, I began to see stars again and to notice new relationships from the perspective of consciousness altered by my recent trauma. The trees—grand and immobile—had assaulted me in an indirect way. What harm a piece of tree might do if it should fall on a human hand . . . touché! . . . all the harm humans have done to the trees . . . such were the revelations of ever-present truths—now seeming so poignant—that appeared in scrambled relationships through the lens of my pain. Lyra had made sure that I would not be distracted from these insights.

When I returned home, an x-ray confirmed Lyra's diagnosis and the emergency room staff approved of the treatment I had received. I didn't mention the "energy-settling" part. The doctor replaced the splint that Lyra made using tongue-depressors and tape with a more elaborate contraption of foam rubber bonded to a flexible metal that I was told to wear for about six weeks, just as Lyra had recommended.

By comparison, the ordeal in the emergency room seemed punitive. There had been a long wait, confusion about my insurance, impersonal and disinterested treatment of my problem. I had taken several labyrinthine journeys to establish my records, to find the x-ray department, and to retrace my steps to the emergency room. Then, the stunning bill! The tongue-depressor splint had been sufficient, I thought. Why did I feel I needed the evidence of an x-ray? My "energies" were quite "unsettled" as I drove away.

The Legendary Witch as Role Model

Neopagan witches think of their craft as the classic benevolent magic, healing and divination that coexisted in preindustrial societies with its counterpart, harmful magic. These practitioners of benevolent magic were numerous among those persecuted as witches. They were enemies of both Christian clergy and professional doctors. By selecting the witch as heroine, today's witches reveal that they feel themselves similarly victimized. They claim the right and responsibility to reclaim authority over their lives from an encroaching and polluting technocracy whose most invasive institutions, in their estimation, are the professions of religion and medicine.

In her first book, Starhawk (1982, 83–85) provided a portrait of the legendary witch that, like a statue of Bruno's art of memory, the Neopagans have imbibed via the imagination, the better to partake of her powers. Starhawk's witch is an old woman, an herbalist and midwife whose healing hands and soothing voice charm away suffering. The blood of aboriginal faery people runs in her veins. On her way to assist a young woman in childbirth, the witch walks through the woods thinking of the tortures suffered by other healers like herself at the hands of the Christian witch hunters. The common lands are being divided; she fears that her own little cottage will be torn down. She has no husband or male relatives to protect her; no longer can she depend on her neighbors, because the priests have turned them against her with their tales of satanic witchcraft. Although a pain stabs at her own heart, she rests only a moment in the forest where she and her mother and grandmother before her gathered healing plants. She stands, makes a magical gesture in the air, and walks on, lonely and afraid, to assist another at a difficult birth.

Starhawk's portrait is an artistic rendering of the historical evidence that pre-modern Europeans linked female diviners and healers with satanic witchcraft and persecuted those who were defenseless. In their divinatory, medical, and religious functions, some scholars believe, the cunning-folk of the sixteenth century were far more important in peasant society than the official clergy (Thomas 1971; Delcambre 1951). Judging from available evidence, these white magicians would probably account for nearly half of those who were persecuted as witches in some areas (Horsley 1979a). In those parts of Europe for which adequate evidence is available—from Lorraine (Delcambre 1951) to Austria (Byloff 1929), from Lucerne (Hoffman-Krayer 1899) to Bremen and Schleswig-Holstein (Heberling 1915; Schwarzwälder 1958)—wise women (and wise men), folk healers, and diviners of peasant societies were indeed numerous among the victims of witch hunts.

Almost every Neopagan thinks of him- or herself as a healer. All "positive-path" magic is intended to heal, that is, to improve present circumstances by restoring lost balance and harmony. More respondents to my questionnaire indicated that they practiced some form of healing on themselves or others (97 percent) than practiced magic (93 percent). Forty-three percent indicated that they practiced nonmedical healing with a group.[1] A little over half of the people working collaboratively described the group as a coven.

The healers reported that they engage in such practices as meditation, using or prescribing vitamins, herbalism, Bach flower remedies,[2] polarity therapy,[3] massage, visualization techniques, affirmations (repeating affirming mental suggestions), use of crystals for healing, and various others. In the "other" category, individuals noted breathing exercises, yoga, mantra (chanting), acupressure, reflexology, hydrotherapy, therapeutic touch, and shamanistic healing, to name a few. (See table 10 for a breakdown of the percentage of respondents who practice each type of therapy (a) on themselves, (b) for others for free, and (c) for others in exchange for payment.)

Many Neopagans who do not practice healing by non-traditional means themselves still maintain a belief in the efficacy of such methods. Ninety percent believe it is possible to heal another being with the will or thoughts. An additional 6 percent gave a qualified positive response, and 5 percent gave a negative one.[4] Slightly fewer (78 percent) believed that it is possible to harm than believed it is possible to heal with the will or thoughts. Many of these respondents wrote marginal notes to the effect that the receptivity of an individual both to healing and to harm must be considered a determining variable in the issue of whether it is possible to affect another with the will or thoughts. Only 10 percent indicated a belief that healing requires physical contact,[5] and 74 percent believed that a transfer of energy is required.[6]

Table 10
Neopagans Who Practice Nonprofessional Healing

	Percentage* Who Practice It	On Themselves Only	On Others for Free	On Others for Payment
Meditation	75.6	39.2	29.6	6.8
Visualization	73.0	25.4	38.6	9.0
Massage	53.9	9.0	38.6	6.3
Herbalism	53.9	17.5	31.1	5.3
Affirmations	51.4	21.7	22.8	6.9
Vitamin Therapy	50.8	30.2	16.9	3.7
Crystal Therapy	40.7	15.3	21.7	3.7
Other**	36.5	12.7	15.4	8.4
Bach Flower Remedies	22.3	10.6	8.5	3.2
Polarity Therapy	19.5	4.2	12.1	3.2

*All percentages are of the total population of 189 respondents
**These alternatives are discussed in chapter 10.

Unauthorized but Authoritative Healers

Like the legendary witches, Neopagans are unauthorized practitioners of healing magic. For them, the most important aspect of healing is empowering people to heal themselves. One need not be authorized by the state or any professional organization to do it. The heart, or spirit, is responsive to enchantment, and the body is susceptible to the healing properties of the plants and minerals, derived from the natural world, that are available to everyone.

Magical healing does not require official authorization. It does require authority that derives from a natural talent, such as clairvoyance, study and magical training, confidence or knowledge that comes as a result of direct experience of suffering, or a well-focused intent to help. Training in covens is intended to strengthen the faculties of will, intuition, imagination, and talent for artistic expression. Advancement through levels of initiation in the more organized covens is based on the capacity to demonstrate knowledge and skill at various types of divination, including interpretation of runes or Tarot cards, astrological prediction, or assessment of energy fields. Coven work involves various artistic skills: writing rituals, music or invocations; performing dramas; fashioning images, talismans, and tools; as well as other artistic abilities. Witches learn to perceive, access, mold, and move energy. Members struggle with the social dynamics of small group psychology and politics. A high priestess or priest who has earned his or her title by demonstrating these many accomplishments wields considerable authority in the eyes of other witches. The fact that each witch is deemed the priestess or priest of her or his own religion means that even the novice enjoys some measure of authority. We have been introduced to Lyra's competence backed by an authority that comes not only from mastery of the Craft of Wicca but the professional credentials of a nurse supervisor. In the following examples we will see that other witches in established covens worked collaboratively (with one another and with hospital staff) to heal a child. Others collected in ad hoc groups to heal one another. One witch acquired the authority to assume control of her recovery from cancer through brief membership in a coven.

Baby Rhiannon and the Tribe of the Phoenix

Members of the Tribe of the Phoenix in Atlanta coordinated their efforts with those of the medical professionals who cared for the baby Rhiannon, daughter of two of the members, who was born in 1985. She was born prematurely by more than three weeks with enlarged organs and dysfunctional kidneys and lungs. Members of the Tribe of the Phoenix told me about their attempts to heal her each time we met at gatherings.

Soon after birth, the baby required a respirator; and when she had grown large enough, she had peritoneal dialysis. On the first evening after Rhiannon was born, the tribe gathered to conduct a healing ritual on her behalf. Because her most serious problem was her inability to make urine, the tribe decided to perform their first sympathetic magic spell at a waterfall, where they raised energy by chanting "Rhiannon heal!" and attempted to direct the energy to the baby. They also attempted to transmit to the baby the reassuring image of her mother who had been separated from her when Rhiannon was transferred to a children's hospital. The day after her birth, Rhiannon's mother signed herself out of the hospital where she was being treated so that she could visit her child.

In the first few days of Rhiannon's life, physicians did not expect her to survive and asked the parents to decide if they wanted to continue vigorous treatment. Shana, the mother, attempted to communicate telepathically with Rhiannon to discover if she wanted to engage in a difficult battle for life. Shana and members of the tribe attempted to communicate to the baby the message they would provide her with energy to draw on if she wanted to try to live; if not, they could understand and let her go in peace.

Shana asked Rhiannon to give her a sign of her wishes. After the child produced a urine output of nearly normal quantity and made her first eye contact with her mother, Shana interpreted these events as a sign that Rhiannon wanted to try to survive. That was the basis for the mother's decision to continue intensive medical efforts. All the members of the tribe felt that they were in telepathic communication with Rhiannon. They told me that they had participated in her fear and pain; several of them assumed her symptoms (not deliberately). Because of these telepathic links, they felt they were able to communicate reassurance and love to the baby.

They set up a telephone network so that they could communicate the progress of the infant's condition daily to all the members of the tribe. Each person, either separately or as part of a group, did rituals each day for several months, often at the waterfall or in the hospital chapel. Other Neopagan groups, some Christians, and even a Native American tribe in Florida prayed for the baby's recovery.

The parents and members of the Tribe of the Phoenix never doubted that the child was receiving necessary medical care that they were incapable of giving. Still, they believed their efforts at spiritual and telepathic healing were in no small measure responsible for the relative success of her treatment.

The hospital staff was generous in their cooperation with these efforts. When the baby's kidneys were failing, the nurses saved the few precious

Baby Witch Needs
HEALING

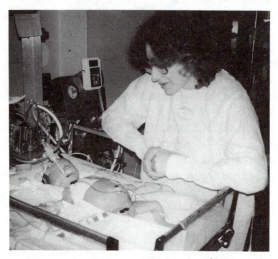

Shana + Rhiannon at Egleston Hosp.
Atlanta, Georgia

Rhiannon Gladell Wilburn, Daughter of
Medicine Hawk + Shana of Shadowlight in Austell,
Ga. was born May 19, 1985 at 4:30 am.
　She was born with cystoxic kidney disease,
under-developed lungs + digestive system. She has
made "amazing" progress (according to the medical
profession) yet is still in need of healing for her
kidneys, lungs, digestive system, and blood pressure.
　If you feel the need, please help!!

More info at Tribe of the Phoenix

wet diapers for the tribe to use in spells of sympathetic and contagious magic in their healing rituals. They agreed also to keep a spirit bag prepared and charged with energy by the group near the baby's unit. During crises, the nurses moved the spirit bag into the bassinet with the baby.

The tribe, for its part, included the medical staff in their healing rituals by sending them energy. The medical staff, in turn, were impressed by the support the tribe offered the parents. The doctors were amazed at Rhiannon's progress, one member of the tribe reported. Nurses and social workers praised their efforts saying whatever they were doing seemed to be working. People in the hospital called her "the miracle baby."

When I last spoke to a member of the Tribe of the Phoenix in 1989, Rhiannon was at home most of the time but had suffered several crises and surgeries. Despite these difficulties, the tribe still believes she is meant to be here. "I feel if she continues to be here she will be a very powerful and wonderful force," one member said.

It is hard to say to what extent Rhiannon's survival is attributable to the efforts of the tribe. Selena Fox explained that magical healing is intended only to provide energy for people to use to heal themselves. The tribe helped the parents and themselves a great deal. The parents benefitted from the guidance and support of the coven while they made many difficult decisions regarding their child's treatment and lived with the difficult consequences. The crisis drew the group together and gave them reason to develop their magical practice, deepen their understanding of how it works, and improve their skills through experience.

The cooperation of the hospital staff was of great benefit to the tribe. The peaceful coexistence of the two very different approaches to the treatment of Rhiannon's dire condition is an interesting example of the way Neopagans may supplement a less than satisfying health care system with the inherent human abilities associated with folk healers. It is also an impressive example of the way covens can provide the support that individuals who are going through crises require.

I had the pleasure of meeting Rhiannon at the Spiral Gathering in the fall of 1989 when she was four years old. Rhiannon initiated the conversation by asking if I would attend the feast that evening. I had the impression that I was speaking with a child seven or more years old. Although her speech was slurred, though only slightly, by the effect of a stroke she had suffered, she addressed me with a surprising clarity and directness. That evening when she was brought to the feast—her first appearance at a gathering—every child in the building rushed to her and piled on top of her. The eight or ten children who had never met her before then sat around her, fascinated, and asked about her unusual physical condition. She answered with serene patience. Rhiannon seems to be unusually well adapted to her infirmities; surely the love and support of the Tribe of the Phoenix has been influential in that regard.

Healing in Ad Hoc Groups of Witches

In 1989 Dolores Ashcroft-Nowicki, a witch from the Channel Islands, a province of Britain, came to the United States to teach female witches to perform a ritual she devised to help women to recover spiritually from rape, incest, and other sexual abuses. Dolores is an internationally well known witch and ceremonial magician. She is director of studies for an international school of Western magic, the Society of Inner Light; she has authored numerous books on the craft, both fiction and non-fiction, and she presents experiential and pedagogical conferences in the United States and Europe.

I was thrilled to take my place among about ten other women and our host Michael Thorne in the presence of this accomplished woman that evening in Queens, New York. I was especially honored because Dolores requested that only women with some initiatory credentials be invited. I recognized only Michael Thorne, our host, and Judy Harrow, who is high priestess of a New York coven and a prolific writer about the craft. Many of us were strangers to one another, yet, the common knowledge and experience of Wicca was the basis for trust and willingness to disclose a part of ourselves that is generally hidden.

The formidable Dolores explained how she had come to the create the "Reconsecration of the Womb Ritual." Institutions of justice fail female victims of sexual abuse miserably, Dolores declared, and there is only so far medical and psychological care can go towards helping women recover from it. Even those who enjoy the loving support of friends and family seem unable to overcome a sense of defilement, a deep spiritual sickness, Dolores remarked. People often refer to the womb as a temple. Why not, like a desecrated altar, reconsecrate a woman's womb? "Everyone of you loving and understanding women is qualified and able to make your sisters whole and clean again. The ritual is simple; it works for anyone who approaches it with love and pure intent. The power of the ritual comes from women's desire to heal one another. Shall I show you how it works?" she asked.

Our host, Michael, retreated and the women tore off jeans and shirts, put on ceremonial robes, and set about the familiar task of assembling the furnishings of a sacred circle. Dolores lost all motherly appearance when she released her long silver hair from its bun and with the quiet competence of an experienced priestess, turned the living room into a sacred temple. "Who will be healed?" she asked, "and who will sponsor her?" Women who were not even sure of one anothers' names deftly washed the hands and feet of the first of several women who would receive the healing. They carried the first volunteer into the circle of women and placed her on the massage table that served as an altar. The reconsecration of the womb was accomplished in less than five minutes. Dolores passed incense over the woman's body, then with salt water she washed her hands and feet and sprinkled her body. She drew down divine force and brought in into contact with the woman's abdomen with the simple words from the script that each one of us held. After anointing the woman with fragrant oil, Dolores declared that not only her womb, but her dreams, thoughts, and all of her body had been made holy again. The sponsors helped her down from the altar and Dolores presented her to the circle of women and declared that our "sister" had been renewed in body, soul, and heart. From that moment onwards the circle of deeply moved strangers felt bonded in a common sense of wonder and mutual respect. Could it be true that each one of us was capable of accomplishing the profound transformation that we had just witnessed? Soon enough Dolores asked who would perform the next healing. With considerable trepidation at first, most of the women either received or gave the healing that evening. We were so surprised by the effect of the simple ritual that when it ended we shared juice and cookies in stunned silence.

Dolores received no payment for her instruction. She gladly gave her experience, creativity, and the gift of confidence in women she had never met because, she said, "there are so many women who need this that I can't get to them all. Do this ritual; modify it if you want to and teach it to others." At the conclusion of each reconsecration Dolores looked the healed woman in the eyes and reminded her of the threefold law by saying, "Now you know what you must do." The threefold law is a system of indirect exchange; the recipient of a kindness passes it on to another who will pass it on to others until eventually a kindness comes full circle. In this way the healer is healed by her or his own healing work.

A year later, March of 1990, I attended a gathering of witches hosted by Judy Harrow. Judy wondered, as I did, if we really could achieve the effect of the reconsecration ceremony lacking Dolores' psychic skill, experience, and authority. So, Judy gathered six witches, not all of whom were initiated formally in a coven, to try it. Only three of us had experienced the ritual. Most of the women were strangers to one another. Once again the common symbolic language and shared traditions put us into rapport. With scripts in hand and, for many of us, knocking knees, we all took turns giving and receiving the reconsecration, even those who had not experienced overt sexual abuse. One woman needed healing following an abortion of a child she desperately wanted. She was ashamed that she was unable to create the economic and social security that is needed to shelter a child. For her motherhood is a way of demonstrating maturity and authority. "Witches take a lot of responsibility. How powerful is my magic if I can't master this?" she asked us and wept. The women agreed that she needed to speak to the spirit of the child. She agreed and asked us to sit in a huddle around her. We listened and wept with her while she explained to her lost child that she wanted it very much but her life and her body were not yet ready. Judy gave her an ear of dried corn as a symbol of the promise of fertility in the future. The woman received it as a profound sacra and declared that she was ready to receive the reconsecration.

Judy announced that I would perform the reconsecration. I was frozen with panic. With my mere first degree initiation I felt embarrassed before Judy who is not only a high priestess but a witch "queen," founder of several other covens that hived off under the direction of priestesses she initiated. Who could say no to such a formidable priestess?

Sure enough, even though I lost my place in the script and I nearly spilled the consecrated oil, at the conclusion of the ritual the woman literally leaped off the altar, danced around the circle, hugging and kissing everyone. The rest of our afternoon's solemn occupation was punctuated with her joyous giggle. Clearly, it doesn't take Dolores Ashcroft-Nowicki to perform that magic.

I attended other performances of the ritual. Even the most self-conscious and halting performance in mundane and unattractive meeting rooms, produced similar responses. I asked some of the women who received the healing to write and tell me how they felt several months afterwards. I received three letters. All said that an initial exhilaration gave way to a new and lasting peace or calm. They said that their lives had taken a new direction. One woman felt a "pushing inside to find the path where I will best be able to help people, animals and the environment."[7] The other women also mentioned feeling empowered and motivated to help others. The three women also mentioned the importance of the "safe space" created by "everyone's sincere intentions," or "the love of the women," or the "power of the desire of the women to help."

Although Dolores requested that the women she taught be initiated, she published the ritual in a book[8] that is accessible to anyone, although it would probably only appeal to individuals having some interest in magic.[9] Many American witches say that to be a witch one need only decide to be. My experience with the womb reconsecration ritual demonstrated that the ability to imagine another's suffering and feel not only compassion but a strong desire (will) to help when disciplined with some magical training and structured by an effective ritual is a valuable resource for healing.

Perhaps not everyone could heal in this way, neither is everyone susceptible to its beneficial effects. One of the women who described her experience in a letter mentioned that she did not feel moved to receive the reconsecration the first time she attended a gathering for that purpose. The mood had been spoiled when a woman was so upset by the experience that she abruptly left. As is true of art, ritual magic depends for its success, in no small measure, on the susceptibility of subjects to the medium. Dolores, the author of the ritual was wise to limit her instruction to initiates of Wicca; those who are not comfortable with its language of symbols could remain unmoved by it, or worse, frightened or offended by it. However, for those who share a religious perspective, such simple efforts to help are a vast and inexpensive source of great benefit.

Alanna's Homemade Cancer Cure

In the case of Alanna, a woman I interviewed at Rites of Spring in 1987, brief membership in a coven gave her the authority to heal herself of cancer. In 1979 she had a hysterectomy and removal of a section of her intestines because of a condition diagnosed as adenocarcinoma. Alanna was not a witch nor a Neopagan at the onset of her illness. Alanna was sufficiently disenchanted with the health care system to consider alternative treatments before she found encouragement in a Wicca coven for her self-sufficiency in managing her recovery.

Alanna could neither afford nor did she desire conventional follow-up care. The failure of her health coincided with an unfortunate separation from her husband, who denied financial or any other assistance to her or their child. Treatment of conditions like hers generally includes chemotherapy and/or radiation. Instead she consulted self-help books and devised a regime that consisted of nutritional supplements of enzymes (most prominently carotene, which she learned in her research is believed to help prevent and cure cancer). As a first phase of therapy, she tried to purify her body with intestinal purges and hot baths to promote the elimination of toxins through the skin. After the purification phase, she undertook a nutrition and exercise program in order to fortify her normal healing process. She ate mostly raw vegetables and fruits and did yoga and breathing exercises, and affirmations. The spiritual phase of her therapy followed all of these efforts.

Alanna met a woman in her yoga class who told her about her membership in a Dianic coven. Alanna became a member of the coven, which stayed together for only nine months, but Alanna continued to worship and do magic alone and with other groups. Her discovery of goddess worship vindicated her beliefs and life-long uneasiness with the patriarchal god. Identification with the female divinity affirmed

Alanna's confidence in her capacity to heal herself. She became interested in occult practices, such as numerology and astrology and *tao* spirituality, all of which helped her to find some meaning for her suffering and some relief.

After about two years of her vigorous self-devised therapy, she read Dr. Bernie Siegel's book, *Love, Medicine and Miracles* (1986), and became a member of one of his cancer patient support groups. She learned to give up her preoccupation with her cancer and her homemade therapy, which by then had become excessive. When I spoke with Alanna, eight years after her diagnosis of cancer, she had given up her self-devised therapy except for health maintenance practices such as yoga, in the conviction that she was healed.

I asked her why she thought the misfortune of illness had happened. She responded by explaining the Eastern notion of *karma*, that actions have repercussions in subsequent reincarnations. There is individual and racial karma, she continued. Illness can occur randomly; an individual may get an illness caused by others, she explained. For instance, the pollution of the environment by some will lead to diseases such as cancer in others. The ordeal of her illness was necessary to her life, she said, because, it caused her to develop strengths such as self-confidence. As a self-conscious and generally depressed person, she had lived in fear she said. (Her voice that day of our first interview was only barely audible). Because she was so alone and without material resources and because she had a son to care for, she was forced to be self-sufficient. "I am completely different now," she concluded. Most importantly, she learned compassion. "The seeds were there," she said, but she learned to understand the suffering of others as a result of experiencing her own.

When I saw Alanna again in the spring of 1989, (ten years after her treatment for cancer began) she appeared radiantly healthy and self-confident. She was offering for sale lovely woolen capes and jewelry that were the products of the burst of creativity that followed the mastery of her suffering.

The Witches' Craft

For the most part, the *craft* of healing operates according to the laws of aesthetics. Success depends on the ability to generate faith within the subject—who must be susceptible to the craft of healing—and the creation of effective symbols that move the person to heal himself or herself. A witch's effectiveness, like that of the shaman and the physician, depends a great deal on her or his symbolic role, the drama of her or his performance, and the use of impressive magical tools.

Although Earil, a witch who incorporates shamanic trance work in her healing practice, warned me before I came to watch her work that instead of seeing a glamorous shaman dancing around in animal hides beating a drum, I could expect to see "a fat woman in sweat pants and no drums!" In fact I was very impressed, as was the patient, by the crystals, incense, the preserved hide of a deceased beloved cat that had been Earil's familiar, and a feather fan with bells, which she used to cleanse and break up blockages in the patient's energy field. For percussion she created a constant "zoop, zoop, zoop" by passing a golden slinky toy from one hand to the other.

A Canadian witch whom I met at Rites of Spring in 1985 reported that in addition to treating cancer and other serious physical ailments with herbal remedies, he and his wife and coven members perform exorcisms for individuals suffering from obsession or possession. These procedures are supplemented with considerable drama—the ceremony is performed in a black room, and everyone wears black robes. Because of these visual clues, he explained, the patient expects something powerful and important to happen.[10] Most witch healers use many tools and props to help them in the task they share with artists—to assemble an effective symbol of feeling, in this case, the feeling of health defined as wholeness and balance.

While *curing* directly alters substances by removing the illness whether or not the result is to place the patient in greater harmony and balance in their world, the craft of *healing* might incorporate the problem into the final product. The sociologist, Talcott Parsons (1951), clarified the many benefits people find in the sick role—for instance, exemption from work or responsibility or entitlement to financial and emotional benefits. Becoming disease-free is not always the remedy that brings a person's life into his or her ideal harmony. For that reason witches never presume to cure an illness without expressed consent.

Selena Fox explained that all healing can boil down to how balanced a person is within her or his life-plan and in relation to the rest of the world. "Sometimes a person appears to be in a diseased state; however, all they're really doing is going through a life passage. That, in itself, is not necessarily a sickness to be conquered . . . [it is] a process to be facilitated." According to Selena a person's growth can be accelerated to help him or her move through the process of becoming. "A stabilization at a new level can then happen, and this can involve growth," Selena said.[11]

Ritual

According to the view that healing is an aspect of personal and ecological evolution, conditions of illness (as well as those of dying) are rites of

Earil, the shaman. Photo included with the permission of Earil Wilson.

passage. They are liminal episodes when the person is neither healthy nor dead, during which the opportunity exists for "mutations."

Ritual is particularly useful, Selena told me, for helping patients release impediments (such as fear or resentment) to healing and for helping them take a perspective on their illnesses, in which they are the heroes or heroines. In the liminality of sacred space, a different understanding of misfortune may be found by the patient. Ceremony promotes letting go of blocks or pains and is addressed to the deep potentials within the self. "A person need not actually be in a diseased state to benefit from healing." Selena continued, "The achievement of an ecstatic mystical experience in rituals, for instance, can result in growth and movement beyond present limitations for anyone, healthy or sick."

Diagnosis

The most important human faculties that the Neopagans named as essential in magic—imagination, will, craft, and to a lesser degree, psychic skills—are useful in diagnosis. Many witch healers are clairvoyant (able to see or feel blockages in energy fields surrounding people or the disease process); others are clairtangent (they intuit problems by touching the patient or something that has been in contact with him or her). Those of us who lack these sensitivities think of them as exceptional (psychic) abilities. Witches learn to develop these abilities and think of them as everyone's birthright. Eighty-nine percent of the questionnaire respondents said they believed it is possible to see auras, although fewer said they were able to do so.

Like Lyra, another witch healer, Sunlion, was able to feel the energy in my broken thumb. There's arthritis building up in there, she discerned by touch, and the energy level in the whole hand is low. After focusing the aim of some energy through a quartz crystal she recommended bathing the hand in hot water with mustard to bring more life force into it.

Others "see," or intuit their diagnoses in the form of pictures or stories. For instance, at a Spiral gathering in 1989, a healer who called himself Flying Horse looked into and beyond my eyes and announced that I had a "box in my head." The image rang true immediately. I understood that he was describing the structure my thinking had assumed as a result of years of academic study. In 1993, Earil said that the box was still there, but probably because my life was more balanced with art as well as scholarship, I'd knocked the corners off the box so that it looked more like an octahedron. She was more concerned about another problem that she diagnosed symbolically as a hole in my heart.

Some diagnoses take on mythic proportions. Because most witches believe in reincarnation, it is possible to explain a problem as part of a challenge that originated in a person's quest to perfect themselves through many life experiences.

Diagnosis is an aesthetic judgement often expressed in terms of the

Flying Horse.

balance of the five elements (fire, water, air, Earth and spirit) within the patient's body and his or her social and spiritual spheres (Shekhinah Mountainwater 1984). A person suffering inflammation, either physical or emotional, might be advised to cool the flames with the waters of compassion and to give direction to the energy with the structure of the solid element of Earth or bring understanding from the thoughtful element of air. A person who is "drowning" in watery emotions might be advised that they lack the assertiveness of fire to balance their passivity or that they need the stability of Earth or the insight of air.

With diagnoses such as these, the healer portrays the ultimate cause of the lost harmony with one's world that rendered the person susceptible to illness, in an effective symbol. The healer gives the problem a face, or character, that makes the diffuse experience of suffering accessible to the patient who can engage it in a battle to win control of the self, or soul. The battle may involve professional medical attention; however, it is subordinate to the overriding object of living out the mythic quest for harmony with one's world. Achieving that balanced state may require psychological or dietary adjustments, relaxation, and adjustment of the aura, or energy field. For the Neopagans, the spiritual component is the most significant.

Healing Starts with the Soul

Sickness may begin on any level—physical, mental, spiritual, or social—and it is important to address all levels in the healing process. However, Selena explained that the spiritual level is the place to begin because there one addresses the divinity within, as well as "who they are" (the soul) on very fundamental levels—the cognitive, emotional, and subconscious.[12] We have seen in the preceding chapter that the Neopagans who responded to my questionnaire share that opinion. More of them believed the condition of the spirit was a more important factor in health (12 percent) than the condition of the body (3 percent), while the majority, (69 percent), believed that the body, mind, and spirit were equally important.

Earil phrases her healings in terms of soul loss; she helps people to discover, in visionary trance states, what part of the soul has been exiled and how to restore it. For instance, she said the hole she saw in my heart was left behind when I removed a part of myself because I believed it caused people to dislike me. The treatment was a trance journey in which she helped me to locate the time and place of the loss. "Now, take that exiled thing, spin it into a string and weave a patch to mend that hole," she advised me. In this kind of healing, the patient requires a refined imagination, I discovered.

For Selena and Earil, the process must begin by removing blocks, such as harbored resentments, guilt, or pain, that limit or prevent people from reaching the potential for healing within themselves. Several years before I experienced Earil's soul retrieval, I visited Selena to see how this kind of healing worked.

A Healing Ceremony in a Cave

When I visited Selena at Circle Farm in 1987, she had temporarily suspended her healing practice because she was devoting all of her energies to defending herself against a suit brought against her by neighbors who were attempting to prevent her from operating her church on her farmland. "If you want to see me do a healing, I'll have to do it on you," she said to me. I didn't feel physically ill, but I had already learned from Selena that one need not be sick to benefit from healing.

One day during my visit to Circle Farm, Selena led me up a hillside to a cave she had recently discovered on her land. There were a few faded remnants of paintings on the wall that she was proud to show me. She invited me to crawl inside a small chamber of the cave just big enough for the two of us to sit. Selena gave me a quartz crystal to put as an offering on a small altar she had created inside the little chamber. She suggested that silently each of us in our own way should call in the spirits of the four directions and the goddess.

Finally she turned to me and said, "I have heard you mention several times that you feel like a horse tied to a post on a short rope." Looking deeply and warmly into my eyes at quite close range, she continued, "You have made some jokes about becoming a bag lady; I think it is a true fear, not a joke. Perhaps we should try to take a different perspective," she said. I wondered briefly when we would get to the healing; however, I quickly forgot what was supposed to happen and became immersed in the conversation. Selena asked about my childhood and about how I had earned a living at various times in my life. She also asked how I felt about work, and what I really wanted to do, and

Selena Fox beside the cave.

what I felt restrained me. At one point she asked me to make a drawing in the dirt. "You will realize your dream of being materially rewarded for work that you enjoy and that uses your talents," Selena assured me. (She told me how moved and impressed she had been by my artwork.) "You are competent; it is your destiny; it will happen." She permitted me to protest at length that it is by no means a simple thing to accomplish and to express my fears that I would not have the luck or support of others, and so on . . . She quietly responded, "Trust me on this one. I see it. It will happen." Then she turned the conversation to practical ways of promoting my artwork. She said she visualized a brochure of colored pictures and told me of groups and organizations to which I should send it.

It began to get cold. "You are part of this Earth," Selena said. "You are sitting inside Her body right now. Why shouldn't you have your material needs met?" she asked. Then she announced that she would leave me alone in the cave awhile. "Form a clear image of yourself well provided for, doing what it is you want to do," Selena instructed. "The Mother will hear you while you sit in her body. Communicate with Her. Also," she continued, "I think when you return home you should do some trance work with the image of yourself as a horse tied to a post, or better still, do some activity within the context of a ritual in which you break free and run. It would help you to destroy that image of yourself as restrained."

After Selena announced that she would wait for me farther down the path and crawled out of the cave, I realized I had just experienced a healing. That was only half of the healing, however—the spiritual part. The physical healing, which was to happen the following day did not take place because I was so busy working with the archives that there was not time.

In the half of a healing I did experience, Selena used many of the elements common to non-Western pagan healings. For example, my healing resembled the curing rites described by Arthur J. Rubel in which folk healers treated *susto*, or soul loss, in Hispanic America (1964). These curing rites included diagnosis (in which the patient's "confession" played a significant part); a drama in which the healer communicated with the patient's soul; and physical therapy, including massage, purification by sweating, and stroking with feathers to remove harmful influences (Rubel 1964).

Selena "divined" the cause of my "illness"[13] and pronounced an authoritative diagnosis: fear of not achieving my life's work. Then she allowed me to confess, that is, to remember or relive the traumatic events that resulted in soul loss. In one case described by Rubel (1964), a woman was struck by her husband with a rock; in another, a man saw his possessions swept downstream off his donkey's back by a strong current.

Selena asked me questions that inspired discussion of how I came to acquire the fears that troubled me (which were more than I realized until that time, I must say). There is opportunity for abreaction in this phase of cure. The patient may reexperience traumatic events in the protected context of healing, during which the healer may reprogram the patient's harmful responses to the events.

Hispanic sufferers sometimes return to the site where the soul loss occurred. Selena took me on a hike through snow-covered hills to sit inside a cave, because she believed I needed to reestablish a connection with the Earth. Among the magical associations with the element Earth are physical matter and material wealth. By bringing me inside the cave, Selena attempted a reconciliation between the material resources of the Earth and myself, who felt alienated from them. In this case, the cave was both a powerful symbol and the substance of material resources for which money is the customary abstraction. Like the Hispanic sufferers of susto, Selena recommended that I make an offering, a crystal.

If there had been enough time, Selena said she would have completed my healing by cleansing and balancing my aura, which reminded me of the way that susto curers scooped away harmful influences from their patients. In fact, Selena often cleanses an aura by combing the area surrounding the body with her fingers or with a feather, as the susto curers did. "Probably I would have done some massage with deep pressure to release tension and accumulated toxins from your muscles, also" she said.

On our hike to the cave Selena made a detour to show me the frame of a sweat lodge. The lodge is covered with blankets in the summer when she performs sweat lodge ceremonies derived from Native American traditions. Beside the frame was a pond (then frozen) into which participants plunge after they sweat. Had it been summer, I would surely have been purified in a sweat ceremony.

Selena told me she often uses Tarot cards as the focus for affirmations. For example, she might suggest that the patient meditate on the strength card—which pictures a woman holding open a lion's mouth—or use it in a ritual to elicit her or his powers to heal or otherwise assume control of circumstances. For me, Selena reinforced my own image of the horse tied to a post.

In another of Rubel's cases, the shirt of a sick child was taken to the location of the dispossession to reconnect the child with his soul by a process of contagious magic. In a similar fashion, Selena put me into intimate contact with the Earth. She had not conducted a healing in her cave before, but she felt that being inside the Earth's body would be beneficial for my specific needs. Selena's healing was sensual and poetic. It embodied the sensitivity and craft of an artist. In a more rustic fashion she assembled the elements of a spell that resembled those Ficino described. Like the Renaissance magicians, she created an effective symbol and conveyed it—in the context of a ritual experience—via the imagination to the image-reading part of me that Western magicians call the soul.

Energy

Ficino described the movement of the substance of magic (pneuma) with the force of love (eros). As we learned in chapter seven, Neopagans describe a similar process as moving energy with the force of the will or intent. Either the magician directly moves or transforms the quality of energy, or inspires another to do so indirectly by resort to symbols.

Illness is one of the sources of the emotional tension that requires catharsis, according to Marett (see chapter seven). The witches would describe the situation this way: much energy is generated from the body in the illness state. When energy is the residue of frustration, fear, pain, and the many unpleasantnesses associated with illness, acts of indirect magic (communication) may be used to transform the *quality* of the energy and divert its flow to the beneficial function of healing.

By direct manipulation, a healer "tunes" a person's energy to a more beneficial vibratory rate. Alternatively, the healer may transmit energy to a patient as a temporary supplement to his or her own healing resources. In the case of the exorcism, described by the Canadian witch, something is drawn out. He called it an obsessing or possessing entity. I asked what it felt like when the entity passed through him. "An icky, squeamish shudder," he responded. He sends the "foreign" energy into the ground, using a steel sword like a lightning rod. His supportive group of magicians then draws any residual energy out of his body and "grounds" it, meaning they release it into the Earth where he believed it would be transformed into more beneficial energy forms.

Love

Selena described the love that is important in healing in words that echo Ficino's discussion of the eros that moves pneuma. "Love is important in healing," she said. "This is not lust, it is divine energy that is channeled. To do this you 'tune yourself'—as with a tuning fork—to get in touch with the divinity within yourself, then you just exude, radiate, and channel love energy. You transmit that high vibration level of the divine, healthy state to the person needing healing. It's catching. When a person is feeling good about himself or herself, the person is in a high vibrational state, and it is possible to trigger it in others just by being in their presence. This divine love," she explained, "is a state of being—not holding anger or hate—I don't know . . . but if I get in that state I'm high and energized for days."

Selena seems to be describing the dynamics Renaissance magicians experimented with: engaging the force of love and orienting the center of the self to the center of the divine universe. Another of the meanings of love—benevolent intent—is significant also. No magic can be accomplished if "perfect love and perfect trust" are lacking, witches say. Many say it is wrong, even impossible, to heal someone if you don't like them. In the estimation of the Neopagans, the healer should be moved by a desire to support, guide and nourish a friend, rather than by a dispassionate interest in solving a problem.

New Moon Healing Ritual at Circle Farm

During my visit to Circle Farm in March of 1987, I took part in the all-day new moon healing in which energy was raised and released over long distances to individuals who had requested healing. The first order of business was to tune the six participants who would be sending the healing energy. Within a sacred circle, Selena made us comfortable lying on the floor with eyes closed to listen to a guided meditation. Whereas Eastern meditation involves experiencing the stillness of the mind at rest, Western meditation keeps the image-receiving and processing part of the mind very occupied. The ability to create internal images is one of the most significant skills that magicians develop. Selena asked us to create clear images of ourselves floating through clouds of each color of the spectrum with all impediments to reaching the state of divine love (such things as illness, fear, and anger) slipping away as we moved from red to violet. With vivid pictures Selena inspired the participants to transform, or tune, their own energy.

In like fashion Selena put us in contact with an external energy source. Her words created visions of the fire from the center of the Earth rising and entering through the feet and mixing with each person's reserve of vital energy, flowing through the body and out the palms of the participants' hands. Those who requested healing for emotional problems, infections, and other relatively minor ailments took a place, one by one, in the center while the circle of healers chanted the recipient's name to drive the circuit of energy from the Earth, through the body and out the palms of the healers' hands which they held near the location of the ailment (for example, near the heart for emotional problems). An immediate resolution to problems was not expected.[14] Giving energy as a gift was intended to "nourish" the ailing ones and help them in their efforts to heal themselves.

After the needs of those present were met, we raised more energy by singing and dancing to the rhythm of Selena's drumming. Then we sat in a circle around a large chalice overflowing with letters requesting healing. Selena instructed us to release healing energy from the palms of our hands into the chalice full of requests. Then one at a time each person held a letter or picture while imagining the transmission of the state of well-being that the group had devoted the entire day's activities to establishing in themselves. The healer's energy vibration must be tuned so that the energy drawn from the Earth will be of a beneficial "vibratory note" (love) when it is channeled through the healer. To ensure greater likelihood of success, each request was treated by three different people.

How do you know if it helped, I wondered. "It's hard to measure," she responded, "because rarely are the results immediate. The intent is only to help, generally in combination with other efforts to heal." Furthermore," Selena said, "it takes a long time to get sick, and recovery must necessarily be gradual as well."

There was one instance, however, when the recipient was affected immediately and profoundly; she passed out. She had been bedridden as a result of a back ailment. When she became unconscious, she was taken to an emergency room. After regaining consciousness, she was able to walk, her pain was gone, and she reported having an out-of-body experience (that is to say, she saw her unconscious body from a distance).

Selena wasn't sure about how healing energy is transmitted over long distances. "The psychic realm operates very differently from ordinary reality, and it is not subject to the same limitations," she explained. However, she permitted me to read her file of letters describing healing responses to long-distance healing.

Selena emphasizes the indirect aspect of the healing magic. Most healing requests come in response to an invitation published in *Circle Network News*. Selena explained that the wording of the request form serves as an affirmation. Just above the place where a signature is requested, is pre-printed, "I signify I am ready to receive the healing." By putting the request for healing in writing, people begin the healing process by affirming their intention to be healed. In this case, direct transmission of energy is enhanced by the indirect operation of communication. Individuals are aware of the date and time of the healing ritual—always on the new moon—which enhances their receptivity as well.

The Patient as Hero

In magical healing of this kind, the experience of the sick person is the most important element in the therapeutic process—more important than the healer's authority, paraphernalia, or technology; more important than the approval of the community (the patient's or the physician's peers); even more important than the disease process itself. Eighty-four percent of the Neopagans said that the resistance of the ill person is more determinative of the outcome of an illness episode than the organism or disease process. The majority felt that the condition of body, mind, and spirit are equally important to health. Following this line of reasoning, healing begins by restoring the patient to a condition of confidence, mental clarity, and connectedness to a vast, inexhaustible source of energy (strength, love, and support), to the community, to the Earth, and even to the universe. The healer offers support for the patient who must do battle for her or his own health and discover the ultimate meaning of the unfortunate condition. The healer is a midwife, a guide, and a support for the patient who is to be the victor or the vanquished in a confrontation challenging the full development of the self.

This role of the witch as "coach" to the sick person may make her or him unpopular, for it is the witch's job to alert the patients to their frailties and to inform them of the errors in themselves, which they must be willing to surmount in order to be victorious in confronting their illness.

Witches do not go into battle *for* the patient as shamans and physicians do, rather they teach their patients and empower them to heal themselves. This may have been the case in the healing practice of European witches, as well. I am aware of no reports that the cunning-folk did battle with spiritual forces on behalf of the patient. Many of them did serve as witch finders, performing rituals to call forth a confession from the person they believed caused illness with malevolent witchcraft.

Present-day witch healers assist patients in their search for the meaning of their illness by relating it to shared beliefs regarding the Religion of the World. Generally speaking, episodes of illness are regarded as challenges. People will become stronger as a result of learning about their frailties and discovering unrecognized powers to heal themselves and will eventually overcome their illness or will learn to accommodate—if cure is not possible—to a new way of being in the world.

Lyra told me that she was utterly transformed—physically, emotionally and spiritually—by the ordeal of recovering from a broken leg. She summarized the meaning she attributed to the accident by quoting from the Book of Shadows: "You must suffer to learn. That experience [of falling] brought me right down to Earth in contact with the Mother Goddess, so that I could learn about Her," she said, "and I learned a lot!" During the process of recovering Lyra's marriage broke up; she changed her residence, lost weight, learned her weaknesses and discovered her strengths, and ultimately met and married a new mate.

It was not until a few years later that she could channel energy for healing again. Ultimately Lyra was grateful for the "lesson" of her illness, she told me, because it deepened her understanding of suffering and helped her to increase her powers, knowledge, and capacity for happiness.

In other words, for witches, illness and other misfortunes are seen as opportunities to improve the self. In this case, the role of hero or heroine goes to the patient; the witch healer—with all her or his talent and competence in visualizing, raising, and transmitting energy—assumes the more peripheral role of interpreter and guide.

Chapter Twelve

Suffering as Opportunity to "Shape-Shift"

L ate in the year of 1974 Andras Corban Arthen, who considers himself a shamanic-witch, thought he was going crazy. It began one day when he felt his mind "just going someplace else" beyond his control and everything around him seemed completely altered. Fear and confusion gripped him at irregular and unexpected intervals throughout the following nine months.

Andras did not consult a health professional. If he presented himself to a therapist with these symptoms and said that he was a witch and did magic, Andras feared—no doubt rightly—that he would have invited more alarm than help. Instead, he interpreted his suffering as "shape-shifting," that is to say, he was enduring the difficult transitional phase of a deliberate magical transformation.

European witches were believed to change their shapes into wolves or other fierce beasts to increase their powers. Shape-shifting is also a significant motif in the mythologies of shamanism. In the cave paintings of the paleolithic era are images of men wearing the skins and antlers of beasts, or appearing to become the beast in some mystic palingenesis.[1] Shape-shifting is in fact a belief in real or imagined transformation that is found in many societies. In European witch-beliefs the "lord of the hunt," a shape-shifter, was significant in the dances and games that were performed to secure plenty of game, often called "the wild ride."

All of these motifs—shape-shifting, the wild ride, and the mystical communion with the beasts and familiars—became linked with the notion of evil in the Christian concept of witchcraft. The Neopagans have restored these images along with that of the witch to their original significance as representatives of inherent powers.

It is often the case that health problems or other misfortunes are

The *Sorcerer* (in which the human and animal merge) drawn by Kathy Pasek from Abbe Breuil's drawing of the original cave painting in *Les Trois Frères* (Ariege), mid-Magdalenian (c. 14,000 B.C.E.).

defined in retrospect as crises of initiation or the alchemists' purification by fire. Andras established the structure of his experience at the outset by defining it as an act of magic, the product of which was to be a revelation of a creative and religious nature, which since that time has inspired thousands of other Neopagans.

Andras resorted to the idea of "shape-shifting" to structure a frightening experience that others would define as pathology. Whereas allopathic medicine aims to restore the person who suffers an illness to the condition of health that preceded it, Neopagans think of illness and health as existential conditions. They apply their magical ideas and training and bring the protective powers of the universe to bear on the

Herne the Hunter, engraving by George Cruikshank, 1843.

challenges of moving into an improved adaptation to their world. In such a process, Andras rearranged psychological and physical systems within himself and created new relationships between himself and his social and spiritual worlds.

His healing involved a transition through an *altered state of consciousness*. He experienced thoughts and feelings that *differed radically* from those he shared with members of the larger society or, for that matter, with other Neopagans. Andras was justified in his fears that he was suffering from mental illness. Madness resembles the shocking breakthrough of an artistic insight. The difference is largely one of consensus, and it is only the outcome that establishes the difference.

Rollo May's description of the creative process corresponds to my experience of it: creativity is an encounter of the intensely conscious human being with his or her world (1975, 54). World, in this sense, means "the pattern of meaningful relations in which a person exists and in the design of which he or she participates" (1975, 50). This definition of creativity relates equally well to the relationship of the magician to her or his world. The magician becomes intensely aware in the experience of gnosis, ecstasy, the hyperaesthetic state, or in the experience

Andras Corban Arthen wears his wolfskin as a symbol of his magical connection with the powers of the beast. The staff bearing the antlers of a deer symbolizes another of his "animal guardians."

of drawing down. Following such inspiration, he or she may be driven— as artists are—to devise an effective symbol of the feelings experienced or knowledge received in that state. The practice of Western magic offers many opportunities to create artifacts of these insights: rituals, songs, poetry, invocations to deities, ceremonial tools, jewelry, and robes, and so forth.

At the heart of the creative process is the break with one's normal self-world relationship, which resembles madness. The experience has been called ''unitary reality'' or ''participation mystique'' because in the throes of it, one feels part of the totality of existence (Neumann 1959).

As we have seen, the Western spiritual tradition—including Wicca—is a repository of techniques and disciplines to aid the magician to achieve just such an experience of intimate connection. Mind-altering drugs may produce the state. Under the influence of mescaline, Aldous Huxley produced an apt description of the experience as perception of "unspeakable and yet self-evident paradox."[2] One's surroundings reveal something unknown, yet in its actual presence, just as it is, it is at the same time something entirely different (Neumann 1959). For example, one might experience such a self-evident paradox while contemplating a sheaf of grain. The plant has been killed, severed from its roots in the Earth. That which drew its life from the rotting things in the soil has become food; this residue of death imparts life force. Life feeds on death. Life and death are one. Participation mystique would entail a direct and deeply moving realization rather than a logical progression to the conclusion that life and death are one, and probably an expansion of that awareness to encompass the dynamics inherent in all of existence. Another example of such an experience would be the transforming insight that resulted from Actaeon's encounter with Diana described in chapter six.

Magical training helps one to invite the creative encounter and to control its impact. However, it also comes involuntarily even to those who have not courted it—as if by grace—as the completion of the gestalt of hard work or search for a solution to a problem (Neumann 1959), or in the heart of suffering.

Nor does the encounter always result in the creative process; the encounter itself is not sufficient. There are levels of intensity ranging from the feeling of being fascinated or spellbound to full possession by a force that is exterior to the normal consciousness. Certain individuals, by virtue of constitutional differences or of the conditions of their lives, are more susceptible to the rapture that is both opportunity and danger.

Jungian psychologists attribute creative insight to a communication of the transpersonal content of the collective unconscious into consciousness. They differentiate those who produce a mental pathology as a result of such a breakthrough from those who do not, more on the basis of the *final outcome* than the qualities of the experience. According to this line of thinking, the altered states of creative individuals are differentiated from neurotics or psychotics by the following: (1) The experience of the creative individual relates to, and may be of benefit to, the collective; (2) the creative person is able to manage the tension between the subconscious and the well-developed mental capacities, or ego; (3) he or she produces an "achievement," rather than neurosis, as a product of the experience (Neumann 1959).

In the mentally ill, the eruption of subjective subconscious content pulls the conscious or ego off center. For creative individuals the breakthrough of novel insights provides the spark that ignites the creative process; it presents the problems for which creativity provides the solution. The creative individual finds a new and better center in the process of generating an achievement, the product of the transpersonal insight (Neumann 1959).

Jungian commentators on the creative experience designate the unconscious or collective unconscious as the source of the content of altered states of consciousness. I prefer to think of the domain beyond society's customary patterns of experience as simply the uncharted territory of all that has not yet been comprehended and classified by that society. It need not reside in any level of human consciousness. The altered states of shamans, for instance, may constitute participation in the awarenesses of animals or plants that may or may not arise from personal or collective unconscious.

The approach of Sergi Shirokogoroff, ethnologist of the Tungus peoples of Siberia, is useful in that he described the shaman's departure from his society's "psycho-mental complex" without such restriction. He described a peoples' psycho-mental complex as those cultural elements which consist of psychic and mental reactions to the milieu. This set of reactions comprises a permanent and definite character (though they vary within a certain range) that defines certain mental attitudes. The psycho-mental complex may be regarded as a theoretical system of a given social unit or of an individual (Shirokogoroff 1935).[3] Despite the fact that the eccentric shamans experience things in altered states of consciousness that are not available to others in their society, they are not to be thought of as mentally ill because they provide insights that relate in a useful way to the larger society. Little by little the shamans incorporate their experience in the formerly uncharted supernatural realm into the psycho-mental complex of their people. It is only through the effective symbols the shaman creates that other members of the society know what lies beyond the ordered psycho-mental complex.

This is also the case with prophets of religious movements and with artists. To put it differently, those who experience radical breaks with consensus reality and are able to create an effective symbol that renders the confusing experience comprehensible to themselves and others are not thought to be mad. When the symbols of those chaotic feelings ring true for others in society they are called art or, in the case of religious revelations, prophecy. In that case, the experience is creative rather than pathological.

The product revealed by these extreme transformations may be some new knowledge of suffering or a religious insight that can be taught or conveyed in behavior or find expression in art work. Andras' experience yielded all three of these products.

Creative individuals are those who possess both visionary capacities as well as strength of intellect and will—to use psychological jargon, a strong ego that permits them to interpret and give form to the numinous experience. We may count Andras among these. By resorting to his skill and knowledge of magic he caused his suffering to yield both healing and creativity.

Andras' Crises

Andras' involvement in Western magic both provoked his crisis and provided him with the resources to transcend it. I first learned about Andras' traumatic descent into the creative process in a workshop he offered at the Rites of Spring gathering in 1985, the theme of which was "The Way of the Butterfly," after the title he gave to his creative revelation. Andras explained to the cabin full of people who attended his workshop that he had experienced a crisis following his conscious decision to change himself and the nature of his magical practice. At the time he was a well-seasoned initiate—into all three levels—of various Wiccan traditions—Welsh, Alexandrian, and Americanized Celtic.

Long before that, Andras had received his original training in magic from his first teachers, whom he calls "Alison and Gordon Mcphersons" (not their actual names). The Mcphersons were members of a family of witches who lived outside of Edinburgh, Scotland. Like many of the witches who objected to Gardner's version of the Old Religion, the Mcphersons claimed to be the inheritors of a long family tradition[4] that differed markedly from Wicca. They did not work in a circle, invoke the mighty ones in the cardinal directions, draw down the moon, perform the ceremony of cakes and wine, nor did they have three degrees of initiation or call the leaders of the coven high priest or priestess.

The witchcraft Andras learned from the Mcphersons is a specific form of pagan magic that they believed developed in the British Isles. They did not think their witchcraft was a religion.[5] The few things the Mcphersons' magic has in common with Neopagan Wicca are working with energy, trance and elemental forces, and the use of a knife as a ceremonial tool. The training Andras received included techniques for inducing deep trance (*fretting*) and for generating and absorbing concentrations of psychic energy (the *farroch*). These techniques could be used to accomplish such things as divination, communing with nature spirits, "journeying to the invisible world," or shape-shifting. The latter is accomplished by creating a *wraith*, a sort of alter-ego, whose shape the magician can assume. As a result of this magic, Andras said he achieved immediate and dramatic changes in himself that he believes would otherwise have taken several years to bring about.

On the autumn equinox of 1969, Andras was initiated by Alison Mcpherson in a ceremony called *witch-making* that differs significantly from Wiccan initiations. His body was marked with *the witch's blane* to distinguish him as an established witch. It proved to be a powerfully transformative experience, Andras said, yet only the first of many shape-shiftings. In "The Way of the Butterfly" workshop he described the elation that he expected other witches also feel when they experience initiation:

> There is a sense of coming home and belonging, and fitting in. Our search has been fulfilled in a way. I think sometimes we get too wrapped up in titles and badges of honor, and names, labeling or defining ourselves in a way that does not allow for much change beyond that. The process of transformation—if we are truly committed to the [magical] work—is something that must go on.

Unfortunately for Andras the Mcphersons moved to the West Coast two years after that first shape-shifting experience. Andras believes the crises he suffered were associated with the disorientation he felt following their departure. He was the only initiate they left behind; he found no one who shared the kinds of "magical/psychic experiences" he shared with them. He was only twenty-two years old, too young he felt to practice magic on his own. He managed to make contact with several Wiccan groups and was initiated into three of them, but many of the people in these groups disapproved of his prior experience. They were particularly skeptical about the absence of the goddess and the Mcphersons' custom of moving counterclockwise in ritual. One woman insisted that he be exorcised because she believed the Mcphersons must be Satanists.

Andras found the Wiccan traditions superficial and insubstantial in comparison to the intense work in which he had collaborated with the Mcphersons. On the other hand, his exposure to Wicca caused him to doubt his former teachers' practices and their authenticity while he was suffering considerable hurt and anger towards them for leaving.

This was Andras' first crisis of confusion, despair and depression that brought his magical work to a stand-still. He found no answers, comfort or guidance from magical colleagues. Many reprimanded him. There should be no fear or "strange stages" such as those which Andras was experiencing, unless he was doing something wrong. Although others confided that they had experienced similar feelings, none could offer any useful advice.

Instead, he found reassuring confirmation of his experiences in books and during a chance meeting with a Seneca medicine man, Peete, who explained the phenomenon of shamanism to him. As a result of that meeting, Andras began to research the popular and scientific literature on the subject. He learned that most of the training he received from the Mcphersons resembled the theories and practices associated with shamanism. Consequently, he began to organize elements of his original training into a coherent system of practice (shamanic witchcraft), and in the autumn of 1975 he founded the Glainn Sidhr Order of Witches.

At the same time he was asked to assume leadership of a more conventional coven. When he attempted to integrate some of the elements of the Glainn Sidhr Order into the workings of this coven, he encountered resistance.

Feeling himself at the center of a whirlwind of conflicting forces, Andras resorted to his magical training to construct psychic boundaries. Boundaries are essential for orienting those who go between the worlds of consensus reality and the uncharted domain of the sacred realm; there are mutually exclusive ways of thinking, feeling, and acting which are appropriate for each. For Andras it was essential to establish boundaries not only between the sacred and mundane realms but among the diverse interpretations of the supernatural domain. He needed to isolate what was uniquely his own from the confusing and often conflicting array of overlapping structures of magical thought and practice in which he was engaged. Not only did the various magical groups disapprove of one another's beliefs and practices, but members within the same groups were moving in different directions. Yet they were reluctant to go their separate ways because of the friendships they had forged.

As a way of accommodating these conflicting desires, Andras founded the Athanor[6] Fellowship as an association of those members of the diverse magical groups who were willing to collaborate. He was successful in providing a common ground where these varied perspectives came together in tolerance and mutual purpose. However, as more of Andras' students joined the fellowship, long-standing personality differences were aggravated. In 1980 he disbanded Athanor and with a few of the original like-minded members, including his wife, Deirdre, reorganized Athanor with a shamanistic witchcraft focus. The establishment of the fellowship was one of two things that helped Andras to heal himself; the other was his knowledge of Western magic, especially the technique of creating the boundary of a magic circle.

Consensus on the nature of the sacred is so difficult to achieve that Durkheim esteemed it the glue that holds the separate members of a homogenous society in the suspension of commonality (1915). Andras stood at the intersection of several overlapping and criss-crossing cosmoses, feeling himself the very hub of discord with no teacher to guide him.

The most overwhelming feeling Andras experienced within the wall he created around himself was the despair of loneliness. At the same time he felt an "overwhelming sense of control, strength, and power," he told us that day of the workshop. However, loneliness and the enormous concentration required to maintain the boundary eventually brought him to a condition in which he felt a willingness to share his most private and powerful magical work with others. By the time he approached the end of nearly ten years of self-imposed isolation, Andras had limited his magical work to shamanistic witchcraft with others in the revised, more homogenous Athanor fellowship. By sharing a little of his private magical work with them, he began to release some of the potentially explosive pressure he felt accumulating within his psychic boundary. The wall had become a prison from which he was starting to escape.

On the spring equinox of 1984 that preceded his crisis, Andras decided to "break down the wall." While he was engaged in this deliberate shape-shifting he experienced another terrifying mental ordeal. There was no teacher who could help him define and structure the episodes of paranoia alternating with rapture. At first he feared that even the members of the Athanor Fellowship could not understand the kind and degree of fear and pain that he was experiencing.

However, his acquaintance with the experiences described by Carlos Casteneda, and his research of shamanism, enabled him to name his experience in terms of the quest of the spiritual "warrior" (Casteneda 1968), or the heroic breaking-apart of the shaman or, in the language of ceremonial magic, the "Great Work" of constructing one's spiritual being or "finding one's true will."

Andras' desire to change himself is not unusual. Many Americans engage in a quest to "find," define or liberate themselves from stale moral imperatives they imbibed during the process of socialization. Therapists are well equipped to help their clients "give birth to themselves," and they are able to buffer the emotional chaos that these transformations of the personality inevitably entail. Andras' ordeal might have been eased by the technological and pharmacological resources at the disposal of therapists. Yet, because Andras was traversing unchartered territory, I think his belief that a professional therapist could not guide him to his destination was well founded. He was creating himself—much as Giordano Bruno had tried to do—as a first, qualifying step towards creating a different version of the American character and a different moral basis for community.

In retrospect, it is possible to define Andras' experience as the breakthrough into the creative encounter—the completion of the gestalt he had initiated when he began to transform himself. Andras stood in the terrifying interval between death to his former self and birth of a revised personality.

Eventually "incredibly beautiful, transcendent, ecstatic states began to alternate with the initial sense of paranoia," Andras explained the day of the workshop.

> Suddenly I would feel, at the deepest level, completely one with the universe, where I felt that I was totally open to everything around me and I experienced myself as part of it. Everything was loaded with meaning. I was able to understand layers upon layers of meaning instinctively and totally—all perfectly crystal clear. Other times when I was experiencing those layers of meaning, it was just too much and I could not understand it. And that's where the paranoia set in. I kept going back and forth between these two similar and yet different experiences of total fear and panic and at the same time total meaningfulness and union. And I just didn't know what the hell to do with it.

In the midst of this psychic ordeal, Andras received an insight. Many people acquire animal guardians in their vision quests, Andras explained in the workshop, and these guardians—the bear, the wolf, or whatever— lend us their powers. "What I did not expect," he continued, "was to receive a butterfly as a guardian." When he was in this trance state, a butterfly came, and she conveyed to him the revelation of a model of spiritual transformation that he named "The Way of the Butterfly." Following his visionary experience of the butterfly guardian, he was able to think of his incomprehensible feelings in terms of the metamorphosis of the caterpillar into a butterfly.

"In a way I'm glad I didn't go to a professional, because I would have cheated myself out of the depth of the experience," Andras said. He refused to name his fear and panic an illness. "I don't mean to discredit psychology," Andras continued, "but I think it was helpful to go through it alone—yet to know I wasn't alone—to know I had around me people who—when I opened myself to them—reacted in a very supportive manner. There were people who were able to love me . . ." Andras paused a moment to choke back tears, then continued, "people who were able to understand . . . see me through. That kicked me so much in the gut, that we need each other."

Following many years of painful trial and error, Andras had succeeded in finding a handful of individuals who shared his religious vision and approach to magic, the Athanor Fellowship. This kind of consensus is a rare and fragile thing. These small intimate groups in which the necessary "perfect love and perfect trust" exist are the most stable structures—although not the longest lasting—in the Neopagan movement. Throughout the 1980s the Athanor Fellowship functioned as a protective enclosure within which Glainn Sidhr witchcraft could evolve. During that time several covens were formed within the larger coven of Athanor. However, twelve years after Andras had reorganized it, the Athanor Fellowship was dissolved on the vernal equinox of 1992, because, Andras explained, its structure was no longer conducive to the development of the Glainn Sidhr Order, which survives intact.

The Athanor Fellowship had been a safety net Andras created for himself. Gradually he began to share his private magical work with them. No doubt the trust that developed inspired him to remove the barrier. His friends and collaborators in the Athanor Fellowship (though none among them had ever experienced what he was going through) "midwifed" him through his shape-shifting when at last he confided in them.

We can all help one another simply by sharing the same symbolic universe and by being supportive, Andras concluded. At this formative stage the Neopagan symbolic universe is under construction and there is little agreement. Where agreement born of common experience or history was incomplete, open-minded acceptance (perfect love and perfect trust) on the part of members of Andras' circle of magical collaborators buttressed the fragile structure of his personality while it shape-shifted.

Andras achieved much more than he set out to. He broke through his shell of isolation and established the desired openness to his circle of fellow-magicians. The Athanor Fellowship strengthened and spawned the EarthSpirit Community, a collection of magical groups comprised of the many participants in the programs Athanor presented, and students of "The Witch's Craft," a course that Andras has been teaching since 1979 at the Cambridge Center for Adult Education. Although Athanor is no more, its progeny, the EarthSpirit Community, is the largest, most organized and productive magical community that I know of in the United States. (A few members work together to continue the work begun by the Athanor Fellowship, evidenced most prominently by how EarthSpirit Community is organized.)

In 1989, the EarthSpirit Community hosted the eleventh Rites of Spring gathering. It attracted the largest attendance ever—about seven hundred people with about four hundred other applicants who could not be accommodated. The group now provides several other gatherings each year. They began in the last two years to publish articles about the national Neopagan community in a professionally edited and produced magazine, *Fire Heart*. All of these services are made possible by the high level of skill and personal strengths of the core of elders of the Athanor Fellowship who worked together for more than eleven years. Andras is a source of inspiration, but the productivity of the group is not attributable to him alone. The group is composed of highly creative, competent and well-educated individuals who are capable of working together in harmony and mutual support. Andras realized his dream— and theirs—for effective collaborative creativity.

The artifacts of Andras' difficult passage—beyond the physical, psychic changes in himself—were insights that he articulated into an accessible paradigm for the central goal of the Western spiritual tradition: perfection of the self.

"The Way of the Butterfly"

Andras crystallized the episodes of his ordeal and ultimate transcendence in three interlocking metaphors of cyclical transformation. He offered them as inspiration and guidance for others in the Neopagan community who are in the same open-ended path of deliberate self-creation.

He compared his shape-shifting to the shaman's crisis of breaking apart. Typically, shamans say that they acquired their exceptional spiritual powers by being broken apart and reassembled, Andras explained. Ecstasy is one of a few techniques for journeying outside of a society's "correct" way of thinking. The shaman's journey—like Andras' experience—embodies both terror and rapture; it is dangerous and enlightening. When the shaman ventures beyond the limits of the psycho-mental complex, he or she enters the uncharted territory of all that has not yet been comprehended and classified by that society along with spirits of diseases, misfortunes, and the angry and unhappy dead. Only the shamans, with the help of their personal spirit guardians, possess the stamina to engage the hostile spirits.[7]

To enter ecstasy and have spirits enter him or her means that the shaman has slipped out of his or her ordinary personality and has become the locus where other possible ways of thinking, feeling, and being in the world may find expression. In this condition the shaman's shape-shifting may be evidenced by moving differently, using the voice differently and, most importantly, thinking and feeling differently. As a result, the shaman will have experiences that are not accessible in ordinary consciousness (Shirokogoroff 1935).

The shaman's journey away from ordinary consciousness and the consensus reality of society is both outward, toward nature, and inward, to the source of all culture. It is a leap into spontaneity, an experience of the world as if for the first time, and on nature's terms, not those of humans.

The shamans risk their lives in dangerous psychic journeys because they hold the promise of novel insights from which they may devise novel solutions to problems, that is, to engage in the creative process.

Andras also related the process of willed self-transformation to cycles of movement around the quartered magical circle in which the elements associated with each of the cardinal directions lend their qualities to the experience. At each place, the powers and magical tools associated with it become available to the magician.

Finally Andras described the third model of transformation, the metamorphosis of the caterpillar into a butterfly. The butterfly-guardian revealed to Andras a model of self-transformation that wove the shaman's myth of shape-shifting and the associations with the quartered circle into the cycle of the butterfly's metamorphosis.

The first stage takes place inside the egg, Andras explained. A small well-defined shape is laid in a safe place, such as the underside of a leaf. In many shamanic traditions, he added, there is the belief that a person's shape includes their "essence" or soul. From a magical point of view, that shape involves the personality and the quality of one's experiences—including those of former lifetimes that can affect current existence. To a large extent one's original shape is defined by the social environment, Andras continues. A sociologist would call this the modal personality into which all members of a society are socialized. Social and political pressures and vested interests tend to keep our shapes limited.

In the way of the butterfly, the first stage is called "Changing Shape." The process of metamorphosis begins where all cyclic movement starts: in the east, the place of dawning light. The east is the symbolic realm of intellectual distinctions; with the blade, one carves boundaries, such as between truth and falsehood. The first step in the magical process of evolution, Andras said, is becoming aware of the limitations and boundaries of our shapes. We evaluate the entire complex of physical traits, behaviors, emotion, ideas, needs, beliefs, and so forth, Andras explained. Then we begin to move beyond the safe haven of the familiar form, prying here and there "like loosening a wet suit, trying to ease out of it." As the shape begins to yield, the witch experiences feelings of excitement, enthusiasm, creative euphoria, and ultimately, a new sense of freedom, release, and change.

The second stage, called "Confronting the Adversaries," corresponds to the south, the element of fire, forceful movement or thrust of the will, and courage and passion. In terms of the metamorphosis of the butterfly, it corresponds to the larva stage. In this frightening stage we confront that which resists change. Fear is activated; conflict and terror characterize this stage. In terms of the shaman's breaking-apart, adversaries are the evil spirits inhabiting the chaos beyond consensus reality. "Most of us instinctively stop when we reach the stage of fear." In fact, Andras was advised to do just that when he turned to his more conservative magical colleagues. This is not a black or white situation, Andras explained. Adversaries are not evil, nor are they necessarily enemies. The adversaries (fears) are simply that which wish us to remain as we are.

For example, in the black and white approach of Christian patriarchal culture, Andras continued, boundaries are clear and rigid, never to be trespassed. What is frightening or illegal is wrong, and all wrongness is associated with the devil. To a certain extent Andras' more conservative Wiccan colleagues reacted similarly. They suspected that he must have done something wrong; magical training is supposed to empower witches to avoid such problems. Often, because magic intensified things exponentially, Andras warned, the fears seem insurmountable. We get the message that it is wrong to try to change. However, Andras, who was moving into uncharted territory and supported by little more than his own hope that he was moving toward some destination other than madness, was able to break through to the next (third) stage, "Going Between the Worlds."

The third phase corresponds to the west, the place of death to form, and to the element of water, the psychic dimension of the self (subconscious, dreams and emotions, including fear). Andras located his mental crisis in this stage. At this point, Andras continued, we overcome the adversaries and break through the cocoon, into the "invisible world" beyond sensory or conscious perception where the witch's psyche is no longer accessible to her or him while it is shaped by the forces of the sacred realm. This is where the transformation occurs. Siberian shamans' descriptions tell of encounters with spirits of the dead shamans who transform them by breaking their bodies apart and inspecting their bones.

Perception expands, Andras said, and we are more open psychically and intuitively. We perceive not only with our physical sense; we can also see beyond the normal or usual shape of things into a dimension beyond the mundane. Simultaneously with these exalted visions, Andras informed us, the witch manifests incoherence, moodiness, depression, forgetfulness, and strange dreams.

This is the experience of the world turned transparent and paradoxical: the shaman's ecstasy, the rapture at the heart of suffering, or the creative encounter. Although the magic circle is drawn between the worlds to contain this encounter with the gods, spirits, ideas, or archetypes of the unconscious, as Andras' experience proves, it may break through in its own time and place.

The experience of going between the worlds constitutes a relationship, Andras learned. If we initiate it, the rest of the universe—the rest of experience—comes to meet us halfway and we merge. At that merging there is transformation and insight.

Andras continued, the fourth phase, "Completing the Circle of Being," corresponds with the north and the element of Earth. The part of the psyche that had been secluded breaks through its cocoon and emerges as a butterfly: "an amazingly beautiful being that can fly and soar, that is light years away from its original shape.'' It returns from the invisible world to reintegrate and transform the rest of the self.

Shamans who describe dismemberment in the supernatural realms say they are put back together in a different shape—the shape of the shaman, which is different from that of ordinary mortals.[8] These are symbols of integration or completion. However, Andras mused, ''If we stop at this point, I think we simply fence ourselves in.'' The process is more accurately one of gradual and constant evolution.

''The pattern is a spiral that repeats itself . . . Each stage builds upon the previous one, creating the stepping stone for the next stage,'' Andras said.

> Once you have gone through the four stages—let's say for the first time—you have now created a new shape, a new ''egg.'' You start all over again. Only the next time you do it, the experience is intensified.
>
> The new shape may become even more fixed [than the original one] because it is so much more powerful. Breaking out of that shape may be more difficult than the first time you did it.
>
> Some people who have gone through that process reach that plateau of integration, and then we tend to slip into ''Well, I'm so spiritual; look at all I've done here; I'm so cosmic. And I've gone through all these wonderful things.'' And we tend to just hang on to it and not want to let go because we perhaps instinctively know that the next time we let go it's going to be harder to do. So the fear and changes are still there, and the process of transformation much more intense, the changes are much more powerful. Presumably, as we follow the spiral pattern of magical evolution, at some point we will get to the point [of completion] that . . .

Andras and the audience laughed together at the ineffable nature of the completion of the spiritual quest for perfection that so few attain. The laughter was gently conspiratorial; the group felt united by the shared belief that it is possible for humans to ''change their shape'' deliberately, and approach the god-like status of creator. They laughed also at the familiar irony that, just as we think we've achieved an evolved spiritual state, the very state we have achieved shows us how little we have actually progressed and how far we still have to go.

Andras then spoke about the importance of community as a support for this process of willed transformation.

> When we consider the fact that we are engaged in this kind of process [open-ended personal transformation] in a culture, a society, a reality that not only frowns on that but negates that kind of individual process of transformation, wants to squelch that kind of process, a society that wants to have very nice, clear defined shapes that are, of course, defined by that society . . .

We've chosen to do something that is not easy. How can we make it easier? I think we do it by connecting with each other, by allowing for that process to happen in relationships rather than in isolation. We need to help one another by creating a context that is supportive and nurtures the process. This has been lacking in the pagan movement. [But] I have noticed in the movement an urge to connect with each other and to find ways to allow such transformation to happen in a reasonably safe place.

How can we as individuals and as a community—however loosely based that might be—support each other in that work? What strategies, processes, institutions, even, can we create? What kinds of insights can we share with each other about what we've done and gone through? We need each other. If we allow it to happen, we have each other.

In the following chapter we will examine some of the efforts Neopagans have made to redefine the terms of relationships and to invent supportive communities such as those Andras advocated.

Andras presented his workshop to many audiences over the last few years and wrote about it in Neopagan periodicals. In 1989 "The Way of the Butterfly" was expressed in a moving ritual in which some seven hundred participants had the opportunity to break through walls of a symbolic cocoon.

A maze that nearly filled a baseball field was constructed of bamboo poles and ribbon. Participants entered through the four gates located at the cardinal directions, selecting the element they most needed to transform in themselves. Following the beat of dirge-like drumming, we made our way through the maze to the center to hear Andras lead a guided meditation in which we were offered images of release from limitation to achievement of each person's full potential. When we opened our eyes to make a labyrinthine return, we saw that the walls of the maze had vanished. Enormous gossamer butterfly kites soared and dived where the walls had been. The ritual, one of the several artifacts of Andras' crises of creativity, was a moving, well-conceived and crafted work of art.

For Andras and others who are seeking to transcend the modal personality derived from their Christian patriarchal culture, there is no clear set of symbols or myths. Andras and the Neopagans are creating a new mythology deriving from their personal experiments. The Western spiritual tradition provides a long heritage of people who have tried to transcend the limits of their culture, but the terrain differs in each age. The "adversaries" change; the episodes in the journey from the former structure into the new one acquire different details. To further complicate matters, the literature of the Western spiritual tradition is deliberately ambiguous. Many of the experiences it treats are ineffable, and as Andras' experience has shown, they are hard to reconstruct from the written word.

American Neopagans are inventing their own tradition, and they are taking shamanism as their model for personal transformation. From this starting point, they are taking a leap into the creation of a new cultural pattern that supports personal initiative in creating the conditions of one's being and one's social life.

In this new model, each person supports his or her fellows in the mystically potent love, so important an element in the Western spiritual tradition. Whether or not the services of professionals—religious or medical—are resorted to, mutually dependent loving relationships within small communities that share a religious perspective are regarded as providing the kind of support that creative individuals require to conceive and manifest their unique vision of themselves and their world.

Chapter Thirteen

Never Again the Burning Times: Cultural Radicalism

The Neopagans feel that the threat of another burning times is ever present. In fact many among them are victims of discrimination and persecution because of their affiliation with this unusual religion. On November 19, 1993, for instance, the home of the Wiccan witch, Micha de Liuda, was burned to the ground along with most of her possessions. She and her former husband called the house that they built themselves on their land, "Great Mother's Love Nature Sanctuary." They constructed the round house with a vulva-shaped door from lumber hewn from the trees that grew on the eleven acres. Being environmentalists, they believed it would be hypocritical to contribute to the profits of the electric company, so the house was lit with natural light and heated by a cook stove. Micha's former husband had been working on a passive solar heating scheme to run his recording studio. There had been hostile encounters with Fundamentalist Christian neighbors from the start. Micha hoped, as many Neopagans do, that with time and patience people would overcome their fear of their pagan ways. However, eventually Micha was moved to file a complaint against some particularly contentious neighbors with the Vermont human rights commission. Soon thereafter, having become a single parent, Micha left most of her belongings behind and took her children to an urban area where she worked as a volunteer for a group called Native Forest Network. She had already worked with EarthFirst, a particularly aggressive environmental group, and had been arrested more than once while working with the anti-nuke movement.

Micha strongly suspects that her house was deliberately torched by her enemies, most likely members of the Wise Use movement that stands on the opposite side of the fence from environmentalists. On the other hand, "some militant Christian activity has been blooming locally," she wrote to her friend Nan Alexander, who reported on the story in *Our Pagan Times*.[1] The night of the fire there had been a Christian conclave in a town about twenty miles from Micha's land; the flier for the event had urged followers to "illumine the night with Christ's righteousness" (Alexander 1993).

If, in fact, the house was destroyed by her enemies, it is hard to know if it was because they wished to punish her for being a witch or an environmentalist, or perhaps for both. In other cases of persecution, discrimination, and destruction of the properties of Neopagans the motivation is more obvious. For instance, in Jonesboro, Arkansas, two Wiccans, Terry and Amanda Riley, were evicted from the premises of their occult supply shop, "Magical Moon," because their Christian landlord, accompanied by two preachers, told them he didn't want the town to be poisoned by unbelievers. Six Christian ministers of Jonesboro who appeared on television called the Rileys Satanists and urged area residents not to rent space to them for occult purposes.[2]

Selena Fox paved the way for the defense of the rights of Neopagans to practice their religion in peace. With the help of the American Civil Liberties Union, she gained legal protection against Fundamentalists and other neighbors who objected to the Wiccan church, networking center, and nature sanctuary she created with her first partner, Jim Allen, on their farm in Wisconsin.

Authorized by state licensure as a minister, Selena had been testifying in courts of law on behalf of other Neopagans for several years before her own battle began. Over the years she achieved considerable success, and the demand for her assistance increased to the point that she asked volunteers to help her with the "Lady Liberty League" referral network that she founded in 1991. Since then, "The Lady Liberty Report" has been published in each quarterly issue of *Circle Network News*. The reports informed Neopagans of assistance given to other owners of occult book and supply stores, including the owners of Dragon Lair in Florida. Someone drove a truck into the little shop and vandalized it. The owner of Gypsy Heaven in Pennsylvania was evicted, as was the proprietor of Moon's Medieval Magic in Tennessee. The Tennessee shop also suffered a bomb threat, and the owner was beaten and accused of devil worship.

Several cases of discriminatory treatment on the basis of religion were covered as well, including the threatened eviction of a Neopagan psychologist from her office, the near refusal to employ a Neopagan nurse, and the firing of a school librarian for supplying a student with a book about Wicca. Many Neopagan parents struggle to prove themselves fit parents despite their affiliation with this unusual religion. With the help of local police forces Neopagans in many states are gaining protection against violence and interference from Fundamentalist

Christians. However, as the movement becomes more visible the attacks become more numerous and more violent.

To make the world safe for themselves and other vulnerable social groups, and to protect the planet against exploitation or destruction, the Neopagans say they must reclaim the power that the legendary witches possessed and use it for a broader purpose than the legendary witches would ever have thought to apply their magic: healing the Earth.

Within a few decades, Starhawk and other feminist witches forged a link between Gardner's Wicca and American social reform ideas that were set in motion in the 1960s. Reclaiming the power to heal the self and the Earth with magic became a prominent theme in Neopaganism.

Andras concluded "The Way of the Butterfly" presentation by naming the pursuit of self-perfection a mere beginning of the ultimate goal of healing the planet.

> The beauty, power, love and caring that is at the heart of what we all do is important for us as individuals and as a community, but it is also important for the planet. We are not just part of the Earth; we *are* the Earth. We are *reclaiming* some of that energy; we are negating the forces of destruction, forces of hate, forces of fear. I think perhaps the most crucial part of our work is to let our magic extend beyond ourselves—beyond all of us as individuals and as community—into the planet, to project that caring love and power. I think before we can do that "out there," really, we have to do it among ourselves.

In Andras' words we find the structure of the Neopagans' cultural radicalism that we will explore in this chapter. The object is the well-being of the planet; the origin is the individual personality. Neopagans are aware that between these extremes, institutions and policies must be transformed. However, the Neopagans feel, as did the "beats" of the 1950s, the "hippies" of the 1960s, and the majority of the mystics of the Western spiritual tradition, that modification of the self and one's way of life takes precedence over the collaborative tasks of political change.

Although many Neopagans are politically involved, their activism occurs at the interface of this spiritual tradition with other secular movements. Essentially, they have more faith that art and poetry (in other words, the power of the imagination) are the most powerful revolutionary forces. The part they are most suited to play is creating effective symbols—including the examples of their lives—to inspire others to work towards a similar vision. "Think globally; act locally," describes their approach to healing not only a society, or even a global society, but the biosphere.

When I encountered the witches and their preoccupation with healing,

I wondered, Who is sick? What is the disease? The "disease," I soon discovered, is "estrangement" or "alienation," and reclaiming is the remedy. Who is estranged and alienated from whom or what? Well, everybody, I found out. We are all alienated from nature and from our human natures. How can the breach be mended? By reclaiming all that was lost to human culture and the natural world over the hundreds of years since "patriarchal culture" established itself. At this point witches offer explanations that strongly resemble those of the matriarchal theorists, such as J. J. Bachofen (1861), Friedreich Engels (1891), and Robert Briffault (1927); and the critiques of modernism, including Karl Marx's "alienation," and Max Weber's concept of the "iron cage" of bureaucracy.

This chapter begins with the story of how the world degenerated into this present "pathological" state and is told in the language of the witches themselves. Then follows a discussion of how Wicca blended with American cultural radicalism in a Neopagan approach to social reform that shares structural constants with the Western spiritual tradition. The witches identify two main time periods as the source of the world's sickness: the displacement of a theoretical matriarchal culture by "patriarchy" and "the burning times."

The Blight of Patriarchy

In the sixteenth and seventeenth centuries Western culture underwent crucial changes that produced the particular brand of "estrangement" that characterizes the "modern world," Starhawk (1982, 185) explained. The persecution of witches was linked to three interwoven processes: the expropriation of land and natural resources (the enclosure of feudal lands); the expropriation of knowledge (the limited access to university education and the professionalization of medicine); and the discrediting of the concept of "immanence."[3] The eclipsed worldview encourages relationships of reciprocity with the natural world rather than domination and supports the possibility of collaborating with the responsive world in acts of magic. The outcome of these political, social and ideological shifts is the "pathology" of estrangement (Starhawk 1982).

However, the roots of estrangement dig deeper into "the Bronze Age shift from matrifocal, Earth-centered cultures whose religion centered on the goddess and gods embodied in nature, to patriarchal urban cultures of conquest whose gods inspired and supported war," Starhawk explained (1982, 5). "'Power-over' relationships (domination) are ultimately born of war and the social and intrapsychic structures that are necessary to sustain mass, organized warfare. Having reshaped culture in a martial image, the institutions and ideologies of power-over perpetuate war so that it becomes a chronic condition" (1987, 9).

The ideological shifts were not accomplished because the winners presented the best description of reality, Starhawk explains, but because of their political, economic, and social utility to influential members in European societies. After the Restoration of Charles II of England, such ideas were termed dangerous "enthusiasms," and a vigorous campaign was carried out by the state, the established Church, and the new scientific institutions against them. By the eighteenth century, the entrenched ideology "legitimized the rising capitalist economy, the exploitation of women and workers, the plundering of nature—and exalted the qantifiable over the qualitative elements of life" (1987, 218).

Starhawk's books offer strategies for *healing* individuals and society of these *pathologies*: (1) to reclaim what was lost—a way of living in relationship with nature, other animals and humans as if they were all infused with a divine life force—that is, revive the consciousness of immanence (by reviving pagan religion); (2) restore the personal power associated with witches and shamans: creativity (pagan magic); and (3) reclaim the power to actively change one's self and world.

The Burning Times

Connection with martyred witches of the past is expressed in these words from a song that was written by a present-day witch:

> The songs are sung to rouse our anger, of martyred Witches gone to the fires,
> But what is served by righteous singing, when all we do is stew in our ire?
> Nine million dead in four hundred years; more in that time simply died of disease.
> Why do we dwell on long-passed dead when we are alive in times like these?
> Rise up Witches, gather your strength, and let your power spread and climb;
> Earth and all Her children need us
> For all now face the Burning Times!
> So if rebellion means to fight a State lost sight of why it was built,
> If heresy's to reject a Church that rules with force or fear or guilt,
> Then let us all be rebels proud, and shameless heretics by creed!
> A tyrant's hand subjects the Earth—more heretic rebels are what she needs![4]

Sing! the singer-songwriter, Leigh Ann Hussey exhorts the pagans; blaming is unproductive. Songs are for rousing anger, an effective technique for raising energy. Like the charge of the goddess, the song urges witches to expect more from life than constant strife and mobilize their powers in acts of rebellious magic if they, and the Earth, would be free of slavery.

Bruno was burned as a witch in the burning times for urging learned gentlemen to hope for more than the constant conflict among contending reformers and to acquire the powers that Starhawk and Hussey encourage witches to reclaim—the creative, visionary capacities—so that they might bring the vision into being. Bruno's concepts remain significant in the social reform ideologies of the Neopagans: love, fulgor, pacifism, and necessary death to the dead world that the Christian reformers created so that a more life-promoting one might be born.

The theme of healing was as significant in the ideologies of the critics of the witch persecutions—most significantly in the teachings of Paracelsus, the Swiss alchemist and physician—as it is to the Neopagans. In the Renaissance, Ficino eased the entrance of the Hermetic texts into Christian Western culture by incorporating the magical techniques into his practice as a physician. And, as we will see in this chapter, all of these themes found vivid expression in the "Rosicrucian Revolution" (Yates 1972) in which the Western spiritual tradition displayed its full repertoire of symbols, philosophy, and techniques.

The Rosicrucian Brotherhood[5]

The Rosicrucian Brotherhood was a Hermetic, cabalistic, secret society that was formed in Lutheran Germany in the early seventeenth century. The fraternity took its name from the legendary founder, a German friar, Christian Rosenkreutz, in the fifteenth century. The Rosicrucian Brothers presented their utopian program as an alternative to the agendas of the Protestant and Catholic reformers. Being fond of alchemy, Rosicrucians expressed their ideas in allegorical rhetoric and often in cryptic pictures.

Although the Rosicrucian movement acquired its name and rich cultural expression in Germany, its roots were in the English Renaissance, principally in the philosophy of John Dee, mathematician and magician. In 1589 Dee visited the English princess Elizabeth, daughter of King James (author of *Daemonologie*), during her reign as the Winter Queen of Bohemia. His philosophy was well received there, and his influence spread into many European countries.

The Rosicrucians tried to unite Dee's occult philosophy, which was inspired by Italian Hermeticism, with English chivalry and German mysticism into a single, ideal Hermetic Rosicrucian state. The Winter King and Queen (Elizabeth, daughter of King James) attempted to realize that ideal in the Palatinate,[6] in their court centered in Heidelberg. There the brotherhood's philosophic literature was published (by De Bray), and their ideas achieved artistic expression in alchemical emblems and magico-mechanical wonders such as moving statues and "speaking" fountains that were created by Salomon De Caus.

The Rosicrucian Brotherhood presented itself in the two anonymous manifestoes as an invisible society. The writers of the manifestoes described themselves as reformed German Christians who used alchemy to intensify their evangelical piety. Comparing themselves to the Jesuit Order, the Brothers claimed to possess a more perfect knowledge of God, Jesus, and nature. They proclaimed the imminence of a great enlightenment, with all the millennial trimmings, and the need for a vast general reformation of the world.

The main occupation of the Brothers was to the sick. In fact, they were to have no other profession—and they were not to be paid for healing. It is perhaps significant to remember that in the early seventeenth century when the Rosicrucians published their manifestoes, university trained physicians were establishing themselves as professionals and attempting to restrict and discredit nonprofessional healers, who, as we have seen, constituted a large portion of those who were persecuted as witches. The Rosicrucian Brothers may have been reacting, at least in part, against the monopolization and professionalization of medicine.

Although they were undistinguished by their dress ("invisible") and preached the charitable healing of the sick, the Rosicrucian Brothers were, nonetheless, elitists in true Gnostic-Hermetic fashion. They invited the "learned" to join them in their world reform mission. Whereas Italian Renaissance magic—with its Orphic incantations, manipulation of flowers, gems, and elaborate drawings to entice the spirits of nature and the stars to descend—was artistic, the magicians of Germany and England, including the Rosicrucians, hitched their reformation to the intellect and science. The ethical issues surrounding the quest for knowledge were a major issue in the planned Rosicrucian Enlightenment.

The Rosicrucians hoped to effect a concordance of all religions and philosophies. Their proposed "more powerful philosophy" (more powerful, that is, than Aristotelian scholasticism) called for a quest for experiential knowledge and reliance on the refined will and imagination of the magus. That is, it should be artistic as well as rational.

Social and religious reforms were, furthermore, the necessary accompaniment to the new science, whose "diabolical" as well as "angelic" possibilities the Rosicrucians foresaw. Perhaps the most striking aspect of the Rosicrucian movement was its insistence on the dignity and worth of the individual and the part he or she is to play in both the divine and worldly schemes.

The Rosicrucian Enlightenment never came to pass. The movement was crushed at the peak of its cultural expression when King James I of England turned against his daughter and—with the League of German Protestants who had been the principal allies of the Palatinate—withdrew his support. Hapsburg troops descended upon the little state; the Thirty Years' War began; and Jesuits set about circulating propaganda that depicted the Rosicrucians as frequenters of witches' sabbaths.

By 1623 Rosicrucianism in Germany had been destroyed by the Counter-Reformation. The Hermetic-cabalistic-alchemical tradition persisted, however, as a significant influence on the new science that was developing. According to some recent historians of the scientific revolution (Berman 1981; Easlea 1980; Yates 1972), the occult philosophy that descended from the Renaissance and filtered through the Rosicrucian expressive culture remained a significant influence on pivotal thinkers such as Francis Bacon, René Descartes, and Isaac Newton. In their private papers, these figures—formerly taken as fully representative of the complete emergence from such "superstition"— reveal the influence of Renaissance occult philosophy. Many of those who were influential in founding the Royal Society expressed their respect for, and even indebtedness to, the Rosicrucian Brotherhood.

Neopagans Build on Inspiration from Earlier Cultural Radicalisms in America[7]

Neopaganism is the inheritor of the exuberant playfulness that American cultural radicalism acquired in the 1960s when the mystical (inward-directed) type of cultural novelty merged with the more pragmatic political (outward-turning) radicalism. When I see hundreds of wildly costumed Neopagans with their brilliant banners, chanting in processions accompanied by drums, flutes, and rattles, going to the ritual circle at gatherings, I am invariably struck by how much they resemble the counter-culture of the 1960s that Roszak (1969) described as a joyous crusade. Marilyn Ferguson called the New Age thinking that was born in that decade a conspiracy; a fitting occupation for people who like to call themselves witches and pagans.

Laurence Veysey, historian of the counterculture of the 1960s, traced its source to the cultural radicalism of the mid-nineteenth century when anarchism, communitarian socialism, and Asian mysticism all appeared more or less simultaneously as different types of cultural radicalism. The essence of the anarchist creed was the opposition to all forms of coercive authority, especially that of the state (Veysey 1973).

The mystical or religious approach has a longer history, as we have seen in the preceding chapters. Both the secular and sacred approaches to cultural radicalism looked to the past for inspiration to find a timeless rather than progressive response to the specter of industrialism (Veysey 1973).

Themes, most of which we have encountered in the Western spiritual tradition, appear in American cultural radicalism: opposition to established agencies of social authority such as governments and churches; the ideal of uncompromising social brotherhood; economic decentralization and self-sufficiency; inner self-development and the search for mental clarity; free thought in religion; the quest for individual or collective states of ecstasy; pacifism; racial and sexual equality; abolition or modification of the nuclear family; belief in a simpler, more natural way of life, for instance in matters of clothing or diet; extreme progressivism in education; and the pursuit of a guru or other enlightened leader (Veysey 1973). All of these themes have a place in Neopaganism, although there is some ambiguity about the Neopagans' relationships with enlightened leaders. Nonetheless, they do seek, appreciate, and respond to enlightened thinkers, as Andras' and Starhawk's exemplary statuses prove. We will explore that issue in more detail in the following chapter.

As heir to both the mystical and the secular approaches to cultural radicalism Neopaganism is a synthesis of both traditions. It takes its worldview from the religious mystics and its style of leadership and community from the anarchists whose communal groups were of the relatively unstructured, low-key variety with a mild, but definite, degree of leadership. The leaders of these secular groups, like those of the Neopagans, ideally "contributed" to the "good vibrations" of the undertakings; they were expected to be impelled by idealism alone, not prestige or power. These relatively formless groups suffered from factional discord, Veysey discovered, and as with most covens, they failed to endure.

The longer survival of mystical groups in comparison with anarchist ones is largely the result of the willing submission to the discipline of a leader or teacher. Elaborate bureaucratic internal structure that went hand-in-hand with the sway of an authoritarian leader produced some of the most stable countercultural environments of the nineteenth and twentieth centuries, particularly the intentional communities that benefitted further—in terms of group survival—from isolation from the influence of the outside world (Veysey 1973).

Veysey found that cultural radicals of both stripes were elitists. We have seen that elitism has been part of the Western spiritual tradition from the beginning: those who refused to strive for perfection—spiritual, in this case, rather than intellectual—would spoil the dream of enlightened polity.

Neopagans have modified the elitism of the Western spiritual tradition by selecting the witch for a culture heroine. They value innate powers to perform magic and honor the simple wisdom that comes from life experience, which at times may be superior to the rewards of education, either spiritual or intellectual. Wiccan elitism crosses ordinary boundaries of social privilege; it acknowledges the possibility that individuals of either gender or any race or social group may possess the powers that they esteem if they only make the effort to develop their innate potentials. Still, the witches see the narrowmindedness of "the mundanes" who take no interest in refining their intellect, imagination and spirituality as the dead weight against which the witches struggle to heal the Earth and against whose persecution they must maintain constant surveillance.

Neopaganism, Descendant of the Counterculture of the 1960s

The 1960s exhibited the qualities of an extended period of liminality. The decade can be seen as the threshold (limin) between the rejection of the former structure and efforts at creating a new one. The organic fusion that many people enjoyed in the 1960s is characteristic of the leveling *communitas* that occurs in liminal phases of rituals and other social processes. Cultural radicals and many others who were disillusioned stood aside from their culture on the threshold of that decade and saw it from a new, more critical perspective.

Roszak named the task of the hippie radicals of the 1960s the "altering [of] the total cultural context within which our daily politics takes place" (1969, 4–5). In this, the cultural radicalism of the 1960s resembled other historical periods of cultural transition when there was a prevalent disenchantment with fundamental assumptions about the nature of knowledge and experience, such as the early centuries of this era that we have already discussed, when the Gnostics devised the Hermetic texts; transition from the Roman Empire into Christian culture (Tiryakian 1974); and the Renaissance and Reformation period. In each case, radical thinkers paved the way back to an experiential approach to knowledge. In these times there was a temporary withdrawal, as if into the potent limbo of a rite of passage for inspiration and a novel vision. The revival of the Western spiritual tradition may be seen as useful in these transitions, "an important vehicle of new expressive symbols and belief systems that aid the restructuring of collective representations of social reality" (Tiryakian 1974).

The 1970s marked the tentative re-entry into a new structure that is still in the process of becoming. Many of the inspirations that occurred to the hippies during that liminal interval of *communitas* can be seen as the "hypotheses" that inspire the "experiments" in which the Neopagans are presently engaged. We will explore many of these in the following chapter.

In the 1960s there emerged a quickening of conscience at the continuing violence in national and international affairs, poverty in the midst of plenty, racial strife and oppression, and other problems. The fundamental worldviews were called into question. The familiar left/right polarity gave way to a quest for a new way of living and for entirely new forms of consciousness. Veysey saw these efforts not as mere shifts or adjustments, but as evolutionary innovations, or even mutations.

Radical dreams of community during the 1960s were visions of an organic fusion of individuals into small, loving groups, like the consciousness-raising groups and covens that developed soon after. There was to be total physical and psychic union—such as that attempted in the enormous groups now attending Neopagan gatherings.

Maximization of consciousness gained a new and wider fashionability. Momentary ecstasy was sought in sex, drugs, and communal fusion. In hallucinogenic drugs many freed themselves for a short while from the their estrangement from the natural world and returned to ordinary consciousness with the conviction that all things are alive, moving and worthy of love and protection. Some went so far as to sacrifice their mental health for this vision. As in the flow of liminality, hallucinogenic experiences afforded the opportunity to review and revise fundamental values. For Veysey, the radical shift from materialistic goals toward simplicity and renunciation was the most impressive and potentially creative aspect of the new vision.

Although the discovery of compassion for a living world went hand-in-hand with a willingness on the parts of the radical thinkers to support the civil rights movement, the counterculture remained largely a white phenomenon, as is Neopaganism. Those who were engaged in the white counterculture were for the most part middle-class youths who had the leisure and resources to contemplate renunciation and fair treatment of others. Blacks had a different, more desperate agenda. Those blacks who are presently disenchanted with "white man's religion" resort to other alternatives; the Muslim religion or the pagan religions of Africa. The few blacks I have encountered in the Neopagan movement, which is theoretically the Old Religion of Europe—not Africa—are expressing an identification with white culture.[8]

The hippies clarified what they had rejected in the mainstream culture and made it the basis for patterned interaction of an anarchistic type— that is, loose, voluntaristic, and practically leaderless. In the 1970s those individuals who shared the hippie style of anarchism (pacifists, feminists, ecologists) and who adopted a stronger mystical approach to their anarchism developed an increasing awareness of common loyalties, values, and beliefs that set them apart from the larger society.

By the 1970s Neopagans had acquired a distinct identity among the progeny of "hippie" radicalism. They sifted through the insights that the ecstatic liminal experiences of the hippies produced and began to embellish and experiment with them. The desire to share information and socialize with others like themselves induced collaboration on projects like publishing newsletters or organizing festivals that unwittingly resulted in a reluctant and amorphous social cohesion. Gardner's Wicca provided a structure for early efforts at collaboration.

Elements of a basic philosophy, or point of view, that Veysey believed remained recognizably constant throughout generations of American cultural radicalism followed a precedent in the Western spiritual tradition, especially as it found expression in the Rosicrucian Revolution: the vision of the simple life; the avoidance of callous masculine aggressiveness in favor of feminine attributes of personality; and the rejection of older established worldviews in favor of the hope that "truth" may be abstracted from all great philosophical traditions and in visionary experiences. As we saw in the preceding chapters, Neopagan gatherings, like former efforts at intentional communities—including that of the Palatinate—express a commitment to geographical and psychic separation from the larger society. "Organic fusion" prevails, and the romantic ideal of bodily liberation reborn in the 1960s finds a haven for expression in covens and at gatherings. Like the efforts of their radical forebears, those of the Neopagans imply an effort to experiment and construct an alternative social order from the individual psyche outward.

Never Again the Burnings

Bjornkin Frievalkyr, a New York City witch, was reminded of the Inquisition when he learned that Pope John Paul II had urged American bishops to combat dangerous departures from normal liturgical practices.[9] The pope's remarks were directed against feminist fringe groups within the church that have taken to worshipping an Earth goddess or "Mother Earth." In the August 1993 issue of *Our Pagan Times*, a newsletter published by a group called "New Moon New York" in Manhattan, Bjornkin remarked that five hundred and seven years ago another pope, Innocent X, initiated the Inquisition by issuing a declaration of war against other "Enemies of the church . . . The church has never been a friend to anyone unless they (the church) could gain power over them, and impress or manipulate their minds and souls,'' declared Frievalkyr (1993, 10).

Neopagans are not alone in their supreme devotion to freedom; it is perhaps the most deeply held value for all Americans. However, the French social philosopher, De Tocqueville, warned that a related aspect of the American character, "individualism," might eventually isolate Americans from one another and thereby undermine the conditions of freedom. Some would say that the destructive potentialities of individualism are already upon us (Bellah et al. 1985). Yet the Neopagans' declaration, "Never again the burning times," implies that individualism has not gone far enough; modern society has become monolithic, and through its unacknowledged state religion—Christianity—insists that there is only one book, the Bible, and one way, the modern, industrial Christian way, to the ultimate good. The Neopagans feel compelled to forestall the return of the burning times by defending diversity. However, if diversity does not promote the effective collaboration that is needed to defend it, how can the entrenched forces of conservatism be confronted? Personal freedom requires social freedom and, where it is lacking, social reform.

Frievalkyr recommends that Neopagans align themselves with others who do not necessarily share their spirituality, but who nevertheless share the egalitarian ideal. Pagans should support pro-choice, gay and animal rights, and the rights of the poor and hungry. Because Neopagans resist the structure and regulation that comes with efficient organization they often do join forces with other groups that are more effective at collaborating than they. The Lady Liberty League has achieved some of its more impressive successes by joining forces with the American Civil Liberties Union, law enforcement agencies, and other more efficient and better endowed organizations.

The Neopagans have something valuable to bring to concerted actions: their motivating symbols and novel visions. The symbols and beliefs we have explored throughout this book may be applied to the purposes of social protest and reform. The idea of a divine Earth inspires ecological conservation and the honoring of all forms of life. Rather than march, accuse, preach, or demand change in grim and angry picket lines, the Neopagans arrange themselves in circles, sing, dance, and harness their vital life force to potent symbols of their idea of a better world. The circle, as an egalitarian social structure, for instance, inspires equal participation. The threefold law promises rewards as the indirect effect of benefits that accrue to others. Within these consecrated circles they invoke deities and the spirits of the elements and raise cones of power to fortify political protests against environmental abuses, racial and sexual discrimination, and other social problems. The circle model unifies spirituality and politics and inspires experimentation with consensus, which we will explore in the following chapter.

The idea of the Earth as alive—mother or lover—and the symbol of the pentagram, or endless knot that connects humans to Earth as well as the vast universe, inspire a broad, rather than local, vision. The Neopagans offer a different vision of time and the repercussions of one's actions than does progress. The notion that instead of moving forward, a lifetime moves through the wheel of the year over and over again in a spiral suggests the impossibility of leaving mistakes or waste "behind." The threefold law inspires actions whose repercussions a social reformer would not mind revisiting when the spiral comes full circle, and a sense of responsibility to those who lived before and those who will be here in the future. The notion of the web mobilizes action for the common good by suggesting that one creature's suffering resonates through all others. If health and well-being, for societies—indeed the planet—as well as for individuals, consist in balance, then inequalities and blockages of the flow of resources will eventually produce pathologies from which none may escape.

As an example of a practical application of the expressive symbols and belief systems we have encountered throughout this book, I offer the response of Inanna, an elder of the EarthSpirit Community, to my question, "How, specifically, do you envision saving the world?"

Inanna Arthen is an artist, musician, and actress who earns her living by working for a non-profit community service organization in Massachusetts. She began by naming some fundamental errors in thinking, then outlined some suggestions and some of her personal efforts to build on the different understanding of the nature of reality that she sees as really being at issue.

> I have felt for a long time that our entire economic system is based on a fundamental error. We have based our economy on the model of the organism instead of the ecosystem. Hence, the economy is seen as "healthy" if it is growing, and the faster it grows, the "healthier" it supposedly is. The essential problem here—that we live in a finite world and cannot grow indefinitely—never seems to be considered seriously by anyone. It's the most massive case of denial I can imagine.[10]

The economic situation is complicated, she continued, by the fact that

> Ultimately, every major problem we have can be traced back directly (and in not too many steps, either) to over-population. The Earth has been over-populated for at *least* several centuries.[11]

Another error of thinking that leads to disastrous behavior she calls

> The "NIMBY" or "Not in My BackYard" syndrome: in which residents of a town where a prison, or sewage treatment plant, or

whatever, is planned set up a ruckus. My proposed solution to this is "IEBY"—"In Everyone's BackYard." That is to say, that every single individual community should be responsible for treating their own sewage, taking care of their own toxic wastes, jailing their own criminals, managing their own trash, housing their own mentally ill, and so on—possibly to the extent of generating their own electricity.

Also you may have heard about "the toilet syndrome": the psychological attitude that when something has disappeared, it's not a problem anymore? That would be a lot harder to maintain if you knew that your waste products and your water supply stayed in the same general location. That's why I'm strongly in favor of septic systems, town dumps and composting.[12]

Of course, Inanna is not the first to identify these fundamental errors in thinking. Like the mystics of the Renaissance and burning times, Neopagans are unique in the depth of their convictions and their foresight. These individuals foresee—with the faculties of the mind associated with magi and artist, most importantly the imagination—repercussions that non-creative individuals generally regard as irrational. Neopagans and other mystics are instead, pre-rational. That is to say, most people do not believe in the problems or the solutions that forward-thinking people envision until they are suffering from them personally. At that point the foresight of the "irrational" few may become rational for more people.

Creative individuals are unique in their approach to social reform most significantly in their willingness to change sooner than others, based on a new ideological position. Like Inanna, they envision some unusual solutions. Inanna shared with me a plan for using technology to live more simply without returning to a harsher existence.

I'd like to set up a grant, and recruit a few very gifted engineering students from, say, MIT to design farm equipment which can be drawn by draft animals but has the power of (or is superior to) tractor-driven tools. Possibly equipment that burns methane or ethanol, which the farmer could produce on his/her own farm from renewable materials, so that the equipment would have extra power for whatever it did (reaping, plowing, whatever) but would be moved around by draft animals. The farmer's expenses would then be reduced from the incredible costs of financing and fueling heavy equipment, to that of maintaining animals and small equipment whose food/fuel he or she actually produced on the farm. The second part of this project would be finding struggling small farmers to test the equipment. Once a few of them had switched over from heavy debts to making a profit, I think the new techniques would be an easy sell.

Another use of technology to aid farmers would be robotized farm tools to assist in the labor-intensive task of diversifying farm crops and using alternative growing methods. (Imagine a robot that could pick potato bugs!) It's all very well to complain about pesticides, but there are "organic" fanatics who'd scream and faint at the sight of a tomato hornworm, let alone the task of spending several hours a day hand-picking them. We need to use small-scale technology to take the drudgery out of intensive farming techniques. If they don't pay, farmers won't—can't—use them.

In short, my ideas for changing agriculture involve making it easier, more fun, and much more lucrative for small farmers to utilize Earth-centered methods. As for big farmers . . . they should go the way of conglomerates. I have no use for "agribusiness" and its hideous abuses.[13]

In response to my question about what she saw as her personal mission, she responded that she sees herself as a steward of the planet, ally of the gods, and destroyer-transformer. She believes magic should be used for protecting the Earth against the threat of developers and industry with "eco-terrorism" if necessary. For example, telekinesis (influencing morphogenetic fields psychically) or magical activation of the biosphere to take over at an accelerated rate could be employed.

We have seen that the style and content of Neopagan ideas regarding social reform have much in common with both the Rosicrucian Revolution and the social reforms expressed in the 1960s in the United States. Viewing the three movements side by side, we discover the structural constants of a Western tradition of social revitalization of a mystical, religious, or artistic type.

The strongest element in the Neopagans' approach is myth-making. Magicians, mystics and artists retrieve from their experiences of gnosis, ecstasy or creative encounters the visions of new and different relationships. They enliven the ideas with art, dance, rituals, poems—and along the way they seek to inspire others, rather than to coerce them, into taking a new perspective out of which different behaviors will theoretically flow naturally. Action begins with the perfection of each person's life rather than demanding that others change. Gradually and peacefully—rather like contagion—the world will change, they hope.

Although this type of cultural radicalism appears benign beside more overtly aggressive—even violent—political efforts to transform society, it is far more radical. Visionaries who involve themselves in these movements are not content to reshuffle resources or reallocate power and authority according to the dictates of existing ideas and social institutions. They challenge "the orderly state" on a very fundamental level—its view of the nature of reality. We have seen that in each place where individuals are accused of witchcraft, they served as the model of what one must not do, or be, in that society. By assuming the title of witch, and by challenging the authority of consensus reality—even if only with ideas, art, and rituals—the Neopagans inspire the kind of fear that results in accusations of malevolent witchcraft. Where fear of witchcraft is combined with the elaborate resources of an established state, Western history has shown, the fear of "burning times" is well founded.

Chapter Fourteen

Coming of Age

W hen he was an ornery fourteen-year-old, Kathleen the Elder's grandson, Zachary, was taken from his home by seven men in the middle of the night. In weekly meetings, Zachary's initiators had prepared him for the rite of passage that he requested. He had been wondering when it would happen; it was the summer solstice of 1991. The men wrapped him in a blanket so that he could not see, and drove him into the wilderness to begin his "man-making." When he was released the boy saw that his captors wore masks representing various aspects of the god including the Green Man (of vegetation) and a fearsome Dark Father. The masked figures directed Zachary to gather wood, enough to burn throughout the night, into a deep canyon-like fissure in the Earth where he would spend the next three days alone, fasting and waiting for a vision. The masked men visited Zachary intermittently to make sure he didn't fall asleep. On the last day the men, including Zachary, cut their fingers to make an offering of blood to the nature spirits. Having survived that ordeal, Zachary didn't need to be told that he had become a man.

Zachary's initiators were Kathleen the Elder's clan members. For several months they collaborated with his mother to plan the ordeal that was to be his rite of passage. Kathleen the Elder's family (her mother's lineage) has practiced a tradition of nature worship and practical magic called *Eld Witan* for twelve generations. When Kathleen's daughter came to her to ask how to initiate her son, they couldn't find much in the family lore because no males had been born in the family for ninety-six years. Thus, Zachary's mother and his seven initiators devised his ordeal based on their research of Native American and other aboriginal initiation practices.

Most of what the men taught him is Zachary's secret, but his mother and Katheen the Elder told me the men taught him the different ways to respect women as lovers, sisters, mothers, and grandmothers. One of his initiators is celibate; some are married, some are unmarried but sexually active, and another is homosexual. His mother thought it was important for him to experience his vigil in the company of men who represented different ways a man might choose to lead his life with regard to women so that Zachary would respect them all. Zachary found that his man-making not only introduced him to different perspectives about relationships between men and women but also transformed his level of maturity by forcing him to be self-reliant.

The American Neopagan movement is three decades old. Many of the originators have married, become parents, grandparents, and senior citizens. To ease these transitions for which they find few resources in mainstream culture, they turned to the Book of Shadows and friends in the Neopagan movement for rites of passage. These rituals mark the boundaries between the physical, social, and spiritual statuses a person has outgrown and those he or she is about to assume. For instance, the gradual, chaotic physical and emotional changes of adolescence may be clarified into a ritual experience such as Zachary's for the purpose of crystallizing the confusing experience into a potent symbolic experience that forces a clear transition. During these rituals the initiate generally receives instruction and support to reestablish equilibrium in the phase of life he or she will enter after exiting the rite of passage. Zachary's mother and grandmother, both of whom are psychotherapists, believe that many of their clients suffer confusion and emotional pain that could have been prevented if they had been provided with clear transitions (in rites of passage) into and through adulthood, such as those that are more prevalent in indigenous societies.

In this chapter we will explore the ways the Neopagans define and mark with rituals the episodes of life and the passages between them. We will also look at the diverse social structures that coexist—not altogether easily—in the national community.

Rites of Passage

The myth of the goddess' descent provides the fundamental truth that it is time, not death, that causes all things the goddess loves and takes delight in to wither and die. After death there is the opportunity to assume a new shape (be reborn). Change is the natural way of the world. The waxing and waning of the sunlight and the seasons of the agricultural year provide yearly rehearsals for beginning, coming to maturity, and descending into the dark fallow periods, only to emerge again in the spring.

Rites of passage serve societies by instructing members how to integrate successfully and to be useful to one another in different ways that are appropriate to each level of maturity. In indigenous societies the rules for social adjustment (the social contract) is conveyed through metaphors of spiritual maturity (knowledge of sacred traditions). Rights and duties are shifted, and social roles are adjusted in the contest of religious rites of passage.

In contemporary Western society the social contract is to a larger extent secular, imparted principally through educational and legal institutions. Graduations mark socially significant transitions as do the achievement of the approved age to begin employment, drive a car, or consume alcohol. Prom night and retirement from occupations could also be considered informal markers of important turning points in maturity. There are few religious rites of passage in mainstream society. Some of the surviving rites acknowledge mastery of knowledge about religion (Bar Mitzvahs and Confirmation) or orient participants to the spiritual aspect that to increasing numbers of individuals seems contingent upon, rather than central to, the transitions of birth, marriage, and death.

Whereas rites of passage in the mainstream are more often occasions for celebration than efforts to transform individuals, all of the Neopagans' rites are overt acts of magic—attempts to create psychological, physical, and social transformation by the shifting of consciousness and the movement of energy. Rather than experiential absorption of ineffable truths about the place of humans in the cosmos, most secular rites of passage are celebrations designed to distract from the confusions and fear of transition. Birthdays of the decades of life are particularly dreaded as representing deterioration and decline from grace embodied in youthfulness and vigor. Rather than the orientations to the coming decade of life these celebrations are occasions for mourning lost youth softened by joking.

The rites of passage devised by Neopagans help individuals relinquish unwelcome attitudes imbibed through cultural conditioning. Like wilderness training, Zachary's initiation created the conditions in which he could discover the personal resources that justify a sense of self-sufficiency, a powerful defense against whatever challenges mature manhood might bring. Helpless dependence on others for protection was revealed as inappropriate to his new condition. Lacking rites of passage such as Zachary's, childish dependence may ripen into uncritical dependence on professionals, such as physicians and lawyers, and on institutions, such as insurance, government, and law enforcement agencies, and burden relationships with friends and spouses. In rites such as Zachary's, terror and suffering open the imagination, in his case to the possibility that he could save his own life. Such a close encounter with death makes its inevitability clear. Whereas the majority of the uninitiated continue to regard it as pathological, catastrophic, or the result of negligence.

Besides initiation rituals, which are rites of passage into spiritual maturity, Gardner's Book of Shadows includes handfasting, which marks a commitment to temporary or permanent marriage, and a funeral. The Neopagans have modified and embellished these and devised others, including wiccaning (blessing and presenting infants to the pagan spirits and divinities to affirm that the child is a product of physical earth), puberty rites, and the transition into old age and death. I have been present at only one wiccaning. I have not been present at any funerals.[1] I attended two puberty rites for males and observed another from a distance. None were as rigorous as Zachary's. I have not attended any for females; these are generally private affairs performed within families or covens. Even divorce or separation of former lovers is occasionally ritualized in a rite of passage.[2] The constantly changing natural world is the model for all rites of passage, and all strive to connect the individual with the larger processes of change in the natural world.

Handfasting

In the ceremony of handfasting, the hands of the couple are tied together as a symbol of the union after the goddess and god are drawn down into each one respectively. The American witches have revised the handfasting ceremony, like most of Gardner's rituals, nearly beyond recognition. For instance the ceremony is used to bind gay and lesbian couples.

Handfasting establishes a relationship that differs significantly from conventional legal-religious marriages. In the latter, the ceremony usually declares that the relationship will endure until death. The handfasting ceremony asks that the couple remain in the relationship as long as the love shall last. It establishes an enduring bond of loyalty, but not necessarily affectional or sexual exclusivity. The couple is bonded as allies, or "soul-mates," for the rest of their lives—including all subsequent reincarnations—whether or not the relationship endures in its present form (in fact, nearly half of legal marriages end in divorce). The vows state that should the relationship become unhappy, the couple promises truthfulness and agrees to part as friends, in love and peace. Handfasting is enduring but not necessarily constant. The ceremony establishes an enduring friendship that may or may not remain as one of sexual and/or domestic intimacy.

Handfasting ceremonies may establish a trial relationship lasting traditionally a year and a day, at the end of which the commitment may be extended or broken. In this case it is an intermediate step to a proven commitment that can withstand the challenge of raising children. Roughly half of the handfasted individuals (sixteen of the thirty-six) who responded to my questionnaire were also legally married; the other fifteen did not have a marriage license.

Many witches have obtained ministerial licenses and can legally confer a marriage license when they perform handfastings. In this way, the Neopagans have liberated themselves from the legal and religious authorities on whom the larger population relies to perform weddings and confer entitlement to a mate's employee and government benefits.

Ordinarily, it is by the authority invested in them by a legal or religious institution that an official is empowered to create a marital union. When two gay men, Nat and Garland, were handfasted at Spiral Gathering of 1990, it was the authority invested in the entire community of about seventy-five celebrants that created a spiritual link between the souls of the couple.

Although they had been sharing their lives for several years, Nat and Garland decided to ask the "Spiral family" to acknowledge their union after it became clear that Nat would die of AIDS within a few years. The community was empowered to create the union (that mainstream society would not acknowledge) by witnessing and thereby legitimizing the union. Also they collaborated in the act of magic that linked the souls of the two men. They wished to be joined through all eternity, although they would soon be separated physically by Nat's death. According to their wishes, Oz focused the intent and imaginations of all who were present on the task of creating an energy vortex running in a circle linking their two hearts in a ring of light.

This handfasting is an example of the strong and significant social cohesion created by the sharing of religion, even when the congregation seldom meets face-to-face. The annual Spiral Gathering is the only occasion when most of the participants see one another. While they received the community's stream of energy Nat and Garland sunk roots into the community. They would need the community, not only to support their union, but to comfort them during the crises that were already upon them, in a way that only that community could—by resort to a common spiritual language. Rather than their consanguinal families or local circle of gay and heterosexual friends, Nat and Garland selected the Spiral family as the most significant social unit—and the only one able to perform a rite of passage (into death as much as relatedness) that is not recognized in mainstream society. In a sense, the couple engaged the members of that congregation, as well as themselves, in an alliance of affinity.

Questions probing legal marital status on my questionnaire yielded the following: 36 percent were legally married; 19 percent were divorced or separated, and 45 percent were never married.[3] Twenty-five percent

Nat and Garland's handfasting.
Photograph included with the permission of Garland Wood.

of the respondents were cohabiting without benefit of handfasting or marriage. The San Diego study yielded a similar breakdown with 13 percent fewer single individuals. Of the nine couples whose handfastings I observed, having children was a significant issue only to one. Six couples did not intend to have children, and for two couples, having children was an unresolved issue.

Croning

In the lore of Gardnerian Wicca, the greatest virtue of the high priestess is said to be her willingness to gracefully surrender pride of place to a younger woman, should the coven wish it, because youth is necessary to the representation of the goddess (Gardner 1954). Many witches condemn this as extinct, sexist, and ageist prejudice. In *The Crone Papers*, a Neopagan newsletter devoted to "the special magick of the elders," retired priestesses praise the wisdom of relinquishing the responsibility to more energetic women. Such graceful surrender is largely the result of effective rites of passage that have been devised to liberate elder women, and less often men, into pride in their condition as expert advisers. These rituals are generally called "cronings." The rite of passage usually occurs at the age of fifty-six when the planet Saturn returns for the second time to its location at the time of birth. Saturn has the astrological significances of Father Time, the teacher and stern taskmaster, a good metaphor for the role attributed to the crones. The Neopagans like to think this rite of passage leads into a period of ease, and well-earned comfort charged with the power and the wisdom of experience.

The "old crone" and "hag"[4] are among the negative images, including witch, whose potential witches like Susun Weed are trying to dignify. With their magic of changing attitudes, they hope to remove much of the sting that they feel is being imposed on aging. For instance, "They're not hot flashes; they're power surges!" the crones say.

The growing population of senior citizens in the mainstream struggles not only to secure entitlement to necessary resources—particularly, medical care—but to affirm the importance of the wisdom and experience they have to offer the young. Those who were present at the inception of the Neopagan movement and matured within it are, without a doubt, possessors of important and rare knowledge and experience. They are an invaluable resource, particularly now that the movement is in need of orientation within its own life cycles.

Preparing for Death

During the same Spiral Gathering at which he was handfasted, Nat prepared himself for death through his participation in another ritual. One day was devoted to a reenactment of Hades' abduction of Persephone into his underworld, the realm of death, where she presided as his queen. In the myth, the Earth becomes barren because Persephone's mother, Demeter, the provider of abundant grain, witholds her bounty while she mourns and searches for her daughter. In the underworld Demeter bargains and wins her daughter whom Hades insists must return each year for a period of time. In the Greek rites of Eleusis the return of the maiden along with Earthly abundance was reenacted to convey to initiates the mystery of resurrection.

In the reenactment at Spiral, celebrants searched for the abducted Persephone so that they could entreat her to return. Celebrants were ferried across the lake (the river of death). They were menaced by Cerebus, the guard dog of the underworld. Having negotiated that barrier, celebrants came one by one before Hades, who was Nat.

For two days, Nat and some helpers traveled back and forth across the "river of death" to prepare the little island for the ritual. There was a throne for Hades, another for Persephone, and several opulent altars. Because I had been given the role of Persephone, I stood in the dark listening to Nat greet each person as they scrambled out of the boat and passed the attacking dog (a man wearing a mask). Nat received them like a cordial host into the realm of death. He enfolded each one in his long black cloak in a welcoming embrace and greeted him or her, "Welcome! How was the journey? Rest awhile and look around." Nat had prepared an opulent display of the treasures that lie under the Earth. He had arranged large, beautiful specimens of stones, minerals, and semi-precious gems, including amethyst, garnet, and quartz, on various altars. There were bleached animal skulls and antlers displayed around them. After allowing some time for their awed inspection, "Hades" urged the initiates onward to stand before the queen of the dead. "Persephone has been asking about you. She will be so glad to see you," he confided to each one.

While attempting to remove the fear of death from the initiates, Nat transformed the descent into darkness and death into the warm homecoming he hoped it would be when he arrived there.

In rituals such as this one, along with the yearly round of sabbath celebrations, Neopagans have the opportunity to approach a reconciliation with the inevitability of death. Neopagans are not alone in finding contemporary culture bereft of healthy ways to approach the end of life. The removal of dying from the home and away from families; complicated medical and legal issues created by technology; dissatisfaction with the type of support offered by the majority religions; the repression of indigenous and alternative spiritualities in favor of institutionalized death practices; and the domination of the professional funeral business over after-death rites, all are criticized as obstacles to the sacralization of death.

On the spring equinox of 1992, Oz founded La Caldera Foundation in Albuquerque, New Mexico, to research the connections between the physical and spiritual experience preceeding and during dying and the changes in states of consciousness accompanying it. The foundation provides access to information, counselling, and personal ceremonial experiences by trained facilitators to guide and coordinate experiences preceding death.

La Caldera's board of directors includes about forty individuals from diverse occupations including health care, nontraditional and indigenous healers (including the Taos Elder, Teles Goodmorning), a cobbler, university professors, an astrologer, and artists. The goal of the foundation is to develop new therapeutic and ceremonial processes to aid those who wish to transform their death experiences. Since its inception, La Caldera Foundation has provided rituals to facilitate grieving and collaborated with other organizations assisting persons who are HIV positive. Some of the members are composing a guide for the passage into death that is relevant to the present age but modeled on the Tibetan and Egyptian Books of the Dead.

Between fifteen and twenty interested persons (most of whom are not yet facing death), including some children between the ages of seven and twelve, meet twice a month to talk and perform rituals. The group operates on the premise that in order to learn to die, one must learn to live well. Each time they meet they ritually address death and remind themselves that it a natural part of life. They support those who are dying and grieve for the death or other loss of loved ones. They try to help one another cope with mundane obstacles to a satisfying life. Also, they experiment with techniques for approaching normal death.

For example, in an effort to learn how to assist the dying, Oz induced a light trance and guided volunteers to the moment before death. She directed them to explore the boundary and consider what others might do to help them cross it. They described the experience and answered questions before Oz gently guided them back into ordinary reality.[5]

In another trance ritual Oz and her partner, Buck, guided a person who is terminally ill with cancer to cross over into death and find an animal guardian. In his vision, a bear approached and welcomed him to climb onto its back. The prospect of being greeted by the bear is, to him, comforting,[6] much as an opulent and welcoming Hades was to Nat.

Two years after Nat and Garland were handfasted, and about a month before Nat died, they came to Spiral Gathering. Nat had already stopped taking all life-extending medications. He was so weak that both men knew the journey from Maryland to Georgia would be heroic and the camping conditions impossible. Nat and Garland retired each evening to the comfort of a motel, but each morning they returned to the counsellors' cabin at the gathering site where Ceil prepared a sanctuary for Nat to say good-bye to his ''Spiral family.'' She padded the bed with a fouton, covered it and the windows with white lace and camouflaged the graffiti-covered walls with fabrics. Nat received good wishes from friends who were not afraid to speak of his dying. Nat and Garland shared hilarious reminiscences with their friends and gave frank descriptions of the ordeal of living and dying with AIDS. Their friends helped Nat sip water and wished Nat an easy passage and great adventures beyond. When it was time to part, it was with promises to rendez-vous at Sawain (Halloween) when the dead are believed to find it easiest to visit the living. Nat assured his friends that he would make his altered presence known at Spiral Gathering next year. The following year his friends kept their promises to welcome him at all rituals, including one devoted exclusively to honoring his spirit. After Nat died, Garland received comfort, although for the most part over long distances, from friends who shared the belief that in a sense death had not parted them and that even a tragic loss is also an initiation.

Neopagan Kinship

Falling into the rhythm of shared ideas about the nature of life passages is one way the diverse membership of Neopagans is solidifying. The shared expectations have a subtle but mild (because the rites of passage are not uniform) standardizing effect. Agreeing to submit to these rites of passage and perform them for one another is one of the ways religion creates social bonds that join strangers together into a community of believers. To some Neopagans these bonds are peripheral, to others they constitute the most significant of their social relationships, surpassing and substituting even those based on kinship by blood (consanguinity).

The relationships established on the basis of the Neopagans' shared view of the place of humans in the cosmos is voluntary. Anthropologists refer to voluntary relationships, those that represent a chosen connection in contrast to consanguinal kinship about which there is little choice, as fictive or affinitive. Fictive kinship involves imitating kinship relationships between people among whom no biological or marital relationship exists. Adoption, for example, "creates a kinship tie by means other than birth" (Bohannan 1992, 98). Because the voluntary alliances that the Neopagans are inventing incorporate some of the functions of family as well as other relationships, they are not considered fictive; they are genuine and original and are considered affinitive.[7] Thus, when Neopagans turn to one another for support and guidance through life transitions they are demonstrating an affinity based on a common perspective on the nature of human life and its part in the larger world (religion).

Affinity in its broader definition means a natural personal attraction, an inherent similarity between things. Generally marriage, as the product of attraction between the spouses and their families, is the substance of affinal kinship. For the Neopagans, and others who have joined together in communes or religious movements, shared ideas—religious or political—are the substance of the sympathy (affinity for one another) that draws them into a social cohesion that is often referred to as kinship.

When I encountered the Reclaiming group at witch camp in California, I had the opportunity to learn about some experimental family arrangements. Two women shared family life with one man; each of them had a child fathered by him. One of the women shared a job as an electrical engineer as well as the care of her child with her "father-in-law" (the child's father's father). Each of them worked twenty of the forty-hour work week, while the other cared for the child. The "wives" were supportive of one another and collaborated easily in domestic responsibilities.

Many members of the Athanor Fellowship began to think of themselves as a family and engaged in a ceremony of union in which they assumed the name, Arthen, that Andras and Dierdre created for themselves when they married. After the Athanor Fellowship dissolved, many members left, some continued to collaborate on EarthSpirit projects, and others cemented their relationship as well as their commitment to shared goals by becoming members of the Arthen family and sharing such intimacies as domestic and child-care responsibilities as well as the family name. Sue Curewitz Arthen told me that on those occasions when most people want to be with family—in times of need or during major holidays, for instance—she wants to be with the Arthen family. "When I need the kind of help for which we have been taught to rely on family, I turn to my friends—who are more than friends, they are my *real* family." Several members of the Arthen family are considering living communally and sharing resources, such as cars and pension benefits, and responsibilities, such as educating the children of their various unions.

In these circumstances, the attracting force of shared religious beliefs creates similar bonds and serves similar functions to those of kinship. The voluntary nature of these bonds makes them intense, although they are fragile because they remain at an experimental stage, and there is little support to sustain them, or even recognize them as significant, in mainstream society.

Human groups organize around kinship to foster cooperation, loyalty, and enduring relationships of reciprocity. Human societies rely on the family to provide such things as their own material needs and those of the young, socialize the children, and transmit such things as property, rights and responsibilities. However, reciprocity, loyalty, and cooperation are increasingly becoming attached to the impersonal relationships of employment and entitlement of citizenship. Because the family is losing its power to mobilize these indispensable social connections in contemporary American society, Neopagans are searching for alternative social bonds to support the exchange of benefits which formerly accrued from kinship by blood or marriage.

The Neopagans are attempting to reinvent kinship based on attractions formed by common beliefs and practicies (affinity) and are held together intimately by their affiliations with covens and other groups, which in turn are organized into diverse social structures, each of which demands a different type of leadership. Because leadership violates the Neopagans' esteemed ideal of egalitarian social structure, there is conflict about acknowledging leadership or rewarding the leaders on whom they rely. As is the case in families, conflict within and among these groups often subverts the purposes of kinship.

In most cases, leadership ideally consists of facilitating collaboration and consensus. We have already seen that Neopagans resist the authority and professionalism which exist in the mainstream institutions of religion and health care. In the new religion of Neopagans, their suspicion of the standardizing effect of bureaucracies, and the hazard of exploitation inherent in them, prevents Neopagans from collaborating sufficiently to strengthen the movement, become a significant political force, or create the social reforms they envision. The more successful of their innovations are those that benefit individuals—healing, modifying the personality, supporting one another through the turning points of life in rites of passage, and the mixed blessing of attracting people into the movement.

Wicca is living-room religion, Judy Harrow claims, and many believe that Neopaganism should not outgrow the living-room. Nonetheless, it has already outgrown its original coven structure and spilled over into a vast congregation of novices for whom there are too few teachers. As a result the rapidly expanding national community is a loosely woven network, studded here and there with large networking organizations.

Structure of Neopagan Congregations

There are basically five types of Neopagan congregations (By congregation I mean a group of individuals who share the religion of Neopaganism, although the members may not constitute a local community): initiatory or lineage covens, such as the Minoan Sisterhood; eclectic covens, which are generally the same size as lineage covens; the shifting congregations that attend gatherings;[8] and the national community consisting of the total of all of these. A fifth type of congregation is the magical lodge or temple. Although this type fits uneasily within Neopaganism, I mention it briefly here because many members of magical lodge groups attend gatherings. Such organizations as the Golden Dawn, for instance, include elements of Christianity in their more ceremonial magic which resembles the Hermeticism and Neoplatonism discussed in chapter six. The hierarchical structure of these organizations is even more complex and rigid than the lineage covens. They are regulated by governing bodies which oversee rigid standards for practice and admission of initiates.

Although they never gather as a unified congregation, we may also think of the thousands of those who learned to practice Wicca by reading books related to Neopaganism (principally, those of Starhawk), as a type of congregation, because they share a body of religious beliefs and practices despite the fact that Wicca was taught by absentee priestesses or priests (authors). Some of those who come to Neopaganism through books experiment and even become adept at magico-religious practices in isolation; they call themselves "solitaries." Others start covens, generally of the eclectic type that will be discussed later in this chapter. Each type of congregation requires a different type of leadership ranging from authoritarian in the initiatory covens to relatively leaderless in the case of eclectic covens.

Initiatory Covens

Initiatory lineage covens, whose traditions are passed on directly from teacher to student, benefit from considerable homogeneity. Graduates of these traditions "hive off" to become high priestesses or high priests of their own covens and pass on the traditions to their students. The social bonds existing in this system are often referred to as kin-based. In fact, the pattern resembles unilineal descent, with knowledge and credentials, rather than common blood, flowing through initiates of either gender from a common source, who is in many cases, Gardner. Each coven is like a nuclear family, headed by a high priestess and, ideally, a high priest also. Each set of covens that hives off from one witch queen is a separate segment within a larger system in which all are inheritors of a common tradition.

There is an internal hierarchy in the lineage covens. Rights to perform certain ritual functions and wear and use ceremonial regalia are awarded according to rank within the three levels of expertise confirmed by initiations. Like matriarchs, the high priestesses in these covens oversee the maturation—spiritual, psychological, and social—of each member.

Judy Harrow, witch queen of Proteus, a lineage coven, included among her jobs as a high priestess[9] such functions as gatekeeper. Because she wants the coven to function like a healthy family, she must see that it is the setting for intimacy, trust, and sharing in which each person is valued. She is responsible for selecting and blending of personalities.

In the role of teacher she conveys the basic symbolic vocabulary of her tradition and guides members to research materials to help them develop special interests and skills. As facilitator she must create an atmosphere in which each person explores his or her special interests and shares them with others.

Proteus is among the traditional covens that incorporate innovations such as the consensus process for arriving at group decisions. Judy is responsible for teaching and monitoring that process in which each person has the opportunity to speak uninterrupted in rounds until all concerns are expressed and responded to, alternatives are invented, and ideally the group invents a solution that satisfies everyone (Starhawk 1987). Rather than taking sides on either/or options, the group engages in a creative process whereby proposals are modified, challenged, and revised (Starhawk 1987). As facilitator, a high priestess requires the psychotherapeutic skills of group process. Judy must hear and voice the emerging consensus and be able to distinguish it from her own preference.

Most difficult is the job of quality control. When she elevates a member to the highest degree, she issues the credentials that qualify him or her to administer his or her own coven. Some do not qualify, even after years of work and study. Largely because the leaders of these intimate covens have considerable responsibility to transmit the heritage accurately, revise it judiciously, and prepare worthy transmitters of it, the size of covens remains small and they reproduce slowly. According to Judy, that is how it should be.

Eclectic Wicca

Eclectic witches believe, as Andras does, that traditional Wicca is too limiting. Five important innovations have arisen in the eclectic groups: (1) the internalization of deity; (2) the deification of the Earth; (3) a concern for "grounding," or connecting, with the Earth; (4) the incorporation of techniques associated with shamanism, and (5) reliance on techniques and metaphors of psychotherapy. The first, the idea that the goddess is not external to but exists within all worshippers (rather than being "drawn down" into a high priestess) is intimately related to the idea that the goddess is the planet Earth itself (the second innovation). Whereas the Renaissance magus was divine by virtue of an ability to connect with the divine universe through the mind, eclectic witches see themselves as divine not only in a spiritual way but in a very material one as well, by virtue of having bodies that are composed of matter originating in the substance of the Earth. In this sense, awareness of inherent divinity replaces efforts to contact external forces.

The third innovation, "grounding," is a symbolic connection with the Earth. Typically, eclectic witches raise energy from the Earth to empower their magical projects. Often this is accomplished by visualizing a root descending from their bodies and sinking into the fiery core of the planet. Through this connection they visualize the fiery energy rising into themselves, then they release it into the reservoir of the circle. At the conclusion of the ritual, they release any residual energy back into the Earth. The eclectic witches see themselves more as conscious conduits of the Earth's energy than generators of it, although they do their share of chanting and dancing to raise energy also.

The fourth important innovation arising from eclectic Wiccan practices is incorporation of techniques for inducing a trance associated with shamans' flight into other worlds and with myths derived from the agricultural worldview. The fifth innovation is that group dynamics are modeled on consciousness-raising groups and group therapy techniques that became prevalent in the 1970s.

The eclectic coven I worked with in Long Island, New York, survived a year and a half with nine members, eight women and one man. Four of the women were visual artists; three were poets; the man was a musician; and one woman worked as an artists' model and as a nurse's aide.

As is characteristic of these covens, the members of the coven agreed that leadership should be shared, but they never achieved a satisfactory solution to the problem that the most dominant members were also more willing to assume responsibility than the less dependable others. Largely because of this imbalance of power, they never achieved the goal of an egalitarian social structure, which is not an unusual outcome for covens such as these which have a high rate of dissolution. The majority of eclectic witches decide to practice "solo," celebrating and working magic in isolation.

Eclectic covens seldom require initiation, and there is no differential access to rights or responsibilities, or acknowledgement of levels of expertise. Members regard all those who are unanimously accepted into the group as a witch on an equal level with more established members. Each member develops and shares special interests—astrology, Tarot, or meditation techniques, for example—which is to say there are no teachers or experts. When members bring skills such as Judy's, the leaderless group has a greater chance of success. More often, as was the case in the Long Island coven, nearly anyone who is interested is welcome, regardless of his or her talents.

Eclectic covens are a distinctly American version of Wicca, whose goal is to provide a foundation for new religion. The flexibility supports innovation, but the lack of experience results in confusion and inefficiency, frequent change of membership, and high rates of failure. The Long Island coven dissolved during the early phase of the creative process when the awkward or inharmonious feelings were identified. With persistence and experience, some eclectic covens are able to reinvent the successes of the lineage covens while avoiding the restrictions of entrenched traditions and the necessity for hierarchy and authority.

The most impressive accomplishments of the Long Island coven were artistic. The ritual structure of creating a quartered circle inspired original invocations of the elements and deities. One member wrote poems, another composed chants, and together the group collaborated on some innovative rituals.

On the evening of the full moon in October 1985, for example, Debbie induced a trance state and led the group in a guided meditation with a political purpose. That year there was a proposition on the election ballot in Bristol, Connecticut, asking, Should the decision of the Supreme Court regarding abortion be overturned? Debbie told everyone to close their eyes and visualize the images her words would create. The group's collective attention was coordinated and focused on the purpose of preserving the rights of women to make their own decisions regarding abortion.

> Remember when time was our time
> And there was CHOICE.
> She Who **Chooses**
> And she who is **chosen**.
> Persephone, Demeter, Hecate.
> Maiden, Mother, Crone . . .

> In the time before beginning were The Daughter and the Mother and The Wise One—Persephone and Demeter and Hecate—those who were birth and life and death. All things paid homage to these Three: She of Death, She of Life and She of Decisions.

> Persephone, The Daughter, cherished the dead: those between life and life. She anointed with blood and fed with pomegranate those she **chose** for birth.

> They came to Demeter, The Mother. She **chose** to nourish them. When time had passed and their time had ceased, Demeter released them from her arms.

> And so they began their final journey: the road to Hecate, The Crone. There Hecate **chose** to send them onward to death, the womb. Once more they were reborn, over and over, around and around in time.

> In the time when beginning had passed and was forgotten, Hecate was seen by men as a withered hag; Demeter a burdened woman; Persephone a thoughtless child.

> Gone was the Triune: the decision-makers, arbiters of the fates of all living kind and kin.

> She who **chose** to give life, men termed a careless teenager. She who **chose** to sustain life, men described as a frantic housewife. She who **chose** to send life to death to rebirth, men condemned as a senile witch.

The daughter was raped. She was dragged against her will into the place of death where she was forced to bring forth life. She had **no** choice. The mother raged and wept and roamed the world. Bereft, she had to bargain with her food for the safety of her child. She had **no** choice. The crone was ignored. She knew, she saw, she spoke of reality and the truth of events. Hers was wisdom garnered from experience, but she fell silent. She had **no** choice.

When time no longer wheeled in cycles with all nature, when time became defined by lines and rules of law and order, men tried to make the choices. It was the choice of men to tell this story in this way. Their beginnings were forgotten, but the women did not forget. They remembered Persephone, Demeter, Hecate. The women were birth and life and death themselves. They remembered and they **chose**.

Remember and Create.
Become She Who is **chosen**
By She Who **Chooses**.
You are Persephone.
You are Demeter.
You are Hecate.
You, the **chosen**,
Are now She Who **Chooses**.
Remember and act[10]

Debbie's invocation illustrates the use of guided visualizations to effect a transformation of consciousness in the minds of receptive individuals in a light trance state. It is also an example of the way American witches revise myths to support their present agendas.

The myths lent authority to Debbie's political perspective and conveyed it in an emotionally and aesthetically moving way. Debbie pointed out that the three goddesses had each been a decision maker and that each had been condemned, trivialized, and derided by "men" (the patriarchy) who ultimately stole their decision-making power from them. Energy was collectively raised every bit as much as by the chanting and dancing Gardner prescribes, although the process was more intellectual or cognitive than biological. Together the witches visualized their passion, fury, and sadness as an energy vortex that would influence the outcome of the proposition in the same way Lady Cybele believed that her grandmother's efforts influenced weather fronts and Lady Boadicea was convinced that the witches kept Hitler out of England.

Beyond that specific issue, the group gained inspiration from symbols of powerful women as "arbiters of fate" to support their ongoing efforts to transcend crippling self-images, such as frantic housewives, hag, or impotent senile old women ("witches").

Eclectic American witches have come to rely on the mythology surrounding the shaman: self-creation, power, and heroic journeys to other realms of reality. Often the shamanic model is combined with agricultural myths. However, the merging of the two approaches to spirituality—the personal quest for power and self-definition with the collaborative lifestyle of the agricultural peoples—is an ambitious undertaking, since individualistic shamanic practice is by nature antithetical to collaboration. Communities have relied on the subordination of individualism to the homogeneity of the group and on submission by most to leadership by a few. How can there be coordination without sacrifice of the potential for full individuation? How can there be a community without leaders, particularly if conformity is anathema to its members? How, in other words, can there be a coven of shamans?

American covens suffer a great deal of chaos precisely because they are attempting contradictory goals: full development of each and every member, effective collaboration, and egalitarian social process.

Nearly every member of the Long Island coven was an artist; had they benefitted from the guidance of someone with experience with group dynamics they might have been able to persevere and move beyond their power struggles.

Starhawk's Reclaiming collective is an inspirational example that with patience, is is possible to achieve full equality through consensus in decision making and the sharing of responsibility. More than ten years ago the collective grew out of the success of a coven that labored several years to create an effective leaderless social structure. Most of the members of this collective continue to collaborate on holding public rituals, teaching, publishing a newsletter, and organizing witch camp (a two-week intensive training workshop for honing skills of magical practice).

For the most part, Neopagans are more successful in the areas of self-development and consciousness exploration and expansion—those aspects of the craft modeled on the mythology of shamanism and the role of the magus in Western spiritual tradition—than in their efforts in community living. The former is easier, almost natural, to individualistic Americans. Distrust of authority is a staple in American culture, although a simple and effective alternative is not forthcoming. Achievement of all of the goals of eclectic covens simultaneously requires a radical reorientation of values, extreme flexibility, and inventiveness. In American Wicca rituals have been turned to the purpose of creating those qualities of mind. When it works the product is a family of affinity that has the potential to take up the slack from the weakening nuclear family.

Serving the Broader Community[11]

Characteristically, people are drawn to the Neopagan movement through books, generally Starhawk's. All count themselves among the estimated few thousand members of the national community of Neopagans who seek teachers, resources, and opportunities to deepen their knowledge, provide healing or protection from prejudice against their religion, and meet others at the large gatherings. They require the support of organizations such as Circle and the EarthSpirit Community, and the administrators of these organizations find themselves overwhelmed by the task of serving such a large and diverse membership in addition to those of their local groups.

For example, the EarthSpirit Community consists of a congregation of thirty, three hundred, or three thousand members depending on the level of commitment and participation of the individuals involved. As the members of the Arthen family, the Glainn Sidhr Order, and the many participants in the gatherings and classes they offer congeal into covens or larger ephemeral congregations at gatherings, a hierarchy develops with organizers overseeing the growth and development of the many members. On the shoulders of those who direct such heavy traffic fall the responsibilities of teaching, counseling, and guiding as well as doing or overseeing the many operational jobs—volunteer manager, record keeper, secretary, fund raiser, event organizer—that are necessary to successfully organize a large group of people. Like leaders of similar organizations, Andras serves his community as teacher, counselor, and advocate. He is also the editor and publisher of a newsletter and the journal, *Fire Heart*. He has represented the national community at the interface with other religions in conferences at the United Nations and the World Conference on Religion.

The Neopagan movement, which is already the largest peripheral religious movement, is growing faster than the providers of training and other services can manage. Members are beginning to require the kinds of services that other religious institutions provide—such as public education, advocacy, outreach—and resources such as community centers, burial societies and cemeteries, publishing houses, health care facilities, and although the anarchistic Neopagans resist it, perhaps professional clergy.

Andras and Dierdre devote from sixty to eighty hours a week to EarthSpirit Community's many projects, for which they receive a modest income and considerable criticism from those they serve, because the community idealizes egalitarianism and believes that it is wrong to accept money in exchange for magical work and teaching. It is understandable that many of the elders in the movement, those with twenty to thirty years of experience, skills, and much valuable knowledge, find they cannot continue to give of themselves to the community, because their commitment to the craft conflicts with their jobs and families.

Gatherings of the National Community

The magical villages that are formed at the gatherings are rehearsals for a hoped-for real future. If they can coexist peacefully and productively during the week or so that they collaborate along different patterns than those which currently exist in the mundane world, participants hope that it may be possible to influence a shift away from oppressive and inefficient patterns found in mainstream culture. For many, attendance at gatherings is nothing more than a wildly imaginative party, a temporary release from the everyday world. For the vast majority, however, there is an urgency in the levity to change (heal) a society believed to be destined to destroy itself and the planet.

The utopia that is "played" at the gatherings is egalitarian. Theoretically, at least, socially necessary work is performed voluntarily, is considered of equal value, and shared equally without regard to sex. However, the utopia is imperfectly realized. There can be no doubt that no one works as hard or long or contributes as much as the planners and administrators. Although participants are expected to volunteer for two-hour (or more) work shifts at gatherings, community meetings are troubled by frustrated efforts to obtain sufficient volunteers to accomplish necessary tasks and by complaints that those who committed themselves never showed up. The delinquents complain of excessive rigidity. The utopia of the Neopagans expresses more effectively what they reject in the mainstream culture—unresponsive authority and rigid structure—than what they would replace it with.

Although the Neopagan community is at a very tentative experimental stage in its effort to create new cultural patterns, it is wrestling with important questions. Can power in the hands of women be truly different from what it is in patriarchal society? Can there be a balance of power based on reciprocity, mutual dependence, and respect? Should sex-based distinctions be dispensed with or redefined? How can individuals be induced to perform socially necessary work without monetary reward or political coercion? How can a community be coordinated without dominance and subordination? How can humans live satisfying lives without damaging the environment?

Neopagans have faith that the social variables—gender roles, division of labor, political authority, economy, religion, and so forth—can be reorganized to constitute a society in which certain classes need not necessarily and universally be oppressed or exploited by others. Society need not be destructive to the natural environment. The work, play, information exchange, and ritual dramas that occur at Neopagan gatherings are experiments with these variables and embody efforts to create a new mythology that will underwrite the realization of their utopia.

Many Neopagans experience a devastating letdown following a major gathering. The experience of community and visions of a better world may fade without the opportunity to keep them alive in a supportive group. Ultimately many risk the danger of sinking back into the rhythm of the prevalent social structure, with all its exposed flaws. A sickening sense of personal inauthenticity occurs because they are unable to devise a way of living in the larger world according to the idealistic visions gained at the gatherings. Confidence in the illuminations gained may erode under the pressure of a prevalent worldview that rejects their religion as deviant. For those who maintain confidence in their criticism of the existing social structure, there is the danger of deepening disillusionment with the world in which they must live and work.

There is danger also in being released in a suspended condition of liminality at the conclusion of the gathering. The old world is discredited, and the task of reforming the world in isolation is ill-defined and overwhelming. The best defense against these hazards is the reinforcement of a stable group.

Those who are unable to connect with a group find reinforcement in communicating—even collaborating on projects—without necessarily meeting face-to-face. One such opportunity is *Moonweb*. Circle Cithaeron, a teaching collective and scholars' circle in Washington, D.C., provides an opportunity for groups and solitary witches in the national community to feel allied in common efforts by performing synchronous rituals. In exchange for the price of postage, Cithaeron sends directions for performing the rituals to subscribers in a publication called *Moonweb*. Most of the rituals are efforts to remedy environmental problems. They send supporting information to enlighten subscribers and inform them of ways to take action in the mundane world as well. Moonweb is an apt description of the structure of these multiple long-distance connections that are reminiscent of the collaborative process described by Lady Boadicea. A common effort is mobilized from the center, radiates outward over long distances, and spreads out in web-like dyadic relationships to each subscriber who then extends the connections locally.

Many established groups offer courses and make seasonal reinforcement available by opening their sabbath celebrations to the public. These are especially prevalent in urban areas.

Much as the Rosicrucian Brotherhood broadcasted the philosophy among the secret elect in their manifestoes, Neopagans communicate via the mail, and more recently, computer networks. There is the constant opportunity to deepen their knowledge by reading the many books that are now available by Neopagan authors.

The Neopagan community is at a turning point and in need of a rite of passage. Neopagans have outgrown the living-room religion. The only ones qualified to initiate them into the next phase of maturity are themselves. In the following chapter we will speculate on the outcome of this turning point at which the movement is too big for its present resources and not yet ready or able to mature.

Positive image of the crone. Drawing from *The Crone Papers.*

Chapter Fifteen
Growing Up or Just Getting Big?

While she poured buckets of water into the toilets in the detention cells of the Brooklyn Criminal Court to see if they all flushed properly, Judy Harrow reflected that working full time as an occupational analyst increases her effectiveness as high priestess. Like most high priestesses, she also devotes about thirty hours a week to her coven work. She who shares the ordinary life circumstances of her congregants is more likely to offer realistic and compassionate advice, she thought, than members of a professional clergy class (especially those who are celibate) who base their teachings on abstract principles rather than on a real understanding of human experience.[1]

Judy is among those who believe that it is inappropriate to accept monetary payment for their services to coven members. Ogaea wrote in *The Crone Papers* that to repay magical teaching or healing with money confounds categories that should remain distinct. Although it is appropriate to pay for secular goods and services with money, it is a means unsuited to the sacred ends of magic. Some things must be done in trust and for love.[2]

In fact, many high priestesses who think monetary reward for teaching the craft is inappropriate accept, or expect, help with domestic responsibilities or child care instead. Others take their pay in power, prestige, pleasure, and pride in the position of high priestess. However, both those who accept monetary payment and those who do not are susceptible to accusations that they perform their craft with ulterior motives: self-serving manipulation, notoriety, sexual gratification, or enhancement of their fragile egos. The transmission of magical knowledge creates a volatile relationship.

Within the family-like structures of covens, social relationships are most influenced by the constraints appropriate to kinship. Like a mother, the high priestess is expected to be wise, compassionate, and just and to ask nothing of her students in return except what mothers expect of their children—that they mature, make good use of her instruction and guidance, and become a source of pride rather than shame.

These bonds may be violated in a number of ways. As in family feuds, resentments between parents and offspring and competition among siblings or between segments of a lineage can develop into personal hatreds, slander, and sabotage. In the intimate settings of covens, witch wars thrive. Witches suspect one another of harmful magic, "zapping" one another (that is, mobilizing a mild charge of unpleasant energy), or trying to restrain one another (as in the bubbling effect discussed in chapter ten). On the few occasions when these things are discussed, such efforts are defended as harmless; after all such magic only speeds up the inevitable effects of the three-fold law, and to restrain another is simply to protect one's self.

Many recognize that although, at least in theory, the high priestess may offer her knowledge and help freely, such gifts incur an obligation to reciprocate. Reverend Jackie Ramirez, for instance, believes that the healer or teacher who refuses payment is egotistical; the student or recipient of healing or teaching deserves the right to free him- or herself of the burden of indebtedness.[3]

The exchange between high priestesses and their coven members lies in the confusing territory between the reciprocity characteristic of the family and impersonal economic transactions. Both efforts to reciprocate and efforts to avoid it compromise the unequal relationship that is always on the brink of becoming one of dominance and submission, such as those the Neopagans despise in the mainstream society. This is one of the blemishes on social cohesion.

Another source of conflict is disagreement about the proper evolution of the movement. Some think the movement is already flawed by uncontrollable progress towards bureaucratization and professionalism. While some would curb the growth, others contend that the movement must mature in order to manage it. Neopagans are afraid of what maturity might cost them. In this chapter we will explore these impediments to progress and try to evaluate the contributions the Neopagan movement has made to its members and to the larger society.

What Constitutes Proper Reward?

The values of creative individuals, including the Neopagans, are at variance with those of the capitalistic consumer economy in which they live. We have seen in chapter five that Ken-Ra was content to receive a modest income for his demanding work as a blacksmith and to give a gift of his own creation each year. In the letter that accompanies these gifts he tells the recipient "I personally want no reward for what has been given to you. Its making was a joy to me. I would not trade that for anything that you could give me. If you are unable to accept it freely, any poetry, song or thing of beauty that you could dedicate to Hephaestus, [the smith god] and turn loose in the world would please me, and him."[4] Ideally, the work is the end, not the means, of fulfillment. However, most landlords do not accept magical tools as payment for rent.

On occasion Neopagans engage in barter to help one another through non-financial means. Because these exchanges have currency only within the movement, they fail to enable priestesses, priests, organizers and artists to practice their vocations exclusively.

In the more impersonal congregation of the national community, the bonds of trust and love are especially susceptible to the influence of the capitalistic consumer economy. Organizers of the gatherings, who are generally also leaders of large organizations, are victims of the full range of accusations to which high priestesses are susceptible as well as suspicion that they are exploiting the Neopagan community by trying to make a profit on the services they provide.

Andras finds that most of the leaders and organizers are "not so much living *off* the Pagan community as they are living *for* the Pagan community." They are so deeply committed to their particular visions for the movement that they have chosen to devote their lives to its evolution, and as a result, most of them have been willing to make very difficult sacrifices for the sake of their ideals.[5] For example, since the Rites of Spring gathering of 1989, Andras, and his wife, Deirdre, have turned away hundreds of people who wanted to attend the yearly gathering. In 1989 almost a third of the seven hundred participants were new to Neopaganism. The core community had difficulty assimilating such a large number of newcomers, many of whom were more curious than devoted to Neopaganism. Because of that unpleasant experience, Andras and Deirdre decided to limit attendance to 450, reduce the number of novices and consolidate the core community. Although a third of their modest income comes from the profits from Rites of Spring, they turn away more than $20,000[6] a year in potential income for the sake of the gathering's integrity.[7]

Paid, Professional Clergy

Unlike most Neopagans, Isaac thinks the hierarchy of clergy and congregation is natural, and it's about time the Neopagan community acknowledged and paid its own full-time professional clergy. He says Neopagan leaders could benefit from the knowledge that previous generations of Christian clergy have accumulated about: budgeting, pastoral counseling techniques, middle- and large-sized group dynamics, and liturgical design.[8]

We have seen that as poets, artists, musicians, ritualists, and visionaries American witches are inventors rather than followers of religious movements. Poet and part-time priestess, Oriethyia believes the presence of professional clergy would stifle the spontaneity and diversity that are Neopaganism's greatest strengths.[9]

Most Neopagans prefer to avoid mainstream religions. Most leaders, on the other hand, believe it is important to gain entrance into ecumenical religious discussions that are presently monopolized by mainstream religions. For instance, Sam Webster, who is a credentialed clergyman (he has a Master of Divinity degree), believes that clergy credentials are needed if Neopaganism is to bring its unique nature-centered spiritual perspective to bear on discussions about such issues as the environmental crisis, minority religions, drug use and abuse, the role of women as clergy, social justice, and world peace. Neopaganism has much to offer, Sam contends, because of its unique teachings of stewardship of the planet and its broad vision that reaches beyond limited cultural horizons.[10] Furthermore, most leaders feel the endorsements by credentialed clergy of other religions may be the best defense against fanatical allegations against which Neopagans struggle to defend themselves.

Without financial support, those who are already serving in leadership roles wonder how they can accommodate the constantly increasing influx of the uninitiated who need and want instruction, counselling, and other services. Andras is afraid that established organizations, councils, gatherings, and publications will continue to fail because of a lack of experience, resources, or other kinds of support. The movement cannot endure if its leaders have to continually reinvent the wheel.[11]

Many Neopagans complain that mass organizations like EarthSpirit Community are making their religion a consumer commodity. By encouraging novices who, do not have the benefit of the one-to-one mentoring that happens in covens, leaders of the movement contaminate the it with the attitudes and processes of the larger society. Many fear that the large organizations disempower the majority who have been conditioned by mainstream culture to be parasitical spectators. At the same time, they are creating a self-serving, self-perpetuating privileged clergy class.[12] Others are afraid that if the movement doesn't adapt to meet the needs of the masses wishing to join, they will go away, perhaps to other religious movements that are the Neopagans' adversaries.

Andras claims it is not necessary to duplicate structures in mainstream society or sell out to patriarchal, oppressive, mainstream religious values. Firming up organizational processes and supporting skilled practitioners, teachers, leaders, and organizers is the natural path of growth and complexity toward the maturation of the Neopagan movement.

What Does Maturity Entail?

Judy Harrow says the movement is mature. It is able to pass its tradition on to the next generation and accommodate appropriate growth through the lineage coven system. Growth that cannot be nurtured in that way is cancerous.[13]

We have seen that the "shamanic-witch" figure, that is the culture heroine and role model for contemporary Neopagan witches, is the conceptual opposite of the European witches' enemy, the established church. Understandably, most Neopagans are reluctant to "lie down" with their legendary enemies and pass through their alien rites of passage to partake of their version of maturity. Characteristically, cults solidify into formal religious organizations by standardizing and institutionalizing the visions that were once innovative; social structure becomes bureaucratic as the religion seeks accommodation with the larger society.

Assuming they were willing to allow the movement to ossify in this manner, would they achieve recognition as peers among established religions? If so, would they gain security and protection, or invite repression as a side-effect of becoming stronger and more visible? We have seen in chapter thirteen that the more prevalent and increasingly favorable coverage in the media coincides with increased opposition by followers of more conservative religions. If they refuse, or are unable to penetrate the higher levels of religious debate, will the Neopagans stunt their own growth, or is it possible to be influential and persuasive in the ways that are more natural for them?

Long before the large influx of novices forced these debates, Neopagans defined themselves as healers. They applied inventiveness, refined by magical training, to healing the self first and then expanding outward to the natural environment, skimming lightly over the broader social milieu. We have seen that the craft provided Andras and others with effective tools for healing themselves. Starhawk provided guidance for achieving love and trust in covens. However, in chapter thirteen we learned that her advise is easier to read than accomplish. The social bonds that stretch across the network of the national community are especially in need of healing.

Although the Neopagans still struggle to get their own house in order, this is also true of other more established religions, whose infirmities are the result of age rather than immaturity. Collaboration could be felicitous for both.

Whether or not Neopagan representatives are welcomed as colleagues by those of more established religions, it seems likely that the movement will survive. It's growth pattern is shape-shifting, however, so we might not recognize it. The basic perspective that humans are not separate but are imbedded in a vast natural world will not cease to be a useful metaphor for life within a now fragile natural environment. That basic religious truth will be adapted much as Starhawk has done, by Neopagans and others outside the movement to new challenges in the mainstream.

Slow organic growth will continue within the coven structure. The lineage covens will preserve traditions, while experiments continue in the more ephemeral eclectic covens. Cross-fertilization will continue at gatherings, which will probably become more numerous, local, and expensive. New organizations will benefit from the experiences of Andras and Selena and other pioneers. Seasoned leaders are already finding ways to hedge their bets. Selena and her husband, Dennis, for instance are acquiring academic credentials in psychology that are marketable in the mainstream as well as being valuable adjuncts to their Neopagan ministry. All who wish to participate will continue to find a level of involvement appropriate for their experience and commitment. Flexibility and diversity are the strengths of Neopaganism.

The unique contribution of the Neopagan movement to the larger society is the gift visionaries bring. As is true of all visionaries, their visions are useful to the extent that they express society to itself with effective symbols. If the symbols do not ring true for a significant number of others in their societies, these individuals are not visionaries at all; social consensus is required to transform a personal hallucination into a prophecy.

We have seen that there is confirmation for the symbols the Neopagans express in their playful rituals, songs, and poetry. The unmanageable growth of the movement is confirmation, as is the evidence that the goddess and the idea of the living divine Earth are being incorporated in other religions and in broader cultural expressions.

Historically, the most conspicuous and powerful symbols created by those outside the movement are the witch and the burning times. As we have seen the long list of improbable traits attributed to witches—including association with animals, night flight, cannibalism, participation in orgiastic rites, emission of light from their bodies, and an inherent capacity for malevolence—amounts to a rejection of human beings by a culture-sharing society. These are qualities more appropriate to animals and unruly nature which mainstream culture seeks to overcome. The accusation of witchcraft expresses loathing both for the human being and nature.

It would seem, therefore, that contemporary witches are discrediting themselves when they claim that they are witches—that is, until we realize that they see animals and unruly nature as necessary elements of culture, rather than its opposite. From that perspective, to attempt to create a culture that removes itself from its source in the natural world and that thinks of human nature as utterly distinct from animal nature is abominable.

As the only culture-creating animals, humans are boundary creatures, both of nature and removed from it. To overcome their animal natures and to carve out a safe haven for themselves, humans began devising more and more effective defenses against the omnipotence of nature. Finally, those who devised the scientific revolution and the Enlightenment were satisfied that they had at last mastered it. However, this required that Europe be purged of witches.

In such times of ideological transition, the Western spiritual tradition emerged, hoping to prepare culture transformers to bring all of their talents—intellect, spiritual refinement to assure pure motivation, along with those gifts more properly associated with the animal nature (imagination, intuition, memory)—to the task.

Even as the witch persecutions were gathering force, one articulator of that tradition, Giordano Bruno, called for some wise witch (Circe, who turned men into swine) to remedy the destructiveness of the Christians with her herbs and enchantments. Even the sinister powers of Circe were better than the Christians' worship of dead things, according to Bruno. The religious reformation and other revolutions of thought contemporary with it erected a firm boundary between the civilized world of humans and the world of nature—and witches. Neopagans, environmentalists, and postmodern thinkers are among those who wonder if humans have traveled too far from their grounding in the natural world. Western culture may be a more sinister enemy than the nature it seeks to control.

Playful rituals, songs and other art works, along with the experiments with covens, rites of passage, and other novel social arrangements, would seem to pose no real threat to American society. However, the witch hunts of the sixteenth and seventeenth centuries proved that in Western society, the crime of witchcraft—daring to be the opposite of right society—to a large degree constituted apostasy from official religion and professional medicine. As the fate of Giordano Bruno indicated, the unauthorized attempt to revise culture, or even to protect one's self from it, frequently encounters brutal opposition.

What the witches claim as their power—and their critics regard as their maliciousness—is *activity* rather than passivity in the face of a perceived need for change (remedy, or healing.) The danger surrounding witchcraft arises from the fact that it is *unauthorized* creativity, and that its methods and ethics are founded in premises that arise from the *natural*, not the social, world.

The contemporary witches remind us of the witch hunts in Europe. They say that like the victims of the witch persecutions, they are healers. We learned in chapter four that about half of those accused of witchcraft—in the places where historical research of surviving documents is available—were, in fact, healers. They also had in common with the other half of the victims of the burning times the misfortune of being convenient scapegoats—defenseless casualties of the economic, political, and religious transitions of that time. With the dismantling of the manorial system, the poor, elderly (mostly women), and otherwise defenseless were displaced from the land. The new commercial ethic and the trend toward cash economy turned neighbors against one another. The accused were also the objects of the crusade on the part of the new ruling class against enemies of the Christian church. By resort to magic, the defenseless tried to defend and avenge themselves as a substitute for impotence and a remedy for anxiety and despair (Thomas 1971). Macfarlane's study of Essex England suggests that after the beggars were blamed for their own misery and turned away, guilt on the parts of the stingy materialized into accusation of witchcraft against the very ones who had been sacrificed in the social reforms from which they benefitted.

When the new witches declare, "Never again the burning times," they remind us that it is easy, almost automatic, to justify unequal wealth and privilege by blaming the disinherited for their own misfortune as well as ours. One astonishingly prevalent pattern, we discovered, is to declare them unworthy because they are inhuman—witches. By assuming the personae of the witch and by reminding us of the burning times, Neopagans urge us to overcome this tendency to blame and destroy the victims of transitions such as the one presently in progress. Rather than kill the messenger, the new witches offer an alternative, one they have been willing to try themselves. By resort to the resources of the Western spiritual tradition it is possible, they say, to perfect the self by enhancing the *natural* capacities of the imagination, will, and craft. As balanced creatures, both at home in one's animal nature and refined by culture, it may be possible to change ourselves and even the near-universal tendency to excuse ourselves by accusing others of being inherently evil.

Appendix

QUESTIONNAIRE
Utilization of Health Care by Magickal Folk

This questionnaire will be evaluated by a human
anthropologist with a small assist from a computer.
Please feel free to give human responses (i.e.: write in
comments or rephrase questions if necessary). Space has
been provided for this purpose; if you need more room,
please use the back of the form.

Definition of terms:

Healing

> Restoration of biological, psychological,
> sociological and/or spiritual well-being.

Professional Medicine

> Healing practice performed by dentists,
> doctors, etc. who would be eligible for
> membership in the A.M.A.

Please answer all questions honestly and to the best of
your abilities. If your response to any question is
"other" please specify in the area provided. Thank you
for your cooperation.

Orion

Name(optional):   Mundane or Given: _____
                   Magickal or Chosen: _____
    If you did not specify it, do you have a Magickal or
    chosen name?   <>Yes <>No

Sex: <> Male   <> Female   <> Androgenous
Sexual Preference: <> Heterosexual <> Homosexual <> Bisexual
                      <> Celibate: <>by choice <>not by choice

Mating Status:
  <> Single   <> Divorced or Separated   <> Legally Married
  <> Handfasted (or other ceremony) <>with <>without a license
  <> Cohabitating <>with <>without formal or written agreement
  <> Significant relationship without regular cohabitation

Education:
  <> High School: <>Finished   <>Did not finish
  <> College: <>Attended   Number of years: ___
                 <>Graduated   Major _____
  <> Technical/Vocational School: What kind? _____
  <> Graduate University: <>Attended   Number of years: ___
                             <>Graduated Degree: _____

Occupation: _____   Field/industry? _____

Where do you live?   City _____   State _____
Type of area: <> Urban <> Suburban <> Rural

Salary range: (per year)
    Personal   Household
      <> $0 to $7000   <> $0 to $7000
      <> $7000 to $15000   <> $7000 to $15000
      <> $15000 to $25000   <> $15000 to $25000
      <> $25000 to $35000   <> $25000 to $35000
      <> $35000 to $45000   <> $35000 to $45000
      <> $45000 or greater   <> $45000 or greater

Political affiliation:
      <> Democrat   <> Republican
      <> Liberal   <> Conservative
      <> Other (_____) <> None

Religious affiliation(s):
  During childhood: _____
  Current religion or Magickal tradition: _____
  Do you worship/celebrate   <>alone? <>with a group? <>both?
  Do you practice Magick?   <>Yes <>No
  Please describe your idea of Magick: _____
  _____

Are you happy/satisfied with your job?   <>Yes <>No <>Somewhat
              ....with your home life?   <>Yes <>No <>Somewhat
              ...with your sex life?   <>Yes <>No <>Somewhat

Utilization of Health Care by Magickal Folk

Do you have medical insurance? <>Yes <>No

Do you belong to a health maintainance group? <>Yes <>No

How many times do you consult an M.D. or dentist?
        each year_____
        in the last year_____
        in the last 5 years_____

Have you ever had any form of psychotherapy? <>Yes <>No
        What kind?_____ How long?____
        Was it successful? <>Yes <>No <>Unsure

Do you ever consult non-medical healers? <>Yes <>No
    If yes, what kinds have you consulted?

Type	Times in last Year	5 yrs	Condition	Was it successful?
Chiropractor				<>Yes <>No
Osteopath				<>Yes <>No
Homeopath				<>Yes <>No
Acupuncturist				<>Yes <>No
Midwife				<>Yes <>No
Massage therapist				<>Yes <>No
Spiritual healer				<>Yes <>No
Crystal healer				<>Yes <>No
Other (_____)				<>Yes <>No

Do you belong to a non-medical healing group? <>Yes <>No
        If yes, what kind?_____

Do you practice any form of non-medical healing on yourself
or others? <>Yes <>No
    If Yes, what kind and for whom?

Type	Self	Family	Friends	Other	For pay?
Meditation					<>Yes <>No
Vitamin therapy					<>Yes <>No
Herbalism					<>Yes <>No
Bach Flower remedies					<>Yes <>No
Polarity					<>Yes <>No
Massage					<>Yes <>No
Visualization					<>Yes <>No
Affirmation					<>Yes <>No
Crystals					<>Yes <>No
Other (_____)					<>Yes <>No

If you could afford it, would you use more professional
medical care than you do now? <>Yes <>No

If health insurance covered it, would you rely more on non-
medical healing than you do now? <>Yes <>No

Utilization of Health Care by Magickal Folk

For the following would you consult an M.D./dentist. or a non-medical healer? If you would consult both, please write "#1" below the one you would consult first and "#2" below the one you would consult second. If you would consult a non-medical healer for any condition, please specify the type of healer.

Condition	M.D.	Non-medical healer	Both	Neither
Cold or flu				
Diarrhea				
Nausea				
Hemorrhoids				
Ulcers				
Childhood diseases*				
Pneumonia				
High blood pressure				
Pregnancy/Childbirth				
Unwanted pregnancy				
Infertility/Impotence				
Persistent headaches				
Impaired vision				
Athletic injury				
Fractured bones				
Sprains				
Hernia				
Severe burns				
Mild burns				
Persistent bad luck				
Trauma				
Anxiety attack				
Mild depression				
Severe depression				
Schizophrenia				
Paranoia				
Venereal disease				
A.I.D.S.				
Tooth ache				
Bladder infection				
Hepatitis				
Diabetes				
Cancer				
Appendicitis				
Kidney disease				
Cardiac condition				
Heart attack				
Other( )				

(*Mumps, measles. etc)

Which is more important for improving health care in this country?

  <> Socialized medicine
  <> Better utilization/availability of non-medical therapies
  <> Both are equally important

Choose one of the following:
    <> Medical treatment is on the whole more effective
       than alternative healing methods
    <> Most non-traditional healing systems are superior to
       professional medicine
    <> Both are equally effective
    <> Each is effective for different conditions

Can you perceive auras?   <>Yes <>No
Or manipulate auras for healing or other purposes? <>Yes <>No
If not, do you believe this can be done?   <>Yes <>No

Do you believe people can make others sick or injured with
their will or thoughts?   <>Yes <>No
Do you believe people can heal others with their will or
thoughts?   <>Yes <>No
Do you believe healing requires physical contact? <>Yes <>No
Do you believe healing requires a transfer of energy between
healer and patient?   <>Yes <>No

Which is most determinative of your state of health?
    <> The condition of the body
    <> The condition of the mind
    <> The condition of the spirit
    <> All three equally
    <> Other(_____)

Which is more determinative of the severity of illness?
    <> Severity of the invading organism/disease process
    <> Resistance of the individual

Do you smoke tobacco?   <>Often <>Sometimes <>Never
Do you smoke Marijuana?   <>Often <>Sometimes <>Never
Do you use recreational drugs? <>Often <>Sometimes <>Never
Do you use visionary drugs?   <>Often <>Sometimes <>Never
Do you drink alcohol?   <>Often <>Sometimes <>Never
Do you exercise regularly?   <>Yes <>No

Place a check beside the foods you normally eat:
    <> Dairy   <> Red meat   <> Poultry   <> Fish
    <> None of the above

How would you categorize your current state of health?
  Physical: <>Above average <>Average <>Below average
  Mental: <>Above average <>Average <>Below average
  Emotional: <>Above average <>Average <>Below average
  Spiritual: <>Above average <>Average <>Below average

Will you donate any of your organs when you die?
    For transplantation?   <>Yes <>No <>Undecided
    To science?   <>Yes <>No <>Undecided

Utilization of Health Care by Magickal Folk

Endnotes

Chapter 1

[1] The word *occult* is derived from the Latin root *occulere* (to cover over, hide, or conceal).

[2] This estimate is based on readership of books published on related subjects.

[3] Valerie Flint (1991, 12) shows that the Early Medieval Christian Church found that rather than condemn pagan magic, it was necessary to retain and transform some of these means for manipulating the environment by supernatural means. The church leaders realized that they were indispensable to society. "There are forces better recognized as belonging to human society than repressed or left to waste away or growl about upon its fringes."

[4] The Kirkpatrick group circulated an eighteen-page questionnaire by mail to Neopagans in the United States, Canada, and Britain in 1983. The majority of the respondents (the number varies per report between 114–151) were from the western United States. Their demographic findings provide data for fruitful comparisons with mine which are gathered mostly from eastern states. I rely for my coverage of this project on an article that appeared in *Iron Mountain, a Journal of Magical Religion* (Colorado: 1984), wherein Kirkpatrick, describes his methodology as "participative sociology." By this phrase Kirkpatrick means that members of the community of witches participated in the project by reviewing the questions and coding the results. To the best of my knowledge this project did not include research by participant observation.

[5] I attended four Pagan Spirit Gatherings; five gatherings organized by the Earth-Spirit Community; eleven Spiral Gatherings; and one each of other gatherings in Pittsburgh, Ohio, California and Upstate New York. In addition, I have visited a group in New Mexico on three occasions, and experienced several seasonal celebrations and workshops each year in the New York area.

Chapter 2

[1] The program was recorded a few days before Halloween in 1987.

[2] Her story is corroborated by other sources. One published confirmation of the story is that of Doreen Valiente in which she includes a testimony by Lovis Wilkinson in her book *An ABC of Witchcraft Past and Present* (New York: St. Martin's Press, 1973).

³ Aelfred: Prilim. 30 in F. L. Attenborough, *Laws of the Earliest English Kings* (Cambridge: 1922). Wihtred 12, quoted in Jane Crawford (1963, 107). This is an obvious elaboration on Exodus 22:18, "Thou shalt not suffer a witch to live."

⁴ W. W. Skeat, *Etymological Dictionary* (Oxford: 1898) s.v. "witch," as cited in Jane Crawford (1963, 108).

⁵ Cunning-folk was a term used to refer to practitioners of practical sorcery. Cunning denotes guile, craft, and skill in deception. It derives from the Middle English *conning*, perhaps from *connen*, to know, Old English *cunnan*. *American Heritage Dictionary* 1993 ed., s.v. "cunning."

⁶ Montague Summers (ed.), *Reginald Scot's The Discoverie of Witchcraft* (London: 1930), 274, as cited in Crawford (1963, 112).

⁷ W. W. Skeat, *Aelfric's Lives of the Saints* (EETS 1881-1900) Sermon XVII, 11. 157f, as cited in Crawford (1963, 111).

⁸ For the roots of the image of the witch in European folklore see Jeffrey Burton Russell (1972). Also worthwhile is Carlo Ginzburg's (1989) interesting theory that the notion of the night flight of witches to the Sabbath with familiar animal spirits and a devil—also resembling an animal—was bequeathed, by way of diffusion, from the shamanistic cultures of Europe.

⁹ My discussion of Gardner, his witchcraft, and his role in originating the current version of the Wiccan religion is based on various sources, including predominantly Gardner's published works along with two different versions of his secret Book of Shadows.

¹⁰ The *grimoire* contains secret alphabets, chants, and recipes for making such things as incense and for performing spells.

¹¹ The coven members were aware that I intended to write about my experiences and observations. The high priestess gave me permission to use my own discretion, but later I discovered some members did not welcome my presence in the coven.

¹² I rely also on Gardner's commentators as they are reviewed by J. Gordon Melton (1982, 105–109), and particularly in Margot Adler (1986), where a summary of Gardner's work and that of this critics and commentators is provided. Adler reviews the thoughts of Gardner's biographer, Jack Bracelin (1960) as well as Doreen Valiente; Raymond Buckland (1971), the priest of Wicca who brought Gardner's Wicca to the New York area; and Aidan Kelly, who researched the private papers of Gardner. Kelly (1991) provides the most thorough study of Gardner's "creation" of the religion of Wicca. See also, an ample bibliography provided by Melton (1982, 106–108).

¹³ Although her numerous critics refer to her as a credulous folklorist, Margaret Murray held a Doctor of Literature degree. She was the first scholar to recognize in the confessions of those accused of witchcraft resemblances to a pre-Christian fertility cult whose horned god was misinterpreted as Satan by the Christians. She is criticized most often for assuming the factual nature of information obtained under torture. Her most vigorous critic, Norman Cohn, discredits her work because she used information in trial records out of context, because evidence of such a cult is lacking, and because she was over 60 years old when she wrote *Europe's Inner Demons* (New York: Basic Books, 1975), 109–120, 123.

¹⁴ Because it is forbidden to give her name to the uninitiated, Gardner calls her "G."

¹⁵ The fivefold kiss is a ritual gesture of marking the points of a five-pointed star on a person's body: the face, breasts, and feet.

¹⁶ Hermetic literature consists of magico-religious texts attributed to the putative Egyptian priest, Hermes Trismegistus.

17 An eloquent expression of this concept is provided by Joseph Cambell (1959, 56-57). "The imprint of the rapture enclosed is suffering . . . is the foremost 'grave and constant' of our science [of mythology]."
18 The basic principle of Tantrism is that a man could achieve realization of divinity only through sexual or emotional union with a woman.
19 White witch is a term denoting one whose magic is good or useful. Their functions generally included healing, foretelling the future, and finding lost things.
20 Lady Boadicea's efforts during world war II is an example.

Chapter 3

1 The major difference relates to Gardner's conviction that witches cannot raise energy from their bodies without a perfectly balanced polarity between an equal number of male and female coven members, alternately placed, in the ritual circle.
2 *Hieros gamos* is a Greek term for a ritual marriage: sacred (*hieros*) sexual union (*gamos*). For a discussion of the origin and function of such rituals see M. Esther Harding (1971, 134-37).
3 The *kore* represents the maiden aspect of the goddess, who, like the moon, is thought to have three phases: maiden (waxing); matron (full); crone (waning).
4 These vary according to the season.
5 Witches believe that magic worked between the worlds affects the mundane world of time and space. "Between the worlds" is an expression that applies to vague unsystematic realms of thought, essentially those of imagination and intuition, where insights and new logical vocabularies are envisioned.
6 Salamanders are imagined to undulate in flames; ondines are small mermaid-like creatures; sylphs resemble small winged fairies; and gnomes are dwarf-like creatures.
7 The Land of Faerie is thought of as a pagan paradise which might be located underground, under water, or on a distant island in the west where the sun descends.
8 I was unable to discover the name of the author who recited her poem at a talent show at a gathering called "Merry Meet" in the fall of 1988.
9 In hieratic city-states, such as Sumer or Egypt, the privileged positions of priests and monarchs were justified by the presumed supernatural or sacred qualities of these individuals.
10 Personal communication, 1988.

Chapter 4

1 Zell's group, the Church of All Worlds, was inspired by Heinlen's science-fiction novel *Stranger in a Strange Land*.
2 A "global culture," such as the Neopagans imagine, would protect and take inspiration from the values, traditions, and experiences of pre-modern societies as well as those of the third world. It would reject the authority of the first world to impose its standards on other societies.
3 George Peter Murdock (1980).
4 This story is quoted from Henry Charles Lea (1883, vol. 3, 388) as cited in Sanford Fox (1968, 12). See also E. A. Wallis Budge, *Egyptian Magic* (London: Kegan Paul, 1899), 3.

5 On the question of whether magic is good or evil, the example of "vengeance magic" that Edward Evans-Pritchard (1937) found the Azande of Africa practicing is enlightening. In retaliation for the death of a relative, the Azande enlist the expertise of a magician to kill the person responsible with a vengeance spell. Although it is hoped that a person will be killed, it is considered good magic because it operates on behalf of the society as a "legal" execution.

6 Irene Silverblatt (1987) tells of one instance in which Christian Spaniards imported this Christian concept of witchcraft to Inca Peru and condemned the women who attempted to defend their culture as witches. As it turned out, these accusations provided the Peruvian women with an ideology of rebellion and a method of defending their culture.

7 Although her grandfather didn't consider himself a witch—because such talents were not linked with witchcraft in those days—Lady Cybele offered this story as an example of the facility with nature that she would consider characteristic of witches.

Chapter 5

1 Barry Singer and Victor A. Benassi, "Occult Beliefs," American Scientist, 69, 1986:49–55.

2 I presented a performance piece that involved story-telling and ceremonial garments that I made.

3 As remarked in chapter 1, when discussing my questionnaire results I occasionally compare them to those of the Kirkpatrick's San Diego group. Both studies relied on self-administered questionnaires, although the San Diego group distributed theirs by mail while I personally administered all but a few of mine. Fifty-three percent of the Kirkpatrick's subjects came from the western United States. From this different geographic perspectives, we can augment and compare my findings mostly from eastern states.

I obtained all comparative statistics describing the national population from the United States Bureau of Census, Statistical Abstract of the United States, 1988, unless otherwise indicated.

All percentages are rounded to the nearest whole or 1/10 percentage point and may not, therefore, total one hundred percent. For greater simplicity I use whole percentages in the text wherever feasible. Where percentages refer only to that portion of the total population that answered a specific question (valid percent), the number of individuals who did not respond is provided in a footnote. Comparisons are made among groups of different sizes: about one hundred and fifty informants for Kirkpatrick, one hundred and eighty-nine in my study, and thousands treated in national statistics. These comparisons are, therefore, only approximate.

4 Thirty-three people did not respond to the question regarding residence.

5 Nine subjects did not respond to the question.

6 Two people did not respond.

7 Judging by the superficial physical appearance of respondents who described themselves as androgenous, I assume they intended to express their rejection of traditional sex roles, rather than biological androgyny.

8 Eleven people did not respond.

9 Forty-six people did not respond.

10 A few Neopagans are able to reconcile Christianity with nature worship.

11 R. R. Marett is quoted by Clyde Kluckholn as a personal communication (n.d.) in Lessa, William and Evon Z. Vogt (1979, v).

12 Based on Current Population Survey.

13 For the most part, I use the terms provided by the informants in their responses to name categories of employment.

14 Thirty-seven subjects did not respond.

15 Personal communication, June 1986.

16 Personal communication, November 1993.

17 Letter November 18, 1993. Hephaestus is the Greek god of the forge. Ken-Ra spoke of his connection with this deity when we first spoke in 1986.

18 Thirty-eight people did not respond.

19 Neopagans who think of themselves as shamans include visionary trance work in their religious rituals, and animal spirits are significant in their supernatural worlds. Gaining power by surviving suffering is a significant theme as well.

20 Dianic witches think of Diana as their supreme goddess, relying on the idea expressed in the Italian La Vecchia tradition described by Leland (1899) that Diana sent her daughter, Aradia, to teach magic to mortals.

21 See chapter 2.

22 The essay is impaired by treating only of males, but it is enlightening nonetheless.

23 In the psychology of Carl Jung the anima is the female inner-personality of a man.

Chapter 6

1 Janet Johnson believes that the inclusion of texts written in the "Demotic" phase of the Egyptian language indicates that elements of earlier Egyptian culture are present (Hans Dieter Betz, 1986, lv-lviii).

2 Hermes Trismegistus is a composite of the Egyptian deity, Thoth and the Greek Hermes. Each was considered the messenger between gods and humans, guardian of the underworld, the embodiment of the moon, and master of magic (Garth Fowden 1986).

3 One of the Arab sources is the Picatrix of Pseudo-Madjriti (d. ca. 1004-7) that provides advice for making talismans (objects marked with magical signs to confer supernatural power) and addressing prayers to the personified planets. In the other, De radii, the author, al-Kindi (d. ca. 873), explained the theory that stars and elements communicate their unique natures to the surrounding world by means of rays, in Ioan Couliano (1984).

4 Although not much is known for certain, the papyri probably came from a single source, a tomb or temple library (Betz, 1986).

5 In these mystery cults initiates experienced ineffable religious truths in secret rites.

6 "Hermes Trismegistus to Tat on the Common Intellect," Corpus Hermeticum XII, (Paris, 1945 and 1954), Vol. I-XVIII, Asclepius and diverse fragments, text by A. D. Nock, Trans. A. J. Festugière. Vol. III fragments extracted from Stobèe, I-XXII, text and trans. by A. J. Festugière, Vol. I, 180-181; Marcilio Ficino, Opera omnia, 2 vol., (Bâle, 1576, 1854), quoted in Frances Yates (1964, 33-34).

7 Author unknown

8 For my review of Renaissance magic I rely predominantly on Ioan P. Couliano (1984); D. P Walker (1958); and Frances Yates (1964).

9 Cabala is a religious philosophy based on an esoteric interpretation of the Hebrew scriptures.

¹⁰ Isaac Casaubon, *De rebus sacris et eclesiasticis exercitationes XVI. Ad Cardinalis Baronii prolegomena in Annales*, in Yates (1964).
¹¹ Orpheus was a poet believed to have founded a mystery religion in the sixth century B.C.E. He is believed to have enchanted humans, beasts, and nature with his songs. Hermetic magicians used surviving texts attributed to his authorship.
¹² This charm is from a magical handbook (Betz 1986, 29).
¹³ I maintain the masculine pronoun throughout the discussion of Renaissance magic because the scholars of the period did not include women in their conception of Renaissance man or man as magus. It is likely that women read the treatises and perhaps wrote some, and may have been devotées of Renaissance philosophy or practitioners of magic. Recognition of this has not been transmitted to us by the writers of the time, however.
¹⁴ *De vita coelitus comparanda, III, Opera omnia* (Basel edition, 1576, 2 vols.) in the *Monumenta politica et philosophica rariora*, series I, 535, quoted in Couliano (1984, 28).
¹⁵ *Commentarium in Convivium Platonis de amore, oratio VI*, cap. 10 (Ficino, 1348), in Yates (1964).
¹⁶ Ficino, *Amore*, VI, 10, *Sopra lo amore o ver' Convito di Platone*, Giorgio Ottaviano (ed.), (Milan 1973, 106), in Couliano (1984, 87).
¹⁷ Giordano Bruno, *Theses de Magia*, XV, vol. III, 466, quoted in Couliano (1984, 91).
¹⁸ According to Plato, whose voice is recognizable and prominent in the Hermetica, the world has a preexistent prototype: the intellectual (noetic) world. The reasoning part of the human soul contains the intelligential model of creation (Couliano 1984).
¹⁹ Bruno was probably inspired by "Egyptian Reflection of the Universe in the Mind," which stated that unless you make yourself equal to God, you cannot understand God. *Corpus Hermeticum* XI, chapter II, quoted in Yates (1964, 198).
²⁰ Bruno, *Theses de Magia* XV, Vol. III, 466 as cited in Couliano (1984, 91).
²¹ Bruno, *Sigillus sigillorum*, II, 2:193 as cited in Couliano (1984).
²² Unlike discourse, which presents its meaning successively, artistic symbolism resorts to images to make a holistic, simultaneous, and integral presentation (Suzanne Langer 1953).
²³ Charles Morgan, "The Nature of Dramatic Illusion," in Langer (1953, 63–64).
²⁴ D. P. Walker (1958, 207) believes that this spell, which was found among Campanella's private papers, was probably actually performed for the benefit of Pope Urban. By "astrologically distilled liquors," I believe he meant that they were distilled during the influence of planets deemed auspicious for the purpose.
²⁵ Religious millenialism is based on the expectation that a thousand-year period (millenium) of holiness, joy, serenity, prosperity, and justice would replace a present period of suffering.
²⁶ Giordano Bruno, *De vinculis*, III, 654, quoted in Couliano (1984).
²⁷ Giordano Bruno, *De gli Eroici furore Dialoghi italiani, con note da, Giovanni Gentile, terza edizione a cura di Giovanni Aquilecchia*, Florence, 1957 (one vol.), pt. II, dial. 5, 1197; L. Williams, *The Heroic Enthusiasts*, (English trans. of Bruno's *eroici furori*), London, 1887–9, II, 114, in Yates (1964, 287).
²⁸ Bruno, *Des fureurs héroïques*, ed. and trans. Paul-Henri Michel. *Les Belles Lettres* (Paris: 1954, I, 4–11), as cited in Couliano (1984, 352).
²⁹ Henry Cornelius Agrippa, *De occulta philosophia, Opera*, "Per Beringos fratres, Lugduni," s.d., Vol. III, 49, as cited in Yates (1964).
³⁰ Giordano Bruno, *De gli Eroici furore*, as cited in Yates (1964, 287).
³¹ *Corpus Hermeticum* (see above, n. 6).

³² Yates (1964, 324) believed Bruno used these symbols in alluding to the secret sect he recommended.

³³ These discussions are presented predominantly in regard to the Hermetic *Asclepius* in his *Articuli adversus mathematicos* and "The Thirty Statues." The latter belongs in a group of Bruno's works, *De umbris idearum*. Both are contained in *Opere latine*, ed. F. Fiorentino, V. Imbriani, C. M. Tallarigo, F. Tocco, H. Vitelli, Naples and Florence, 1879–91 (3 vols. in eight parts). Facsimile reprint in 1962 (Friedrich Fromman Verlag Gunther Hoolzboorg, Stuttgart-Bad Cannstatt), as cited in Yates (1964).

³⁴ Gardner claimed that the charge of the goddess came to him through the Book of Shadows that he acquired from Old Dorothy's coven. Doreen Valiente claimed to have composed it from inspirations gained from the writings of Crowley (*The Book of the Law*, the chapter devoted to the Egyptian goddess, Nuit.) It seems likely to have derived ultimately from the devotional literature associated with a cult of Isis that was contemporary with the writing of the Hermetic literature. The Greco-Egyptian Isis was the product of fusion of the Egyptian Isis with Greek goddesses including Demeter and Aphrodite. One inscription recovered from Memphis contains a similar declaration in the first person: "I am Isis, the ruler of all land . . . I separated earth from heaven. I showed the stars their paths. I ordered the course of the sun and the moon." The preamble to Gardner's charge claims the goddess was called by many names including Aphrodite and Isis and other goddesses including some Celtic names. In like fashion, a hymn to Isis that was possibly written in the first century, praised her as an omnipotent, all-embracing goddess whom the whole world adores under a myriad of different names. Like Diana, Isis promised to teach the people magic (Fowden 1986, 45–51).

³⁵ Giordano Bruno seems to have seen it as a more impersonal force, like gravity, and quite separate from affection (Couliano 1984).

³⁶ Giordano Bruno, *De gli Eroici furori*, (see above n. 27.).

³⁷ Giordano Bruno, in *Opere latine* (see n. 33) Vol. II(i), 179 ff.

³⁸ Ibid. Bruno was probably accusing the Christians of abusing magic (laws of eros) to manipulate the masses into turning against one another, whereas Bruno used the same magic to inspire pacifism.

³⁹ Legends of the Burning Times tell that witches made their pentacle (inscribed plate) of wax so that they could be destroyed in the fire should anyone discover them and try to use the magical tool as evidence against them (numerous personal communications).

⁴⁰ Percy Bysshe Shelley, "The Witch of Atlas" in *The Complete Poetical Works of Percy Bysshe Shelley*, George Edward Woodberry (ed.), (Cambridge, MA: The Riverside Press/Houghton Mifflin, 1901), 273, 277.

⁴¹ One of Bruno's enemies, Mocinego, declared to the Inquisition that Bruno "revealed a plan of founding a new sect under the name of philosophy." Mocenigo, *Documenti della vita di Giordano Bruno, a cura di Vincenzo Spampanato*, (Florence: 1933), quoted in Yates (1964, n. 5, 312). Other informers claimed that the sect was called "Giordanisti," Angelo Mercati, *Il sommario del processo di Giordano Bruno, (Citta del Vatincano: 1942), 61; cf. in Yates (1964, n. 6, 312).

⁴² The legend of the garter is recounted by Katherine Kurtz (1983).

⁴³ Geomancy is a system of divination from signs obtained from the earth. Neopagans practice it today by interpreting lines and dots randomly drawn on the ground or on paper.

[44] For further research into the nature of the Hermetic works as documents for Pagan Gnosticism in the early centuries C.E., the reader is referred to A. J. Festugière, *La Revelation d'Hermes Trismegiste*, Paris: 1950-4 (four vol.), in which the author reconstructs the social and religious atmosphere of that period. Other useful works are: C. H. Dodd, *The Bible and the Greeks*, (London: 1935); Fowden (1986); J. R. McL. Wilson, *The Gnostic Problem*, (London: 1958).

[45] A. J. Festugière, *La Revelation d'Hermes Trismegiste*, *Ibid*. Vol. I:iff.

[46] Francis Bacon, "Novum Organon," Vol. 4:109, 62-63, 97; and "Of the Dignity and Advancement in Learning," Vol. 4:298, both cited in J. Spedding, R. L. Ellis and D. N. Heath (eds.), *The Works of Francis Bacon*, 7 Vols., vol. 4 (London: 1858-61; reprinted Friedrich Frommann Verlag, 1963), 298 as cited in Yates (1979).

Chapter 7

[1] These principles are published on the back cover of *The Kybalion: A Study of the Hermetic Philosophy of Ancient Egypt and Greece* (Georgia: Tri-State Press, 1908, 1988).

[2] Aleister Crowley, a British magician began the convention of adding a "k" to magic to distinguish it from stage magic that is strictly illusion.

[3] The word *energy* derives from the Greek *energes, energos*, meaning active, at work: *en-*, at, plus *ergon*, work. These, in turn, derive from the Indo-European root *werg-*, meaning to do. The Old English, old High German, and Greek versions of the root all mean work as well (*American Heritage Dictionary*, 1993, s.v.)

[4] The only other exception is Jeanne Favret-Saada's (1980, 114) description of the effect of bewitchment she observed in a French mountain region as the power of magical force (powerful language) to mobilize vital force. Transmission of vital force by touch gives one "a good dose of magic electric shock."

[5] My piece of the web ended up in the lining of a banner I made for a collective art project for world peace.

[6] Francis Hutchinson, *Historical Essays Concerning Witchcraft*, 1718, vii.

[7] Personal communication, 1984 and 1989. Susun is a high priestess of Dianic Wicca and founder of the Wise Woman Center in Vermont where she teaches herbalism and women's spirituality. She has published books on her approach to herbal healing. (See Weed 1989.)

[8] Merlin Stone, Opening Ceremonies of the New York Goddess Gathering, 1989.

[9] The wooden wand, the tool used to focus the magician's will, was hidden as a broom handle by persecuted witches, the new witches say.

[10] Lyra, a nurse and magical healer. Personal communication at Rites of Spring 1985.

[11] However, only 57 percent of them could do so themselves. Another 47 percent believed it is possible to manipulate auras, but only 37 percent believed they were capable of doing so.

[12] The communication with plants to this effect is described in chapter 8, but here we should note that the witches believe one need only stand in the presence of living trees, animals, and plants to restore one's own energy from their resources.

Chapter 8

[1] In her revised edition of *Drawing Down the Moon* (1986), Margot Adler wrote that in the seven years since the original publication of her book festivals have completely changed the face of the Neopagan movement.

2 Often the size of a gathering is limited more by the size of available camping accommodations than popularity.
3 Kirlian photography captures the energy fields surrounding plants and animals.
4 Both of Starhawk's first books are in their second edition and have been translated into German.
5 Personal communication, Sally Cook, 1985.
6 The social dynamics operative in sacred space (*liminality*) will be discussed in the following chapter.
7 "Ms. Manners' Official Guide to Etiquette and All-Around Appropriate Behavior at Pagan Gatherings," was distributed at the registration desk. It included advice for appropriate behavior at rituals ("Don't touch other peoples' ritual tools"; "Don't throw cigarette butts in the ritual fire"; and such things). Advice about sex included the following: "Among Pagans, nudity is not an invitation to have sex"; "If you have a sexually transmitted disease, please be responsible and discuss this with your partner" (free condoms were provided).
8 This ritual is described elsewhere by Neopagan priestess, Oz, in "An Insider's Look at Pagan Festivals" in *Witchcraft Today: The Modern Craft Movement*, Charles S. Clifton (ed.), (St. Paul: Llewellyn Publications, 1992).
9 Lyrics of "Ain't No Mountain High Enough" by Nicholas Ashford and Valarie Simpson, © 1967, reprinted by permission of Jobete Music Company, Inc.
10 See chapter 5 for a discussion of the ritual of drawing down the moon.
11 Lyrics of "Ain't No Mountain High Enough" by Nicholas Ashford and Valarie Simpson, © 1967, reprinted by permission of Jobete Music Company, Inc.
12 *Ibid.*
13 Oz, whom I numbered among the BNPs above, told me that she danced with the men to embody the god (personal communication, 1994).

Chapter 9

1 Michael Harner has written about a technique involving drumming at specific rates to induce "S.S.C." (Shamanic State of Consciousness) in *The Way of the Shaman: A Guide to Power and Healing* (New York: 1982). His Center for Shamanic Studies publishes a glossy magazine, *The Shaman's Drum*, and offers workshops.
2 Jeff Rosenbaum (1987).
3 Victor Turner used the term *liminoid* to describe the displacement of the potency of liminality from the domain of communal rites into the more individualistic and optional genres of the arts and leisure activities associated with the postindustrial societies. For a discussion of this concept see Turner (1982, 32–33).
4 The Andromeda ritual was presented by Dahna and Sior of Tennessee at Spiral Gathering in 1986.
5 By this term Bellah means the tradition of government by representation rather than the specific legacy of the Republican political party.
6 Jeff Rosenbaum (1987).

Chapter 10

1 Although it is a controversial point, Neopagans generally believe it is unethical to ask for payment for the performance of any magical work.
2 Allopathic medicine is a term denoting official or professional medicine.
3 Iatrogenesis is a process of creating illness while attempting to alleviate it.

4 Robert J. Blendon, ScD. (1989, 2–10) reported some of the findings of the survey initiated by *HMQ* and conducted by Louis Harris and Associates, in conjunction with the Harvard School of Public Health in late 1988.

5 The *Time/CNN* poll was conducted by Yankelovich, Clancy, and Schulman, and it was discussed by Horowitz and Lafferty (1991, 68).

6 In guided imagery, the therapist helps the patient to imagine the desired healing with the expectation that the body's natural healing processes—including those of the immune system—will respond by accomplishing the envisioned healing. The Neopagans call the same mental states visionary trances, and they use them to effect all manner of psychic transformations, most of which would be described as healing.

7 Nineteen people did not respond.

8 Twelve people did not respond.

9 Sixty-two percent of these indicated that they make one or two visits per year. Fifty-nine percent indicated that they had some psychotherapy (fifteen people did not respond).

Seventy-four percent indicated that they would rely more on *non*professional medicine if it were available and if medical insurance covered it (9 percent did not respond); 73 percent of my respondents had medical insurance; 25 percent belonged to a health maintenance group (5 percent did not respond).

10 Nine people did not respond.

11 Seventy-seven percent of the Neopagans responded that they drink alcohol, only 16 percent do so often, another 61 percent sometimes (twelve people did not respond). Fifty-nine percent of the general population indicated that they were users of alcohol between 1974 and 1985. It is difficult to infer from this any comparison of the relative quantity or frequency of alcohol consumption.

Seventy percent of the Neopagans indicated that they are nonsmokers (twelve people did not respond); in the larger population, 68 percent of those over the age of eighteen reported that they do not smoke tobacco.

12 Eight people did not respond.

13 Statistics on the use of tobacco, alcohol and marijuana by the national population are from the U.S. National Institute on Drug Abuse, *Main Findings from the 1985 National Household Survey on Drug Abuse.*

14 This is, incidentally, an impressive example of perseverance in a problem of group dynamics. It is a strong group that could survive such a confrontation intact.

15 To my knowledge, no forces or beings are thought to keep an account of deeds and their rewards and punishments.

16 Fifteen people did not respond.

17 The reader is referred to Paul Starr's sociological and historical study, *The Social Transformation of American Medicine* (1982), for a discussion of the unusual process by which physicians established and protected their exalted position in American society.

18 The third eye is a space at the low center of the forehead where the center of psychic vision is considered to reside. This idea was adopted from Eastern spirituality.

Chapter 11

1 Twenty-nine people did not respond.

2 Bach flower remedies are made by allowing the essence of flowers to infuse water.

Theoretically the healing properties of the flowers are ingested by drinking a few drops of the solution.

3 Polarity therapy involves manual manipulation of the electomagnetic energy field of the body.

4 Ten people did not respond.

5 Ten people did not respond.

6 Fourteen people did not respond.

7 An anonymous letter.

8 *Daughters of Eve*, (London: Aquarian Press, HarperCollins, 1993).

9 There is a difference between learning magic by reading a book and by personal instruction. Those of us who were instructed by Dolores observed gestures and such things as timing and the arrangement of the space that are not conveyed in writing.

10 Personal communication, anonymous witch, 1985.

11 Personal communication 1987.

12 Personal communication, 1987.

13 Illness is a subjective experience of discomfort that is not necessarily accompanied by the objective biophysiological evidence of disease.

14 However, by the next morning Selena's husband, Dennis, experienced relief of the pain in the region of his jaw that the group had tried to heal.

Chapter 12

1 Palingenesis is an experience in which the soul of one being may move into or merge with that of another.

2 Aldous Huxley, *The Doors of Perception*, (London and New York: 1954), 17.

3 I think the concept of the psycho-mental complex corresponds to the interpretive grille (a person's or social unit's prescribed process of thinking and feeling) that in more complex societies changes over time in response to political and social pressures (see chapter 6).

4 Andras said the Mcphersons showed him photographs and portions of letters that corroborated to his satisfaction their belief that the tradition of witchcraft had existed in that family at least as long ago as the sixteenth century (personal communication 1994).

5 The Mcphersons felt that to make a religion of the numinous forces they worked with would be "a self-serving hedge against the fear of the unknown that belittles the powers inherent in the universe" (personal communication, Andras Corban Arthen, 1994).

6 Athanor is an alchemical term for a vessel in which diverse elements are blended.

7 I believe that spirits may be described as personifications of truths, worldviews, theories, or ways of thinking and feeling.

8 For example, shamans may be given an additional bone or an iron skeleton (Siberia) or be filled with light (Tierra del Fuego) or with quartz crystals (Australia).

Chapter 13

1 *Our Pagan Times* is the newsletter of the Neopagan group, New Moon, New York. Nan's story appeared in the December 1993 issue, Vol. 3, No. 12.

2 Peter Plumley, "Jonesboro Part II: The Rileys Take Manhattan," *Our Pagan Times*, December 1993, Vol. 3, No. 12:4–5; and Gerrie Ortaz, "Lady Liberty League Report," *Circle Network News*, Spring 1994, Issue 51:7.

³ By immanence Starhawk (1982, 185) means that all of the natural world, including people and all species of plants, animals and minerals are infused with a divine force, "the world and everything in it is alive, dynamic, interdependent, interacting, and infused with moving energies; a living being, a weaving dance."

⁴ Leigh Ann Hussey, "Burning Times," from the audio cassette, Homebrew, Berkeley, CA: 1988.

⁵ I rely for most of my data in this section on Frances Yates (1972), and all references, unless otherwise noted, are to this source.

⁶ The Palatinate was a state of the Holy Roman Empire ruled by a count (the Elector Palatine). It consisted of two territories that are presently known as Bavaria and Rhineland-Palatinate (Yates 1972).

⁷ For my discussion of American radical thought I rely on the historical works of Howard Kerr and Charles R. Crow (1983); and most prominently, Laurence Veysey (1973).

⁸ I encountered one group of blacks, The Church of the Universal Forces of Columbus, Ohio, who think of themselves as part of the Neopagan movement. Lady Isis, leader of that group, is a priestess of Voudon. I attended the "Pantheistic Gathering" they sponsored in 1985. It brought together an assortment of individuals I had not encountered at other gatherings, including Christian faith healers and many Voudon practitioners. All of the group rituals were derived from the Voudon or Santeria religions. Less than half of the fifty people who attended were black.

⁹ Alan Cowell, "Pope Condemns 'Nature Worship' by Some Feminist U.S. Catholics." New York Times, July 3, 1993.

¹⁰ Personal communication, letter from Inanna Arthen, October 24, 1989.

¹¹ Inanna Arthen, 1989.

¹² Inanna Arthen 1989.

¹³ Inanna Arthen, 1989.

Chapter 14

¹ However, Selena described a ceremony that resembled an exorcism, in which she escorted the remnants of the spirit of a young man who committed suicide out of the realm of the living.

² When a couple is handfasted their hands are temporarily tied with cords. Separation may be symbolized by untying the same cords. One couple shattered a ceramic pot at the start of their handfasting to dissolve former unions.

³ Fifty people did not respond.

⁴ Feminist scholar, Mary Daly, valorized these terms by selectively reviving parts of their etymological heritages. Crone may be interpreted to mean "the long-lasting ones," who like crows [old crows] make oracular utterances. Because "hag" derives from the Greek hagios, meaning holy, women may be honored by the epithet. GYN/Ecology; Metaphysics of Radical Feminism, (Boston: Beacon Press, 1978), 14–16.

⁵ Buck Rhodes, "Journeying to Death," La Caldera Communique, October 1992, Issue 2, 3.

⁶ Oz, personal communication, August 1993.

⁷ The Latin affinis, meaning "neighboring, allied by marriage," is the justification for this use. The American Heritage Dictionary of the English Language, s.v., (Boston: Houghton Mifflin, 1981). This meaning derives from the Old French,

meaning closely related. *The American Heritage Dictionary of the English Language*, s.v., (Boston: Houghton Mifflin, 1981).

8 Although about a half to two-thirds of the congregation at any particular gathering return nearly every year—constituting a core group—there are many others who attend only occasionally. Consequently, the congregation at each gathering is unique.

9 Judy Harrow,"On Being a High Priestess," *The Crone Papers*, March 1990, Vol. IV, No. 2:8–11.

10 This is an abridged version of Debbie Light's invocation.

11 Much of this discussion comes from an article, "Pagan Clergy" in *Fireheart*, No. 7, 1993. Along with Andras, others contributors were Sam Webster, an experienced ceremonialist and teacher who holds a Master of Divinity Degree; Judy Harrow; Isaac Bonewits, the originator and administrator of the Ár nDraiocht Féin, order of Neopagan Druids; and Oriethyia, a poet who favors an inventive (eclectic) approach to the craft.

Chapter 15

1 "Pagan Clergy, Part II," *Fireheart*, No. 7, 1993.

2 Ogaea, "Consistency and Money in the Craft," *The Crone Papers*, Vol. II, No. 6:8.

3 "Money as an Exchange of Energy," *The Crone Papers*, 1988, Vol. II, No. 5:12.

4 Ken-Ra, letter of congratulation to recipients of the magical tools he makes and presents as gifts (1994).

5 "Pagan Clergy, Part II," *Fireheart*, No. 7, 1993.

6 The admission fee for the Rites of Spring gathering, which lasts six days, is about $250 for cabin accommodations, all meals and access to all events. This is characteristic of most gatherings.

7 "Pagan Clergy, Part II," *Fireheart*, No. 7, 1993.

8 "Pagan Clergy, Part II," *Fireheart*, No. 7, 1993.

9 "Pagan Clergy, Part II," *Fireheart*, No. 7, 1993.

10 "Pagan Clergy, Part II," *Fireheart*, No. 7, 1993.

11 "Pagan Clergy, Part II," *Fireheart*, No. 7, 1993:69.

12 Judy Harrow, "Pagan Clergy, Part II," *Fireheart*, No. 7, 1993.

13 "Pagan Clergy, Part II," *Fireheart*, No. 7, 1993.

Bibliography

Adler, Margot. 1986. *Drawing Down the Moon: The Resurgence of Paganism in America.* Boston: Beacon Press (originally 1979).

Alexander, Nan. 1993. Untitled article. *Our Pagan Times.* December, Vol. 3, No. 12.

An Doile, Murtagh Adhamh. 1984. "Shamanic Initiation and Neopaganism." *Circle Network News,* Winter, Vol. 6, No. 4. Mt. Horeb, WI.

Anderson, Robert M. 1979. *Vision of the Disinherited: The Making of American Pentecostalism.* London: Oxford University Press.

Anodea, Judith. 1984. "Shamanism and Faerie: Pressing Through the Portal." *Circle Network News,* Winter, Vol. 6, No. 4. Mt. Horeb, WI.

Arthen, Andras Corban. 1988. "From Roots to Dreams: Pagan Festivals and the Quest for Community." *Fire Heart, a Journal of Magick and Spiritual Transformation,* Spring: 18–23.

Ashcroft-Nowicki, Dolores. 1993. *Daughters of Eve.* Hammersmith London: Aquarian Press, HarperCollins.

Bachofen, Jacob J. 1861. *The Mothers, Myth, Religion and Mother Right: Selected Writings.* (Trans. by Ralph Manheim.) London: Routledge & Kegan Paul, 1967.

Bednarowski, Mary Farrell. 1983. "Women in Occult America." In *The Occult in America: New Historical Perspectives.* Howard Kerr and Charles L. Crow (eds.). Chicago: University of Illinois Press, 177–195.

Bell, H. Indris. 1948. *Egypt from Alexander the Great to the Arab Conquest.* London: Oxford University Press.

Bell, Jessie Wicker. 1974. *The Grimoire of Lady Sheba.* St. Paul, MN: Llewellyn Press.

Bellah, Robert N., Richard Madsen, et al. 1985. *Habits of the Heart: Individualism and Commitment in American Life.* Berkeley: University of California Press.

Berman, Morris. 1981. *The Reenchantment of the World.* Ithaca: Cornell University Press. Reprint. New York: Bantam Books, 1984.

Betz, Hans Dieter (ed.). 1986. *The Greek Magical Papyri in Translation.* Vol. I: Texts. Chicago: University of Chicago Press.

Blendon, Robert J. 1989. "Three Systems: A Comparative Study." *Health Management Quarterly,* First Quarter Vol. XI, No. 1:2–10.

Bohannan, Paul. 1992. *We the Alien.* Prospect Heights, IL: Waveland Press.

Bonewits, P.E.I. 1971. *Real Magic: An Introductory Treatise on the Basic Principles of Yellow Magic.* Berkeley: Creative Arts Book Company.

Boyer, Paul and Stephen Nissenbaum. 1974. *Salem Possessed.* Cambridge: Harvard University Press.

Brennan, Noel-Anne. 1984. "Shamanism: A New Old Path." *Circle Network News* Winter, Vol. 6, No. 4. Mt. Horeb, WI.

Briffault, Robert. 1927. *The Mothers: The Matriarchal Theory of Social Origins.* New York: Macmillan.

Briggs, K. M. 1982. *Pale Hecate's Team: An Examination of the Beliefs of Witchcraft and Magic among Shakespeare's Contemporaries and His Immediate Successors.* New York: The Humanities Press.

Brody, Howard. 1973. "The Systems View of Man: Implications for Medicine, Science and Ethics." *Perspectives in Biology and Medicine,* Autumn 1983. Chicago: University of Chicago Press.

Bureau of the Census 1988. *1987 Statistical Abstract of the United States* (108th edition). Washington, D.C.

Burr, George Lincoln. 1889–1890. "The Literature of Witchcraft." *American Historical Association Papers* IV:3:235–266.

Butler, Jon. 1979. "Magic, Astrology and the Early American Religious Heritage, 1600–1760." *The American Historical Review,* Vol. 84:173–187.

Byloff, Fritz. 1929. *Volkskundliches,* 40, 30–31. Quoted in Horsley, 1979a.

––––––. 1934. *Hexenglaube, and Hexenverfolgung, in den osterreichischen Alpenlandern.* Quoted in Horsley, 1979a.

Campbell, Joseph. 1959. *The Masks of God: Primitive Mythology,* rev. ed., New York: Penguin Books, 1969.

Cassell, Eric. 1976. *The Healer's Art: A New Approach to the Doctor-Patient Relationship.* New York: J. Lippincott.

Casteneda, Carlos. 1968. *The Teachings of Don Juan: A Yaqui Way of Knowledge.* Berkeley & Los Angeles: University of California Press.

Cochrane, Glenn. 1970. *Big Men and Cargo Cults.* New York: Oxford University Press.

Cohn, Norman. 1975. *Europe's Inner Demons: An Enquiry Inspired by the Great Witch-hunt.* London and New York: Basic Books.

Corcoran, John X.W.P. 1984. "Celtic Mythology." *New Larousse Encyclopedia of Mythology,* (Introduction by Robert Graves. Trans. by Richard Aldington and Delano Ames, and revised by a panel of editorial advisors from the *Larousse Mythologie Generale,* edited by Felix Guirand, 18th impression.) London: The Hamlym Publishing Group.

Cornett, Larry. 1987. "Magick: Will Applied in a Quantum Universe." *Aurora Borealis,* Vol. II:1:3, January, Canada.

Cotta, John. 1968. *A Trial of Witchcraft.* New York: Da Capo Press.

Couliano, Ioan. 1984. *Eros and Magic in the Renaissance.* (Trans. Margaret Cook.) Chicago: University of Chicago Press. (reissued 1987).

Coulton, George G. 1924. *The Death Penalty for Heresy from 1184 to 1921 A.D.* London.

Crawford, Jane. 1963. "Evidences for Witchcraft in Anglo-Saxon England." *Medium Aevum* 32:2:111–112.

Crowley, Aleister. 1926. *The Book of the Law (Liber al vel Legis)*. Pasadena, CA: Church of Thelema.

Delcambre, Étienne. 1951. *La Concept de la sorcellerie dans le duché de Lorraine au XVIe et XVIIe siècle*. Quoted in Horsley, 1979a.

Delumeau, Jean. 1977. *Catholicism between Luther and Voltaire*. London: Burns & Oates.

Demos, John 1982. *Entertaining Satan*. New York: Oxford University Press.

de Tocqueville, Alexis. 1969. *Democracy in America*. (Trans. by George Lawrence), J. P. Mayer (ed.). New York: Doubleday, Anchor Books.

Diethelm, Oskar. 1970. "The Medical Teaching of Demonology in the 17th and 18th Centuries." *Journal of the History of the Behavioral Sciences* 6:3–15.

Dixon, Roland B. 1908. *Some Aspects of the American Shaman*, JAFL, XXI (Jan.–March):1–12.

Douglas, Mary. 1970. *Witchcraft Confessions and Accusations*. London: Tavistock Publications.

Durkheim, Émile 1915. *The Elementary Forms of the Religious Life*. (Trans. by J. W. Swain.) New York: Free Press, 1965.

Easlea, Brian. 1980. *Witch Hunting, Magic and the New Philosophy: An Introduction to Debates of the Scientific Revolution 1450–1750*. New Jersey: Humanities Press.

Ehrenreich, Barbara and Deirdre English. 1973. *Witches, Midwives, and Nurses: A History of Women Healers*. Glass Mountain Pamphlet No. 1. New York: The Feminist Press.

Eliade, Mircea. 1964. *Shamanism: Archaic Techniques of Ecstasy*. (Revised and enlarged edition translated by Willard Trask. Bollingen Series LXXVI, second printing.) Princeton: Princeton University Press, 1974.

———. 1975. "Some Observations on European Witchcraft." *History of Religions* 14:149–72.

———. 1976. *Occultism, Witchcraft and Cultural Fashion: Essays in Comparative Religion*. Chicago: The University of Chicago Press.

Ellwood, Robert Jr. 1973. *Religious and Spiritual Groups in Modern America*. Englewood Cliffs, NJ: Prentice Hall.

Engels, Frederick. 1891. *The Origin of the Family, Private Property, and the State*, 4th ed. Moscow: Foreign Languages Publishing House.

Eran. 1986. "The Physics of Magik." *Converging Paths: Newsletter of the Georgian Tradition*. Fall Equinox, Vol. 1, Bakersfield, CA.

Estes, Leland I. 1983. "The Medical Origins of the European Witch Craze: A Hypothesis." *The Journal of Social History* 17:271–284.

Evans-Pritchard, E.E. 1937. *Witchcraft, Oracles and Magic Among the Azande*. Oxford: Clarendon Press.

Farrar, Stewart. 1983. *What Witches Do: The Modern Coven Revealed*. Washington: Phoenix Publishing Company.

Favret-Saada. 1980. *Deadly Words: Witchcraft in the Bocage*. (Trans. by Catherine Cullen.) Cambridge: Cambridge University Press.

Febvre, Lucien. 1973. "Witchcraft: Nonsense or a Mental Revolution." In *A New Kind of History*. London: Routledge & Kegan Paul, 185–192.

Ferguson, Marilyn. 1980. *The Aquarian Conspiracy: Personal and Social Transformation in the 1980s*. Los Angeles: J. P. Tarcher.

Firth, Raymond. 1954. "Social Organization and Social Change." *Journal of the Royal Anthropological Institute* 84:21–20.

Flint, Valerie. 1991. *The Rise of Magic in Medieval Europe*. Princeton: Princeton University Press.

Fowden, Garth. 1986. *The Egyptian Hermes: An Historical Approach to the Late Pagan Mind*. Cambridge: Cambridge University Press.

Fox, Daniel M. 1985. "History and Health Policy." *Journal of Social History*. Pittsburgh: Carnegie-Mellon University.

Fox, Sanford. 1968. *Science and Justice*. Baltimore: The Johns Hopkins University Press.

Fox, Selena. 1984. "Shamanism: A New Old Path." *Circle Network News*, Winter, Vol. 6, No 4. Mt. Horeb, WI.

———. 1987. *Circle Guide to Pagan Resources*. Mt. Horeb, WI.

Frank, Jerome D. 1963. *Persuasion and Healing, a Comparative Study of Psychotherapy*. New York: Schocken Books.

Frazer, Sir James. 1907. *The Golden Bough*. London: Macmillan.

Frievalkyr, Bejornkin. 1993. "Never Again the Burnings." *Our Pagan Times*, (August) Vol. 3, No. 8:5,10.

Galbreath, Robert. 1983. "Explaining Modern Occultism" In *The Occult in America*, H. Kerr and C. Crow (eds.). Chicago: University of Chicago Press.

Gardner, Gerald. 1936. *Keris and Other Maylay Weapons*, B. Lumsden Milne (ed). Singapore: Progressive Publishing Company.

———. 1954. *Witchcraft Today*. London: Rider & Company. Reprint. New York: Magickal Childe, 1982.

———. 1959. *The Meaning of Witchcraft*. London: Aquarian Press.

Geertz, Clifford. 1973. *The Interpretation of Cultures: Selected Essays by Clifford Geertz*. New York: Basic Books.

Geertz, Hildred. 1975. "An Anthropology of Religion and Magic." *Journal of Interdisciplinary History* 6:83–87.

Ginzburg, Carlo. 1989. *Ecstasies Deciphering the Witches' Sabbath*. (Trans. by Raymond Rosenthal.) Turin: Guilo Enaudi Editore, 1991.

Gluckman, M. 1965. *Politics, Law and Ritual in Tribal Societies*. Oxford: Blackwell.

Godbeer, Richard. 1992. *The Devil's Dominion; Magic and Religion in Early New England*. Cambridge: Cambridge University Press.

Graves, Robert. 1948. *The White Goddess: A Historical Grammar of Poetic Myth*. New York: Farrar, Strauss, & Giroux, 1981.

Gray, William G. 1984. *Concepts of Qabalah, Sangreal Sodality Series*, Vol. 3. York Beach, ME: Samuel Weiser.

"The Great Goddess." 1982. *Heresies: A Feminist Publication on Art and Politics*, Vol. 2, No. 1, Issue 5, Revised Edition.

Haekel, Josef. 1958. "Kosmischer Baum und Pfahl." *Mythus und Kult der Stamme Nordwestamerikas*, WVM, VI, n.s.1:33–81. (Quoted in Mircea Eliade 1974.)

Halifax, Joan. 1979. *Shamanic Voices: A Survey of Visionary Narratives.* New York: E. P. Dutton.

Hansen, Chadwick. 1900. *Witchcraft at Salem.* New York: Braziller.

———. 1983. "Andover Witchcraft." In *The Occult in America: New Historical Perspectives,* Kerr, Howard and Charles L. Crow (eds.). Chicago: University of Chicago Press.

Hansen, Joseph. 1900. *Zauberwahn, Inquisition, und Hexenprozess in Mittelalter und die Entstehung der grossen Hexenverfolgung.* Aalen: Scientia Verlag, 1964.

Harding, Esther. 1971. *Women's Mysteries, Ancient and Modern.* New York: G. P. Putnam & Sons.

Heberling, Richard. 1915. *Zauberei und Hexenprozesse in Schleswig-Holstein-Lauenburg.* Zeitschrift der Gesellschaft für Schleswig-Hosteinische Geschichte, XLV:116–247, esp. 117–125.

Hill, W. W. 1944. "The Navaho Indians and the Ghost Dance of 1890." *American Anthropologist,* XLVI:523–27.

Hirst, Paul. 1982. "Witchcraft Today and Yesterday." *Economy and Society,* Vol. II, No. 4 (November):428–448.

Hoffman-Krayer. 1899. *Luzerner Aken zum Hexen-und Zauberwesen.* Schweizeisches Archiv für Volkskunde 1899, III:22–40, 80–122, 189–224, 291–329.

Horowitz and Lafferty. 1991. "Why New Age Medicine Is Catching On." *Time,* November 4:68.

Horsley, Richard A. 1979a. "Who Were the 'Witches'? The Social Roles of the Accused in the European Witch Trials." *Journal of Inter-Disciplinary History* 9:689–715.

———. 1979b. "Further Reflections on Witchcraft and European Folk Religions." *History of Religion* 19:71–95.

Howard, Mike. 1989. "The Hermetic Traditions," *The Cauldron: Pagan Journal of the Old Religion,* Autumn, Caemorgan Cottage, Cardigan Dyfed, Wales.

Hubert, Henri and Marcel Mauss. 1972. *A General Theory of Magic.* (Trans. by Robert Brain.) London & Boston: Routledge & Kegan Paul.

Huizinga, John. 1950. *Homo Ludens: A Study of the Play Element in Culture.* Roy Publishers. (Boston: Beacon Paperback ed., 1955.)

Hultkrantz, Ake. 1981. *Belief and Worship in Native North America.* Syracuse: Syracuse University Press.

James, King I. 1603. *Daemonologie.*

James, William. 1897. "What Psychical Research Has Accomplished." In *On Psychical Research,* Gardner Murphy, Robert D. Ballou, and William James (eds.). New York: Viking Compass.

Kehoe, Alice Beck. 1936. *The Ghost Dance: Ethnohistory and Revitalization.* New York: Holt, Rinehart and Winston.

Kelly, Aidan. 1991. *Crafting the Art of Magic, Book I.* St. Paul, MN: Llewellyn.

Kerr, Howard and Charles L. Crow (eds.). 1983. *The Occult in America: New Historical Perspectives.* Chicago: University of Illinois Press.

Kieckhefer, Richard. 1976. *European Witch Trials: Their Foundations in Popular and Learned Culture*. Berkeley and Los Angeles: Routledge & Kegan Paul.

Kirkpatrick, R. George. 1984. *Iron Mountain, a Journal of Magical Religion*. Florence, CO: Artemisia Press.

Kittredge, George Lyman. 1929. *Witchcraft in Old and New England*. New York: Russell & Russell, 1958.

Kluckhohn, Clyde. 1944. *Navaho Witchcraft*. Cambridge: Harvard University Press.

Konner, Melvin. 1991. "We Are Not the Enemy: A Medical Opinion." *Newsweek*, April 5, Vol. 41.

Kraemer, Heinrich and Jakob Sprenger. 1487-1489. *Malleus Maleficarum*. (Trans. by Rev. Montague Summers.) London: Pushkin Press, 1928.

Kreiger, Dolores. 1979. *The Therapeutic Touch: How to Use your Hands to Help Heal*. New Jersey: Prentice-Hall.

Kroeber, A. 1952. *The Nature of Culture*. Chicago: University of Chicago Press.

Kurtz, Katherine. 1983. *Lammas Night*. New York: Ballantine Books.

Langer, Susanne, K. 1953. *Feeling and Form: A Theory of Art Developed from Philosophy in a New Key*. London: Routledge & Kegan Paul.

Larner, Christina. 1981. *Enemies of God, the Witch-hunt in Scotland*. Baltimore: The Johns Hopkins University Press.

_____. 1984. *Witchcraft and Religion, the Politics of Popular Belief*. Alan Macfarlane (ed.). Oxford: Basil Blackwell.

Larsen, Stephen. 1976. *The Shaman's Doorway*. New York: Harper & Row.

Laszlo, E. 1972. *The Systems View of the World*. New York: Braziller.

Lea, Henry Charles. 1883. *The History of the Inquisition of the Middle Ages*. 3 vols. New York. Reprint. New York, 1955.

Leach, Edmund (ed.). 1967. *The Structural Study of Myth and Totemism*. London: Tavistock Publications.

Leland, Charles Godfrey. 1899. *Aradia, or the Gospel of the Witches*. New York: Hero Press, 1971.

Lenman, Bruce and Geoffrey Parker. 1980. "Judicial Revolution." Cited in Larner 1984, n.3.

Lessa, William A. and Evon Z. Vogt. 1979. *Reader in Comparative Religion: an Anthropological Approach*. 4th ed. New York: Harper & Row.

Lévi-Strauss, Claude. 1963. "The Sorcerer and His Magic." In *Structural Anthropology*. New York: Basic Books.

Lewis, I.M. 1971. *Ecstatic Religion: An Anthropological Study of Spirit Possession and Shamanism*. New York: Penguin.

Lex, Barbara. 1977. "Neurobiology of Ritual Trance." In *The Spectrum of Ritual: a Biogenetic Structural Analysis*, d'Aquili, Laughlin et al. (eds.). New York: Columbia University Press:117-151.

Light, Deborah L. 1985. Unpublished guided trance meditation.

Linton, Ralph. 1943. "Nativistic Movements." *American Anthropologist*, XLV:230-240.

Luhrmann, T.M. 1989. *Persuasions of the Witch's Craft*. Cambridge: Harvard University Press.

Macfarlane, Alan. 1970. *Witchcraft in Tudor and Stuart England, a Regional* and Comparative Study. London: Routledge & Kegan Paul. (Reissued by Waveland Press, 1991.)

Malinowski, Bronislaw. 1948. *Magic, Science and Religion and Other Essays.* Boston: Beacon Press. (Reissued by Waveland Press, 1992.)

Mandrou, Robert. n.d. *Magistrates et Sorcièrs en France au 17e siècle.* In Stone, Lawrence, "Disenchantment of the World." *The New York Review of Books,* December 12, 1971:17–25.

Maple, Eric. 1962. *The Dark World of the Witches.* London: Robert Hale Ltd.

Marks, Elaine and Isabella de Courtivron (eds.). 1981. *New French Feminisms: An Anthology.* New York: Shocken.

Marett, Robert R. 1909. *The Threshold of Religion.* London: Methuen, 1914.

Marwick, M. G. 1952. "The Social Context of Cewa Witch Beliefs." *Afika* 22, No. 2:120–135 and No. 3:215–233.

Marx, Jean. 1914. *L'Inquisition en Dauphine: Étude sur le développement et la répression de l'hérésie et de la sorcellerie du XIVe siècle au début du regne de François Ier.* Paris.

Mauss, Marcel. 1950. *A General Theory of Magic.* (Trans. R. Brain, from *Sociologie et Anthropology,* Paris 1950, originally "Esquisse d'une théorie générale de la magie" [with H. Hubert] in *L'Année Sociologique* VII [1902–3] 1904, 1–146.) London: Routledge & Kegan Paul, 1972.

May, Rollo. 1975. *The Courage to Create.* New York: W. W. Norton & Company.

Melton, J. Gordon. 1982. *Magic, Witchcraft and Paganism in America: A Bibliography.* (Compiled from the file of the Institute for the Study of American Religion) New York: Garland Publishing Company.

Michelet, Jules. 1862. *La Sorcière.* Paris: M. Didier.

Middleton, J. and Edward Winter, (eds.). 1963. "Witchcraft and Sorcery in Lugbara." *Witchcraft and Sorcery in East Africa.* London: Routledge & Kegan Paul; New York: Praeger.

Midelfort, H. D. 1971. "Witchcraft and Religion in Sixteenth Century Germany." *Archiv für Reformationsgeschichte* 62, 2:266–278.

––––––. 1972. *Witch Hunting in Southwestern Germany.* Stanford: Stanford University Press.

Monter, E. William. 1969. *European Witchcraft.* New York: Wiley.

––––––. 1971. "Patterns of Witchcraft in the Jura." *Journal of Social History,* IV (Fall):11–25.

––––––. 1976. *Witchcraft in France and Switzerland.* Ithaca: Cornell University Press.

Mooney, James. 1896. "The Ghost Dance Religion and the Sioux Outbreak of 1890," *14th Annual Report of the Bureau of American Ethnology, 1892–93,* Part 2. Washington, D.C.

Muchembled, R. 1978. *Culture Populaire et Culture des Élites.* Paris: Flammarion.

Murdock, George Peter. 1980. *Theories of Illness, a World Survey.* Pittsburgh: University of Pittsburgh Press.

Murray, Margaret. 1933. *The Witch-Cult in Western Europe.* London: Sampson, Low, Marston & Company.

Nachtigall, Hurst 1976. "The Cultural Historical Origin of Shamanism." In

Realm of the Extra-Human, Agents and Audiences, A. Bharati (ed.). Mouton Press.

Nadel, S. F. 1952. "Witchcraft in Four African Societies." *American Anthropologist* 54:18-29.

Needham, Rodney. 1978. *Primordial Characters*. Charlottesville: University of Virginia Press.

Neumann, Erich. 1959. *Art and the Creative Unconscious: Four Essays*. (Trans. Ralph Manheim.) Bollingen Series LXI, Princeton: Princeton University Press.

Notestein, Wallace. 1911. *A History of Witchcraft in England from 1558 to 1718*. Washington, D.C. Reprint. New York: Russell and Russell, 1968.

Obeyesekere, Gananath. 1981. *Medusa's Hair: An Essay on Personal Symbols and Religious Experience*. Chicago: University of Chicago Press.

Parsons, Talcott. 1951. *The Social System*. New York: Free Press, 1964.

Raschke, Carl A. 1980. *The Interruption of Eternity: Modern Gnosticism and the Origins of the New Religious Consciousness*. Chicago: Nelson-Hall.

Regardie, Israel. 1985. *The Middle Pillar: A Co-Relation of the Principles of Analytical Psychology and the Elementary Techniques of Magic*. St. Paul: Llewellyn Press.

Rose, Elliot. 1962. *A Razor for a Goat: A Discussion of Certain Problems in the History of Witchcraft and Diabolism*. Toronto: University of Toronto Press.

Rosenau, Pauline Marie. 1992. *Post-modernism and the Social Sciences: Insights, Inroads and Intrusions*. Princeton: Princeton University Press.

Rosenbaum, Jeff. 1987. "The Festival Movement." *Changeling Times*, No. 00011, June 1987, Ohio: The Association for Consciousness Exploration.

Roszak, Theodore. 1969. *The Making of a Counter Culture: Reflections on the Technocratic Society and Its Youthful Opposition*. New York: Anchor Books.

Runyon, C. R. 1978. No title. In *The Crystal Well*. Chula Vista, CA: Labrys Foundation, 22-23.

Russell, Jeffrey Burton. 1972. *Witchcraft in the Middle Ages*. Ithaca and London: Cornell University Press.

———. 1977. *The Devil: Perspectives on Evil from Antiquity to Primitive Christianity*. Ithaca: Cornell University Press.

Rubel, Arthur J. 1964. "The Epidemiology of a Folk Illness: Susto in Hispanic America." *Ethnology*, 3:268-283.

Schwarzwälder, Herbert 1958. *Die Formen des Zauber-und Hexenglaubens in Bremen und seiner weiteren Umgebung, vor allem wahrend des 16. und 17. Jahrhunderts*. Heimat und Volkstum: Bremer Beitrage zür niederdeutschen Volkskunde: 3-68. In Horsley 1979a.

Sebald, Hans. 1978. *Witchcraft: The Heritage of a Hersey*. New York: Elsevier.

———. 1980. "Franconian Witchcraft." *Anthropological Quarterly* 53:173-187.

Shekhinah Mountainwater. 1984. "Healing with Tarot." *Circle Network News*, Fall, Vol. 6, No. 3:13. Mt. Horeb, WI.

Shirokogoroff (Shirokogorov), Sergi M. 1935. *Psychomental Complex of the Tungus*. London: Kegan Paul, Trench, Trubner & Company.

Silverblatt, Irene. 1987. *Moon, Sun, and Witches: Gender Ideologies and Class in Inca and Colonial Peru*. Princeton: Princeton University Press.

Sonderberg, Peter. 1985. "Rituals as Theatre: An Introduction." *Circle Network News*, Summer, Vol. 7, No. 3. p. 14. Mt. Horeb, WI.

Spiro, Melford. 1966. "Religion: A Definition." In *Anthropological Approaches to the Study of Religion*. New York: F. A. Praeger.

Starhawk. 1979. *Spiral Dance: A Rebirth of the Ancient Religion of the Great Goddess*. San Francisco: Harper & Row. 10th Anniversary revised ed., 1989.

———. 1982. *Dreaming the Dark: Magic, Sex and Politics*. Boston: Beacon Press.

———. 1987. *Truth or Dare: Encounters with Power, Authority, and Mystery*. San Francisco: Harper & Row.

Starr, Paul. 1982. *The Social Transformation of American Medicine*. New York: Basic Books.

Stone, Lawrence. 1980. "A New Interpretation of Witchcraft." In *Witches and Historians: Interpretations of Salem*, Marc Mappen (ed.). Huntington, NY: Robert E. Krieger Publishing Company.

Stone, Merlin. 1976. *When God Was a Woman*. New York: Harcourt Brace Janovich.

Summers, Montague. 1928. Introduction to the Translation of the *Malleus Malificarum*. London: Pushkin Press.

Talking Stone, Kurt. 1993. "Never Again the Burnings." *Our Pagan Times*, August, Vol. 3, No. 8.

Thomas, Keith. 1971. *Religion and the Decline of Magic*. New York: Charles Scribner's Sons.

Three Initiates. 1908. *The Kybalion: A Study of the Hermetic Philosophy of Ancient Egypt and Greece*. Clayton GA: Tri-State Press, 1988.

Tiryakian, Edward (ed.). 1974. *On the Margin of the Visible: Sociology, the Esoteric, and the Occult*. New York: John Wiley & Sons.

Turner, Victor. 1974. *Dramas, Fields, and Metaphors: Symbolic Action in Human Society*. Ithaca: Cornell University Press.

———. 1982. *From Ritual to Theatre: The Human Seriousness of Play*. New York: PAJ Publications.

Tylor, E. G. 1871. *Primitive Culture*. New York: Harper Torchbooks, 1958.

Valiente, Doreen. 1973. *An ABC of Witchcraft Past and Present*. New York: St. Martin's Press.

———. 1978. *Witchcraft for Tomorrow*. New York: St. Martin's Press.

Veysey, Laurence. 1973. *The Communal Experience: Anarchist and Mystical Counter-Cultures in America*. New York: Harper & Row.

Waite, Arthur Edward. 1961. *The Book of Ceremonial Magic*. Reprint. New York: The Citadel Press, 1970.

Walker, D. P. 1958. *Spiritual and Demonic Magic from Ficino to Campanella*. London: The Warburg Institute, University of London, 1969.

Wallace, Anthony. 1956. "Religious Revitalization Movements." *American Anthropologist*, 58:264–81.

Webster, Paula. 1975. "Matriarchy: A Vision of Power." In *Toward an Anthropology of Women*, Rayna Reiter (ed.). New York: Monthly Review Press.

Weed, Susun. 1989. *Wise Woman Herbal, Healing Wise.* Woodstock.

Whitehead, Alfred North. 1925. "Science in the Modern World." *Lowell Lectures.* Reprint. New York: Free Press, Macmillan, 1967.

Wilner, Eleanor. 1975. *Gathering the Winds: Visionary Imagination and Radical Transformation of Self and Society.* Baltimore: Johns Hopkins Press.

Wilson, Monica. 1951. "Witch Beliefs and Social Structure." *American Journal of Sociology,* LVI:307–313.

Wind, Edgar. 1958. *Pagan Mysteries in the Renaissance: An Exploration of Philosophical and Mystical Sources of Iconography in Renaissance Art.* Revised and enlarged edition, New York: Norton and Company, 1968.

Worsley, Peter. 1968. *The Trumpet Shall Sound: A Study of "Cargo Cults" in Melanesia.* 2d. Aug. ed. New York: Schoken Books.

Yarros, Victor S. 1921. "Contemporary American Radicalism." *International Journal of Ethics,* XXXI:353–54.

Yates, Frances A. 1964. *Giordano Bruno and the Hermetic Tradition.* Chicago and London: The University of Chicago Press. Reprint. Chicago: Midway, 1979.

_____. 1966. *The Art of Memory.* Chicago: University of Chicago Press.

_____. 1972. *The Rosicrucian Enlightenment.* London and Boston: Routledge & Kegan Paul.

_____. 1979. *The Occult Philosophy in the Elizabethan Age.* London: Routledge & Kegan Paul.

Zaleski, B. 1988. "What is Your Most Politically Incorrect Fantasy?" *New York Times Book Review,* April 10:14.

Index